A Study of Malignant Narcissism

A Study of Malignant Narcissism offers a unique insight into malignant narcissism, exploring both its personal and professional aspects and constructing a theoretical framework that renders its origins and manifestations more accessible.

With reference to his own family dynamic and to 45 years of professional experience, Richard Wood explores the psychology of malignant narcissism, positing it as a defence against love. The book first offers an overview of existing literature before examining relevant clinical material, including an analysis of Wood's relationships with his own parents. Wood presents vignettes illustrating the core dynamics that drive narcissism, illustrated with sections of his father's unpublished autobiography and with his patient work. The book makes the case for malignant narcissism to be considered a subtype of psychopathy and puts forth a framework setting out the key dynamics that typify these individuals, including consideration of the ways in which malignant narcissism replicates itself in varied forms. Finally, Wood examines the impact of narcissistic leadership and compares his theoretical position with those of other clinicians.

This book will be of interest to clinical psychologists, psychoanalysts, and psychotherapists, as well as all professionals working with narcissistic patients.

Richard Wood, PhD, is a psychoanalytically oriented clinical psychologist based in Ontario, Canada, with over 45 years of experience. He was educated at Cornell University and Wayne State University.

'*A Study of Malignant Narcissism* is an essential contribution to the growing literature on dangerous personalities and the destruction they cause. Courageous, searingly honest, and deeply moving ... A rare combination of compelling biography and crucial work of science, this is essential reading for our disordered times. An invaluable work of wisdom and experience.'

Ian Hughes, *Senior Research Fellow, MaREI Centre at University College Cork, Ireland*

'This fine book offers a marvellous combination of often hair-raising raw experience with thoughtful, illuminating reflection and insightful commentary. Dr Wood throws much needed light on character formation and function, defensive deformation of personality, ... and resilience. This is a courageous, timely, well written, important book.'

Dr Brent Willock, *Founding President of the Toronto Institute for Contemporary Analysis, Canada*

'With superb prose, Dr. Wood provides a scholarly and informative description of the characteristics and behaviors of individuals with narcissistic personalities ... For anyone wanting to learn about psychopathy and malignant narcissism, and how this knowledge might apply to autocratic leaders, this is the book to read.'

Graeme J. Taylor, MD, FRCPC, *Psychoanalytic Fellow of the American Academy of Psychoanalysis and Dynamic Psychiatry and Professor Emeritus, University of Toronto, Canada*

A Study of Malignant Narcissism

Personal and Professional Insights

Richard Wood

Routledge
Taylor & Francis Group

LONDON AND NEW YORK

Cover image: Colin Anderson Productions pty ltd / Getty Images

First published 2023
by Routledge
4 Park Square, Milton Park, Abingdon, Oxon OX14 4RN

and by Routledge
605 Third Avenue, New York, NY 10158

Routledge is an imprint of the Taylor & Francis Group, an informa business

British Library Cataloguing-in-Publication Data
A catalogue record for this book is available from the British Library

Library of Congress Cataloging-in-Publication Data
Names: Wood, Richard (Psychologist), author.
Title: A study of malignant narcissism : personal and professional insights / by Richard Wood, Ph.D.
Description: 1 Edition. | New York, NY : Routledge, 2022. | Includes bibliographical references and index. |
Summary: "A Study of Malignant Narcissism offers a unique insight into malignant narcissism, exploring both its personal and professional aspects and constructing a theoretical framework which renders its origins and manifestations more accessible. With reference to his own family dynamic and to 45 years of professional experience, Richard Wood explores the psychology of malignant narcissism, positing it as a defence against love. The book first offers an overview of existing literature before examining relevant clinical material, including an analysis of Wood's relationships with his own parents. Wood presents vignettes illustrating the core dynamics that drive narcissism, illustrated with sections of his father's unpublished autobiography and with his patient work. The book makes the case for malignant narcissism to be considered a subtype of psychopathy and puts forth a framework setting out the key dynamics that typify these individuals, including consideration of the ways in which malignant narcissism replicates itself in varied forms. Finally, Wood examines the impact of narcissistic leadership and compares his theoretical position with those of other clinicians. This book will be of interest to clinical psychologists, psychoanalysts, and psychotherapists, as well as all professionals working with narcissistic patients"-- Provided by publisher.
Identifiers: LCCN 2022004625 (print) | LCCN 2022004626 (ebook) |
ISBN 9781032160597 (paperback) | ISBN 9781032160580 (hardback) |
ISBN 9781003246923 (ebook)
Subjects: LCSH: Narcissism. | Psychology, Pathological.
Classification: LCC BF575.N35 W66 2022 (print) | LCC BF575.N35 (ebook) | DDC 616.85/854--dc23/eng/20220511
LC record available at https://lccn.loc.gov/2022004625
LC ebook record available at https://lccn.loc.gov/2022004626

ISBN: 978-1-032-16058-0 (hbk)
ISBN: 978-1-032-16059-7 (pbk)
ISBN: 978-1-003-24692-3 (ebk)

DOI: 10.4324/9781003246923

Typeset in Times New Roman
by Taylor & Francis Books

To my spouse, Mary Walton, whose inspired love made this book possible and to my mentors, Dr. Kenneth Davidson, Dr. Paul Lerner, and Dr. Ray Freebury whose warmth, gentleness, and wisdom helped me become human.

Contents

Preface

This is a book that I have known I would have to write eventually. While most of the ideas that inform this book declared themselves to me in my 40s as I struggled to make sense of my own experience with my family and, of course with my patients, it was always a book I planned to dedicate myself to once I had substantially retired. This is a piece of work that I have both looked forward to and dreaded. I knew that if the book was to be understood it would require me to share my inner life with frightening candor. While I am very open with my friends and my loved ones, finding deep sharing very meaningful and sustaining, my circle of intimates is relatively small and very familiar to me, allowing me to navigate my way through my world in a way that feels mostly manageable.

A work of the kind that I am embarking upon, however, requires me to open doors to any who would choose to read what I have written. Doing so feels like an enormously uncomfortable venture and a very unsafe one. Off-setting what I can only describe as an imposing sense of trepidation is my hope and – compellingly – my conviction that what I have come to understand will better enable others to more deeply appreciate the human condition that defines us.

After some deliberation, I have had to admit to myself that I cannot adequately disguise case file material in a way that would ensure, to my satisfaction, that not only would patient identity be protected, but that patients could not recognize themselves when they read this book. I appreciate that many other authors have quite usefully and instructively included case or clinical material in their discussion of clinical entities. Much of this material has been helpful to me personally in my learning journey. Now that I am faced with the task, however, of incorporating my own work with patients into my text, I cannot conceive of doing so in a way that would not cause potential harm to a patient who comes to realize that I am talking about him or her. Even given prior permission/approval and a chance for a previous patient to review material I have written; I am well aware that with the unfolding of any attention this book receives there may be unintended consequences for such people that neither I nor they can foresee. As a consequence, I will only talk about broad patterns or generalities that seemed to typify the two major groups of patients that I worked with – narcissistic personality disorders and the people that they impacted.

Finally, I have deep concern about the impact such an intimate look at a psychologist's personal struggle and his inner world might have upon those many people with whom I have worked over 40 years of practice. Inevitably, alarming and disconcerting for some, possibly shattering idealizations that people relied upon to help them heal and, perhaps simultaneously, affirming of their own humanity and the many variegated forms through which humanity expresses itself. Equally prominent for me is my awareness of those people who might choose to seek help for themselves in the future who might be dissuaded by a frightening view of a therapist's pain.

So, all in all, not such an easy work to consummate.

Psychotherapy itself, in my view, is an immensely personal undertaking, requiring a therapist to repeatedly draw upon their own experience and their own trauma to better understand a patient. Doing so demands endless – and probably always flawed – self-examination side-by-side companion personal therapy that punctuates the life of a therapist. The process is necessarily messy, ambiguous, and imperfect. Even with the support of intermittent psychotherapy of one's own and peer collaboration, a therapist can expect that he or she will inevitably lose their way many, many times during the course of their work. Sometimes patients evoke counter responses in a therapist that the therapist finds too deeply disconcerting to contain. Sometimes patient trauma activates the therapist's own traumatic experiences, immersing the therapist in a process called vicarious re-traumatization. Or sometimes the therapist's difficulty with their own lives at a particular point in time means that doing their job – listening, empathizing, understanding – becomes exceptionally challenging. Potential sources of compromise for a therapist are endless. Not all of them, even with extensive training, can be anticipated. Unless a therapist is possessed of exhaustive self-knowledge and exhaustive knowledge of the human condition – which none of us can be – a continuing commitment to try to know ourselves as well as we can is the best that any of us can do. This is the work of a lifetime and it is always incomplete, but without it there is little chance that we can recover ourselves and help the people we are meant to help when we get in over our heads. Getting in over one's head with greater frequency than one would like, I would maintain, is a constant of therapeutic work.

Even with a reasonable (but certainly always imperfect) understanding of who we are, where we come from, and what we have come to be, any of us, whether we are therapists or not, must still face a profoundly challenging struggle as we attempt to alter patterns and defenses that define us. Absent such an imperfect understanding – and for many people all but the most superficial look at the self is too painful to bear – relative blindness renders the possibility of becoming more caring, more generative, and more loving human beings that much more remote.

I believe that because the imperfect and messy process of looking at the self can be so disruptive, much of modern mental health initiative has become variably programmable, relieving therapists of at least some of the uncertainty and discomfort more extensive investigation of the self can create. Within the context of programmable work, therapists enjoy the benefit of more or less knowing what they are to do during each session. Therapist focus is on objectively reproducible technique. Programmable interventions also seem to be particularly amenable to numeric evaluation of therapy success. Both therapist and patient, then, have the reassurance of being able to confirm progress, session by session, towards realization of certain identified goals. Because programmable therapy tends to be short-term in nature, there is often not time to get stuck in the intricacies of either the patient's or the therapist's psyches. Therapeutic intervention is highly replicable and is ordained by clearly elucidated steps that define process. It is a good companion to an age that demands declarative answers and numeric verification.

It is argued by many in our contemporary surround that which cannot be quantified cannot be science; that that which cannot realize objective verification through vigorous research paradigm cannot produce real scientific data. But unless we look at what is happening inside us, we ignore who we are. Numbers can only capture some of these realities; words, it seems to me, do far better. Words, then, become the core tools and the essential means that we have to rely upon to make sense out of the self. Words can capture nuance, variegation, and complexity of thought and feeling in a way that still eludes algorithms and quantification. Imagine trying to construct even a relatively brief interaction with a friend that encompasses ambiguities of intent, feeling, and thought that play themselves out through gestures, facial expressions, and spoken words with a series of numbers or formulas. How does one assign a number to insouciance? Or to irony? And how would one convey the potentially complex mix of emotions implicit in eye rolling? To my mind, words represent the best means that we have – and the most precise – to approximate, to share, and to explore phenomenology. And even with the wonderful precision and explanatory power of words, we can never fully describe or define our internal realities – not until even more effective tools than words present themselves to us. Using words, we construct models and suppositions of what we think takes place in people, displacing them with better models and better suppositions as we seem to deepen our awareness of ourselves. The study of phenomenology progresses, much like any other science, through a series of insights, reappraisals, missteps and new clarifications. It may feel more ungovernable, more chaotic, and more elusive than other branches of science, particularly the physical sciences, but I'm not sure that it is. In the end, as Mark Twain famously suggested, what we know may ultimately be limited by our inherently flawed capacity to be honest with ourselves.

Our best but inevitably continuously changing grasp of phenomenology will have to marry itself to wonderfully, spellbindingly complex interactions with epigenetics, genetics, brain function, biochemistry, and the dynamics of disease and healing.

As an aside, I should emphasize that I do feel programmable and evidence-based psychotherapeutic interventions, like cognitive behavioral therapy (CBT), make a significant contribution to mental health remediation, though perhaps not to the extent that we once believed that they did. Importantly, they offer an alternative to the risks of intense self-exploration that render intensive, extended self-awareness work unsuitable for many people; they create a therapeutic milieu that is more tolerable for many therapists; they facilitate training of greater numbers and greater varieties of therapists; and, not inconsequentially, they make a more affordable form of psychotherapy (because it is generally shorter-term in nature) available to greater numbers of people than extended self-awareness work can. Programmable work also affords people the opportunity to engage in limited self-exploration within the context of a relatively safe paradigm. Its major drawbacks are its capacity to address mental health problems characterized by severity, chronicity, and long-term risk. I would also say that it is less well equipped to provide us with the full range of tools and conceptualizations that we need to more meaningfully extend our understanding of who we are. Intensive self-awareness work is better equipped to do the latter, but it can produce painful, disorganizing confrontations with the self that may be catastrophic for an individual to bear. Great care has to be taken in its application. Because it is often (though not exclusively) long-term in nature, it also tends to be much more costly than various forms of programable symptom relief intervention.

Both approaches are valuable, then, and both are possessed of limitation. And both approaches, of course, represent legitimate approaches to science. It also has to be said that, at present, there are many forms of mental health challenge which neither approach can adequately address, even with the help of psychotropic medication.

The microcosm of the two therapeutic worlds I have just referenced offers us a portrait of what I think we see in the larger world around us. I would say that we appear to live in an age in which problems – particularly human problems – demand simplistic conceptions consisting of soundbites that belie the extraordinary complexity of the issues we are trying to make sense of. Binary thinking and binary choices seem to reassure us. Truth can only be true if it is simple and, one might add, visceral and therefore easily accessible. Problems must be actionable and solutions realizable through a series of declarative steps imbued with moral imperative. We must have the one right or true way to do a thing rather than admit the bewildering array of alternatives and ambiguities which real-life complexity creates for us. Complexities and ambiguities confuse us and frighten us. We'd much prefer the comfort and reassurance which "simple truths" seem to afford us – even if, in adhering to them, we cause damage to ourselves, to others (including other species), and to our planet. Voices which cry for change and for a more accurate representation of reality are often met with outrage, indignation, denunciation, and even attempts to obliterate.

We cling to the truths we create for ourselves with ferocity and tenacity. Those who favor ceaseless exploration and curiosity about the self and about the world around them (and much of humanity does) are felt to create jeopardy for those who don't. The inherent tension between these opposing forces within human nature has the potential to be constructive, enhancing either growth or stability in orderly turns. When appreciation of nuance and complexity becomes too prominent or moves ahead too rapidly or in a seemingly ungovernable fashion, human nature finds itself locked in combat with its fractious parts. Combat is real – moral, psychological, economic, and physical. Old forms of thought and being which define old identities face compromise. Safety is forfeit. Means of distinguishing friend versus foe and good versus bad are rendered more tentative. And the self loses the underpinnings and moorings that it relies upon to insulate itself against the inherently chaotic and disordered inner world we must all somehow find a way to live with. It seems that more of our inner lives we wall off to make ourselves safe, the more dangerous it becomes to tolerate knowing the self. The struggle to find ways to feel safe with our inner world appears to be a core human conflict.

I would suggest the war we wage within ourselves has escalated in modern times. I would also say that we risk annihilation if we do not find the means to know ourselves better – however imperfectly, but better. Every age probably perceives its struggles in epic proportions and every age might wish to say of itself that it is the best and the worst of times. Never, it seems to me, has humanity shown such promise and never has it been so close to its own end. It is my hope that in sharing some of the darkness in my own soul and the souls of those close to me in my family of origin I can help – even if only in a very limited, incremental way – to extend our willingness to examine who and what we are. I can make no claim that the models of the human psyche I piece together here are necessarily accurate representations of the phenomena I have attempted to capture. At most - assuming they are possessed of any value at all - they can only be approximations that, hopefully, will give rise to further discussion which refines and elaborates them in a more useful manner. This is a book about phenomenology – the study of our inner worlds - that treats me and four members of my family of origin as the objects of its study. The subject of this book is narcissism or, more accurately put, narcissistic personality disorder (NPD). NPD may express itself in a variety of ways and with varying degrees of severity; my exclusive focus in this work is on one particularly virulent or extreme form of NPD, which has sometimes been referred to as "malignant" narcissism. My clinical experience tells me that NPD is a continuum; it is my view that less virulent forms of NPD can be seen to share many of the characteristics and psychodynamics of malignant narcissism, differing largely in the degree to which they manifest themselves. I recognize that many clinicians might disagree with my perspective. I'm also very cognizant that my clinical experience, while extensive in terms of years, necessarily represents only a small clinical sample of the ways in which narcissism expresses itself and the causes that lead to its development.

For ease of reference, I will use the terms malignant narcissism, narcissism, and NPD interchangeably, though I am very much aware that not all narcissism and NPD, though destructive to self and others, is imbued with the measure of malevolence l am attempting to investigate. It must be emphasized that some people who qualify for a diagnosis of NPD appear to be capable of leading relatively successful and productive lives, depending upon the metric that one applies. I also very much recognize that healthy narcissistic experience has its own constructive contribution to make to the human developmental process. In entitling my book "*A Study in Malignant Naarcissism*," I hope to remind the reader that I am looking at an extreme variant of NPD. Malignant, unfortunately, carries with it connotations of pejorative judgement, but it is so compelling as a descriptive term I have decided to use it. I am not the first clinician to employ the diagnostic construct malignant narcissism (see, most prominently, Eric Fromm and Otto Kernberg, among others). Like other writers, I have constructed my own understanding of what malignant narcissism means based on both personal and clinical experience. The reader will see for him or herself whether my grasp of this particular facet of the human condition is possessed of any value.

As I noted earlier, this is a book I have always known I would have to write and that I had planned to write some time in my early-ish 70s. From my point of view, the center stage that Narcissistic Personality Disorder has occupied in recent years did surprise me, though perhaps, in retrospect, it should not have. It was never my intention to write about a particular individual or series of individuals, but rather to try to more deeply investigate what narcissistic personality disorder is. My preference was that I could have written a book about narcissism without it finding itself center stage in the midst of a maelstrom of controversy. But Narcissistic Personality Disorder is a profoundly important human phenomenon that has both served humanity well in some respects during the course of its evolution and, much more latterly, created potentially devastating future outcome for virtually our whole planet. Whether I would wish it so or not, it is timely that we intensify our efforts to understand such a pivotal variation of the human character.

From one perspective, malignant narcissistic personality disorder must surely be seen as a core form of human evil. It would appear to play a very important and at times central role in the various forms of suffering that we cause one another. In addition to as yet poorly defined biological and genetic factors, I would maintain that it can be a consequence of devastating early suffering that gives rise to terrible distortions of the human character. From this vantage point, it is neither good nor bad, but, rather, a variation of the human character, like any other, that demands respect, compassion, and perception. Indeed, the devitalization of the human spirit it occasions imposes a lifelong agony and spiritual deadness upon those who must live with it. While an individual enduring NPD would rarely describe themselves as damaged, preferring instead to portray their destructiveness as strength, the torment that endlessly invades their day-by-day life must eventually become acutely transparent to any who would look.

I will not personally reference contemporary figures in this book. There are many contemporary figures, I believe, to whom the term Narcissistic Personality Disorder could be applied. To make the book about one or a select few individuals would defeat its purpose. The reader will see, however, that aspects of the literature on malignant narcissism and related concepts does engage clinicians' assessment of Donald Trump. My focus when I review this portion of literature will direct itself towards a description of the formulations that clinicians propose rather than on commentary they make about Trump. Side-by-side the rest of the literature review, the review chapter will help set the stage for the reader to critically evaluate my ideas. It also permits me, in the final chapter of the book, to compare and contrast my ideas with those of other clinicians.

And so, I begin, for me, a perilous journey.

Acknowledgements

First and foremost, I owe a great debt of thanks to my wife for her extraordinary patience in reviewing endless drafts of this book and for her seemingly limitless forbearance as she gently nudged me to structure content in a way that would make the book more accessible to my readers. She, more than anyone, knows my story intimately. While I'm aware that it was difficult for her to read about many aspects of my experience with my father, she persisted, allowing herself to be drawn into some of the darkest corners that I explore, emerging from them to offer insight and demand clarification where it was needed. Thank you, Mary, for your companionship during what might otherwise have been an overwhelming journey had it been undertaken without your presence.

I must also express a debt of gratitude to the numbers of people who took the time to review the manuscript, often providing me with painstaking editing that must have required hours and hours of effort on their part. My old friend Dr. Timothy Gilmor, with whom I shared the mentorship of Dr. Paul Lerner and who has remained a dear friend throughout much of the entirety of my professional life, was one such person. Another long- standing friend, Dr. Brent Willock, also invested an enormous amount of time and energy in reviewing the manuscript and in helping me work with it. His contributions, like Tim's, were deeply valued. So, too, were the contributions of relatively new friends, Dr. Donald Edwards and Dr. Susan Andresen, whose acquaintance I made subsequent to my relatively recent move to Stratford, Ontario. Like Tim and Brent, without hesitation they shouldered the task and moved through a somewhat imposing manuscript that I know Don, at least, found troubling to confront at times. It is my hope that my friendship with both of them and their partners will continue throughout my remaining years. Two other long-established friends, Don Duprey and Gia Levin, also indulged me by reading my manuscript, offering their own appraisals and thoughts. I also have to extend special thanks to my dear friend Ron Barzso, who read through the book several times and passed it out to numbers of friends.

Old friends whom I had the pleasure of reconnecting with, Dr. Ray Freebury and Dr. Graeme Taylor, not only took the time to read this book, but commented on it extensively and wrote reviews. And, finally, I owe a considerable debt of thanks to my colleague and long-standing friend, Joel Kumove, for his thoughtful appraisal of the work.

I also reached out to total strangers – other mental health professionals whom I knew shared my deep concern about the terrible risks that dangerous personalities, like malignant narcissists, create for us when they assume positions of power and leadership. Dr. Ian Hughes was one such like-minded person. Having read his book, Disordered Minds, I could guess that we would hold important common ground with one another. I was right. Ian was not only receptive to my request to read a manuscript from someone he had never heard of, but demonstrated himself to be extraordinarily generous, proving to be not only a careful editor, but a source of support, affirmation, and encouragement. I would wish that our work will continue to lead us in similar directions in the future so that we might work together again. His presence in my life has been an unexpected gift. Other mental health professionals – Elizabeth Mika and Harper West took the time to read parts of the book and offer their comments. I express my gratitude to them as well.

I also want to extend special thanks to the editors at Routledge – Susannah Frearson, Kate Hawes, Jana Craddock, and Ellie Duncan – who took an immediate interest in my book, saw some promise in it, and undertook to publish it. With your encouragement, the book became more than it was. It's very much been a pleasure to work with all of you.

And lastly, I want to express my deep appreciation for my "new" family member, Melanie Ryan, for her extraordinary support. Without her willingness to rescue her mother and me from the terrors of working with a Word document converted from PDF format, I'm not sure this book would have ever made its way to the publisher. Thank you for your patience and encouragement.

Chapter 1

Establishing an Attitude of Skepticism

Relying on memory to accurately capture one's early, formative experiences may be a fool's errand predicated, as it has to be, upon unappreciated misconception, misapprehension, and reality bending distortions as one attempts to protect the self from early insults. Acuity of remembered perception must always be co-mingled with formidable limitations. While it can plausibly be argued that the subjective realities that define contemporary inner narratives and experiences are the only "realities" that a therapist can legitimately deal with, there is recognition that the subjective realities that define us now may not correspond in the ways that we think they do with our early experience. At the moment, differentiating what actually happened to us from what we think happened is, essentially, an insoluble problem. The more we know about memory – and the impact that trauma has upon memory – the more uncertain we must be about what we think we recall. We are left to grope in the dark with a bewildering array of memories, images, feelings, and variously successfully articulated experiences that we believe, with varying levels of conviction, tells us who we are.

As with any scientific endeavor, we begin by cataloguing what we think we see, establishing points of reference and putting the remembered past and the actualities that seem to define the present together as best we can, always reminding ourselves that both past and present (for the present is subject to the distorting impact of defenses as well) must be viewed with skepticism. At times, we have the advantage of watching a childhood as it unfolds and seeing somewhat more directly (but always imperfectly) the effect that a given set of circumstances has upon varieties of individuals. At other times, we may even have the benefit of longitudinal study that spans years, if not decades, of a given individual's life. Gradually, from a morass of gloriously imperfect "data" (some psychologists, at least, are said to love ambiguity), patterns begin to emerge that seem to enjoy various forms of validity confirmation – some from number science and some from carefully articulated accounts of the human endeavor. And gradually, cautiously, we began to invest incremental confidence in the science that emerges, always remembering we must be prepared to replace old ideas with better ones.

DOI: 10.4324/9781003246923-1

When meaningful patterns begin to define themselves, we cling to them much as a drowning man might cling to a life raft. We need them to be true in order for our world to feel safer. As the scales fall from our eyes and we begin to recognize their inadequacy, or feel it, we are cast adrift again to re-forge other, hopefully better, explanations that will confirm for us there is order in the world after all. The desolation one feels as patterns, laboriously constructed, begin to fail us is, to say the least, extraordinarily disconcerting. Will we ever be capable of finding meaningful answers? Are the answers that we have found for ourselves the best that we will ever be able to devise – and if that's true, how will we survive our ignorance? The wait for new answers – models that better approximate the human experience – can take years or even decades. Drifting around in the wilderness of one's own thoughts and feelings seems interminable, and interminable engenders potentially suffocating despair. When new ideas finally do begin to present themselves, particularly when they are integrated into seemingly elegant patterns that appear to possess enhanced explanatory power, we are besotted by them, desperate, as we are, for means that allow us to pull ourselves away from the darkness. Elegance and coherence co-mingled with terrible need make such ideas hard to resist. Scientific skepticism ought to compel us to stand back from our creation and question it, but in so doing we evoke jeopardy for a self that is loath to give up the bits and pieces of order it has discovered. We must be ever mindful of this vulnerability if we are to test our ideas adequately and if we are to spur ourselves further into uncharted territory. For me, the answers that I pieced together and the models that I laboriously assembled into pleasing patterns felt like lifelines without which my psychic survival would not be possible. The tension between the desire to invest in them and the need to divest oneself of them when appropriate was ever present. One had to willfully remind oneself to resurrect skepticism. The struggle to do so was certainly not always successful.

I remember all too well the mixture of intense trepidation and anticipation when I entered graduate school. I would be talking to people and taught by people who knew about and understood the human condition; they could help support me in my heretofore hapless efforts to know more about myself and others. But such "knowing" would come at a cost. It meant that I would have to allow myself to be known. Very dangerous territory. Like so many other graduate students in clinical psychology (although I was convinced my own position was far more precarious than theirs), I imagined the immensity of my pain and my disordered interior would be both so transparent and so repellent I could expect to be quickly turned away. The pain I carried also meant that I was only capable of limited work effort and of episodic successes, sometimes confirming talent and sometimes deconstructing it. The etiology of the up and down course typifying my work ethic was beyond my means of apprehension at the time. I secretly and shamefully concluded this particular pattern represented moral failing. The frustration of my mentors seemed to confirm episodic disappointment and disapproval, apparently reiterating my self-appraisal. I was unable to recognize that my teachers were truly as perplexed as I was, probably because they lacked conceptual frameworks that have become commonplace in psychology today. It did not occur to me, in other words, that the state of their knowledge was imperfect. There were glorious moments when I saw that was so, but, reflexively, I always turned any misgivings against myself.

As my graduate experience elaborated itself into years, I continued to feel confused – or probably, more accurately, astonished – that I had not been rejected. The sense of precariousness that had characterized the early part of graduate school persisted in succeeding years, in part because I did not see myself becoming a "knowing" being in the way that my teachers were and, in no small part, because I still failed to recognize that any of the answers I acquired through reading or through clinical experience and supervision were, essentially, only approximations, each of which was possessed of limitations and flaws that I mistakenly attributed to my own stupidity or backwardness. It was only with the passage of time that I recognized that I, like everybody else, was required to endure the painful solitude that I think we experience when we finally acknowledge there are no absolute answers – only imperfect ones. I wanted someone else to simply tell me how everything worked in the human psyche. I had to face the contentious and painful reality that if I wanted to know, I would have to make my own journey, admitting each step of the way the best I could do was a better idea.

I implore the reader again to remember that the ideas contained in this book are only approximations of reality, approximations that may be extended if they prove worthy, but will most certainly be changed or dismissed as we come to know more about ourselves.

I also want the reader to be aware that the ideas that I present in this book about narcissism represent the culmination of many, many other people's work. I am building on their shoulders and am deeply indebted to them, not only for the literature that they produced, but for the personal endeavor that so many of my clinician colleagues undertook, either directly or indirectly, to help me grow and learn.

Many of these contributions are described in the literature review chapter which follows this one. In that chapter, I have tried to capture clinicians' efforts to understand the dangerous form of personality organization that this book concerns itself with. Following completion of the literature review, the reader will see that I do not incorporate references to literature, with few exceptions, in the chapters that follow. I very much wanted to create a narrative that is uncluttered by repetitive literature citation; my intention is to draw my readers' attention to the ideas and the extensive clinical material in the text, which, hopefully, I have managed to present in clear and accessible language.

I am inviting my readers to take a very visceral journey with me, one that I know may render the book hard to read for some people. As the book unfolds, I will be exposing people to disturbing experiences that I endured which are meant to elucidate what it felt like to grow up in a narcissistic surround. I not only want the reader to see and hear about what happened; I want them to feel it. Only by being visceral can this book capture the distorting impact narcissists have upon the people close to them. In each chapter I have presented a series of experiences and vignettes that, although they may seem disconnected, are intended to incrementally provide insight into the nature of narcissism. If at various points along the way people find themselves confused and lost, their confusion, perplexity, and perhaps distress will serve to help them better appreciate what my own experience was like. The "voice" that the reader will find me using to represent my younger self is often an intellectualized one, very much reflective of my desperation to make sense out of all the chaos around me and inside me. At various other points, my despair, my horror, my helplessness, and my repugnance with the changes that were unfolding inside me will obviously eclipse the intellectualized or clinical tone that I attempted to establish for myself as a younger person and that I relied upon to protect me. If people can endure the companionship that I offer them – a kind of emotional partnership with me and with my childhood and young adult self – my hope is that the reader who persists will be rewarded with a depth of understanding of narcissism that would otherwise elude them. I believe that what I endured is not only indicative of what happens to family members exposed to a narcissistic other, but to much larger groups of people that may fall under the narcissist's sway, including nations that they lead.

Chapter 2 provides an extensive literature review of salient commentary clinicians have offered with respect to our evolving grasp of what I am referring to as malignant narcissism. It will not attempt to describe conceptual work clinicians have undertaken in their efforts to understand forms of narcissism that fall outside the dangerous personality I'm attempting to investigate.

Chapter 3 will focus on my relationship with my mother, whose own formidable and ultimately lethal psychological liabilities rendered her exquisitely vulnerable to my father's depredations. Her struggles for cohesion, for identity, and, ultimately, for survival were a deeply poignant part of my growing up experience.

Chapters 4 through 6 direct their attention towards a series of vignettes that are meant to capture some of the core dynamics that I believe drive narcissism. Each chapter builds upon the ideas that the previous chapter explored, though not always in an obvious way. Because the dynamic forces that characterize narcissism are entwined with one another, it was not possible to discuss each dynamic as a separate, discrete entity. Invariably, describing one set of dynamic themes implicates others. I have done my best to avoid repetition as I look at various facets of narcissism, but I have to beg the reader's indulgence because, in order to explicate new constructs, I have to reference older ones I have already examined.

Chapter 4 is a foundational chapter in the discussion of narcissism. As I review a number of searing experiences with my father, I begin to explore what they mean. Towards the end of the chapter, I consolidate my reflections on both my father's behavior and my own internal responses to it into a number of important questions.

Chapter 5 investigates the nature of my father's "friendships." I identify various facets of his narcissism that shape the way that he relates to people.

Chapter 6 returns to a theme, via further vignettes, introduced in Chapters 3 and 4: my father's need to obliterate other personalities and other voices, replacing them with a version of his own. Chapter 5 also returns to another theme identified in the first two chapters: the apparent inclination of some of the people in my father's sphere of influence to incorporate his voice and his perspectives as their own with an almost celebratory zeal.

Chapter 7 calls attention to growing similarities between my father's manifestations of cruelty and those I recognize in myself. The parallels between his inner life and mine are felt to provide damning evidence of my own compromise. I document my growing fear that my humanity, like his, will eventually be displaced by the ugliness I see accruing inside myself

Chapter 8 reviews two different kinds of psychological damage that were prominent in my response to my father's narcissism. The first was clinical depression and the second complex post-traumatic stress disorder. I discuss the dynamics of both extensively, closely examining the ways in which each manifested themselves in my father's life and in mine.

Chapter 9 looks back at my father's growing up years and young adulthood through the lens of the two extensive autobiographical statements he provided me. The autobiographies themselves have not been included in the body of my work because they are so lengthy. I have excerpted significant parts of them in the narrative that Chapter 9 provides. I was deeply appreciative of my father's willingness to construct these portraits of his life; they allowed me to penetrate narcissism and to piece together a far more deeply compassionate view of him, which was very much welcome, allowing me to reframe some of the anguish he had caused. I think there was a part of him that wanted me to know who he was, where he came from, and how he had come to be the man that he was. The autobiographies, in their original form, however, are also obviously self-serving; entirely absent in them is any indication of his awareness of the injury that he imposed on the people around him.

Chapter 10 makes the case that Narcissistic Personality Disorder (NPD) is best understood as a subtype of psychopathy. I take strenuous issue with the DSM-V conception of psychopathy and of NPD, elaborating upon my reasons for doing so. In this chapter I acknowledge the ambiguities and challenges of the diagnostic process.

Chapter 11 provides a synthesis and an elaboration of all of the ideas about malignant narcissism in the book into a single framework that attempts to formally conceive the compelling and most often destructive dynamics that typify individuals manifesting this extreme form of narcissism. It is intended to capture the general case, rather than being a reference to my father's experience. It is meant to set the stage for the two chapters that follow, which also broadly reference the issues they are attempting to address rather than focusing on my father's dynamics specifically.

Chapter 12 considers the ways in which malignant narcissism replicates itself, sometimes by manifesting itself in other forms of psychopathy. I remind the reader of the important similarities that emerged between my psyche and my father's as I was progressively exposed to his narcissism. I spend the greatest portion of the chapter, however, describing my patients' responses to the influence of a narcissistic other. Various mechanisms of transmission of psychopathic traits are outlined in some depth. I also extensively describe various patterns of psychological injury people living in a narcissistic surround sustain. Characterization of injury and of injurious dynamics unfolds against the backdrop of what healthy human psychic development can look and feel like.

Chapter 13, moves from consideration of injuriousness narcissism occasions for family members and friends to investigation of the impact that narcissistic leadership has upon the governed. Extending what one sees in the family context to the context of a larger entity, like a state, produces a model of narcissistic leadership marked by brutality, toxicity, incitement to violence and hatred, inflammation of bigotries, generation of conspiracy theories, blunting of citizens' humanity, and movement towards an increasingly psychopathic national culture in which bullying and endemic fear progressively overwhelm decency. Quality of thought faces compromise; intellectual endeavor and truth both endure murderous erosion.

Chapter 13 also attempts to make sense of our susceptibility to narcissistic leadership, identifying numbers of potential factors that seem to contribute to our willingness to be led by this damaged and very damaging group of people.

Finally, Chapter 14 attempts to compare and contrast my conceptions with those of other clinicians. In the process, my intention is to delineate my formulation of malignant narcissism with greater clarity.

Chapter 2

Literature Review of Malignant Narcissism and Related Constructs

A literature review of the sort that I am about to embark on now, like many another literature review, offers a microcosmic view of how we acquire knowledge and of what scientific process looks like. The reader will feel each of the practitioners I reference in this chapter struggling with challenging realities that they're attempting to capture. Each new theory, each new conceptualization potentially moves one closer to a more accurate appreciation of the complex phenomena one is attempting to understand. Some ideas will eventually prove themselves to be detours that turn one away from a closer approximation of truth; some may strike one as deeply insightful, even epiphanous, only to disappoint as more knowledge accumulates; and some that may impress one as inelegant or as perplexing will show themselves possessed of great merit upon better acquaintance. The reader will probably find him or herself feeling that many of the formulations and perspectives of the clinician writers I review seem contradictory or even impossibly at odds with one another. With the passage of a great deal of time and as ideas are repeatedly tested, real knowledge begins to build. Even though many, many very qualified people have attempted to understand what I refer to as malignant narcissism, this is still very nascent science. We have a very long way to go. If the various contributors to the subject matter, including myself, help us better appreciate important facets of the material we have been studying, our work can be said to be successful. Each of us builds on the efforts of others, sometimes in ways that are quite apparent to us and sometimes without full awareness of the impact that other scientists and other ideas have had upon us. It's a slow process, often a very confusing one marked by lots of blind alleys and misdirection, but, in the end, after a great deal of extensive work, a very rewarding undertaking.

This literature review will confine itself to consideration of psychological constructs relied upon to understand a particularly destructive and dangerous form of personality organization that has a profoundly pathological impact upon the affected individual and those people that he interacts with, whether it be on a personal, familial, societal, or governmental level. You will see that some practitioners are reluctant to tie the pathological form being described

DOI: 10.4324/9781003246923-2

to a particular diagnostic entity, preferring instead to try to identify markers that help us appreciate when a given individual has become dangerous; others clearly do see the damaging personalities they're describing as extending from recognizable diagnostic categories. Some of the practitioners I reference will largely direct their attention towards catastrophically damaging pathological leadership; others will focus upon the broader implications (not just in a leadership context) of the processes that they're trying to understand.

Psychoanalyst and psychologist Eric Fromm began a serious conversation about malignant narcissism in his 1964 book, *The Heart of Man*, that has extended from that point in time up to the present. It is a conversation that has waxed and waned since Fromm presented his original ideas, becoming somewhat more focused and garnering more intense interest over the last five or six years. Some, like myself, would argue that this is such an important subject and, in many ways, such a neglected one, that we must now of necessity turn more energy and attention towards it.

For Fromm, as was true of Freud, narcissism was an inherent part of the human condition and one that mankind could never hope to entirely eclipse, in spite of man's efforts to humanize himself and grow. Fromm conceived of growth as a progression from narcissistic preoccupation with the self to a state in which, increasingly, humankind was ever more mindful of the needs of others and evermore capable of generativity and love. The process, as he imagined it, was an imperfect one that never allowed one to fully escape one's preoccupation with one's own importance.

Simultaneously, Fromm considered that each individual's absorption with their own significance was biologically necessary for survival in a competitive world; without a compelling investment in oneself one could not find the will to struggle and to assert his right to exist against the pressing needs others could be expected to express. Saintliness, Fromm pointed out, might represent an idealized conception of the human spirit, but saints could not be expected to last very long.

Narcissism, Fromm believed, was felt to grow out of the infant's symbiotic attachment with the mother figure in the very earliest or pre-Oedipal phase of development. In the very first part of its life, it could only know its own wants and needs, the fluctuations of its own biological realities, the gratification/satiation that life provided, and the frustrations that it imposed. Within this framework, the infant was said not to have awareness of the outside world and, in particular, of the existence of other people, or, in analytic language, of other objects. It was only as the child came to painfully recognize its separateness and the existence of the world outside itself that the child could be said to step away from its narcissistic engagement with itself (what Fromm and others have referred to as primary narcissism). Differentiating self from the rest of the world meant that the child was free to divert the energy it invested in itself towards building attachments with others. As this process of differentiation unfolded, the child learned to attend to others' needs and to identify with them as an effective means of managing in a world he or she could not entirely control. The child might remain narcissistically involved with his own needs, but now an awareness of others and the importance of addressing their needs had evolved as well. The stage was set for the child to begin to transcend his primary narcissism as he became more prosocial and collaborative. Parenthetically, Fromm recognized that humans were equipped with a multiplicity of drives and different forms of energy rather than two primary drives; these views led him to re-conceptualize the meaning of the various critical developmental phases Freud described (narcissistic, oral-receptive, oral-aggressive, anal-sadistic, phallic, and genital).

Within Fromm's conception, narcissism appeared to refer to broad dynamic forces: man's inclination to over-estimate his own value and, simultaneously, his propensity to exist within a closed world that fed upon itself, one defined by his own perspectives, thoughts, feeling states, and needs to the exclusion of others' realities and the realities of the world that existed around one. Life, then, was a balancing act, pitting mankind against the seductive urge to over-invest in the self and in the self's subjective realities, on the one hand, and humanity's willingness, on the other, to embrace the world of people and events outside oneself. Fromm emphasized that "whatever the different manifestations of narcissism are, a lack of genuine interest in the outside world is common to all forms of narcissism" (1964, p. 67).

Fromm distinguished two forms of narcissism: benign and malignant. Benign narcissism, as its name implies, was seen to be a potentially constructive, creative narcissistic force. Fromm believed that as man made a narcissistic investment in the importance of his work and his achievements, the scope and extent of such narcissistic attachment was naturally self-limited by the work that one had to do to realize a desired accomplishment. Work mitigated narcissistic investment, in other words, reminding a creator that output was only possible through disciplined, sustained effort. It could not occur simply because one wished it to. The frustration inherent in such effort served to remind one of one's own constraints, tempering burgeoning hubris in the process. Fromm recognized that there was at least one important exception to his view that benign narcissism was curtailed by the effort of achievement; he cautioned that narcissism occasioned by conquest could not be considered benign. One had the sense that he was not entirely satisfied with his formulation of benign narcissism, but felt that it was nonetheless sufficiently important as a construct to try to articulate.

Malignant narcissism, in contrast, was defined by output that was highly – and one could say exclusively – valued because the creator saw himself as inordinately special. Valuation of one's productions was not mitigated by the demands that achievement requiring hard work could impose. For the malignant narcissist, something was good simply because it came from him or was of him. In such a context, reality was inconsequential. All that mattered was that one's view of oneself as ascendant or superior could be maintained.

Fromm described malignant narcissism as "not self-limiting, and in consequence is crudely solipsistic as well as xenophobic" (p. 74). The malignant narcissist could be expected "to isolate himself increasingly in narcissistic splendor" (p. 74). Being malignantly narcissistic meant that one was profoundly alone, in an echo chamber of one's own making.

In other sections of his chapter on narcissism in which he did not appear to be explicitly referring to malignant narcissism, Fromm suggested that grossly inflated estimates of one's talents and one's achievements was an inherently self-defeating undertaking. The bearer must continuously fend off contradictory voices and perceptions lest their appraisal of self face jeopardy – the caveat being that narcissistic self appraisal was unrealistic and therefore all too vulnerable to criticism. Criticism, in turn, was expected to produce rage fed by fear that diminishment of the self's special status would feel catastrophic. Overvaluation of the self could only be supported by an expanding sense of grandiosity and omnipotence that had to be continuously augmented to hold countervailing voices and forces at bay. Other voices and other realities had to be discredited to protect the self from the devastating realization that its own acts of imagination were essentially barren.

If burgeoning grandiosity and omnipotence unfolded in a personality possessed of unusual assets, such a personality might eventually consolidate inordinate power. Inordinate power meant that opposition could be annihilated and that the narcissist could bend reality to suit his own distorted interpretations. Delusional beliefs could become realities that the narcissist compelled those around him to enact, providing him, in the process, with confirmation that his power was limitless and that what he thought must be real simply because he thought it. Fromm referenced personalities like "the Egyptian pharaohs, the Roman Caesars, the Borgias, Hitler, Stalin, Trujillo" who had become "gods, limited only by illness, age and death" (p. 63). Fromm reflected that such a human contingency was "madness, even though it is an attempt to solve the problem of existence by pretending that one is not human" (p. 63).

Presuming that Fromm regarded personalities like Hitler's and Stalin's as a form of malignant narcissism, one further understood that, from his perspective, such personalities contained the seeds of their own destruction because they are at war with the dictates of reason and love. Reason offended grandiosity and love was precluded by narcissistic failure to experience others as separate beings deserving of respect. Escalating overvaluation of the self and escalating omnipotence must inevitably create failures for such personalities that would jeopardize the omnipotence they require to feel safe. Should mounting evidence contradict the realities they tried to impose on others, Fromm thought that compromised omnipotence was likely to produce potentially lethal depression. It was as a result of often poorly articulated, but nonetheless formidable depressive potential that the narcissist was driven to safeguard omnipotence at all costs. In this formulation one hears echoes of other authors (see, for example, Mika, to be discussed shortly) who regard malignant narcissistic adjustment as precarious and, ultimately, as fatally flawed, destined to end itself in personal disintegration.

Fromm did not attempt to articulate clinical causalities or life experiences that could set the stage for the development of malignant narcissism beyond identifying pre-Oedipal attachment as creating a pan-human narcissistic substrate that everyone could be expected to be exposed to as part of the developmental process. He did, however, in one interesting passage identify mother fixated men whose mothers directed contempt towards the father, demonstrating a clear preference for the son. Consequently, such men developed the conviction they were better than father and better than any other man. Fromm concluded that "This narcissistic conviction makes it unnecessary for them to do much, or anything, to prove their greatness" (p. 98). He added that these men's entire self-esteem was embedded in their relationship with a woman, from whom they required unconditional, limitless admiration. While not specifically a formulation of etiology for malignant narcissism, his comments are worthy of mention here because they mirror, to a degree, Kernberg's conception of causative factors contributing to the development of malignant narcissistic personality organization (see the discussion about Kernberg that follows below).

Fromm believed that pathological narcissism could manifest itself in large groups of people just as it could in individuals. Fromm referred to such narcissism as "social narcissism," believing that "it plays as a source of violence and war" (p. 75). He pondered the seeming contradictions between personal and social forms of narcissism. How could individuals sacrifice personal narcissism to become part of something larger? Fromm concluded that:

> the survival of the group depends to some extent on the fact that its members consider its importance as great as or greater than that of their own lives, and furthermore that they believed in the righteousness, or superiority, of their group as compared with others.
>
> (p. 75)

Investment in group narcissistic identity offered people the energy to serve the group and to make severe sacrifices in its behalf.

In Fromm's conception of social narcissism, identification with the group that allowed its members to see themselves as superior or special in some form might represent "the only – often very effective – source of satisfaction" (p. 76) for those members of society deemed to be economically and/or culturally impoverished. Consensus about group values was often confounded with reason, the former imparting a sense of rationality to group choice. Reason was seen to be a casualty of group narcissism as was scientific attitude (critical thinking, robust skepticism, and attunement to reality), which Fromm thought imperiled the group's narcissistic belief system. "Lack of objectivity and rational judgement" were the "most obvious and frequent symptoms" (p. 81) of the pathology of group narcissism.

Fromm cautioned that "The highly narcissistic group is eager to have a leader with whom it can identify itself" (p. 83). Such a group could be expected to project its narcissism onto the leader. Fromm tells his readers that "in the very act of submission to the powerful leader, which is in depth an act of symbiosis and identification, the narcissism of the individual is transferred onto the leader" (p. 83). Dynamics that applied to individual narcissism also applied to group narcissism. Narcissistic injury that the group sustained or criticism directed towards it could be expected to evoke rage, the desire to annihilate, and revenge.

Malignant narcissism is only one of three processes in a triad of processes that Fromm identifies which eventuates in human evil or what he calls the "syndrome of decay" (p. 33). The first leg of this triad is orientation towards death (necrophilous) rather than life (biophilia). Fromm's grasp of death orientation implies not just a preoccupation with various manifestations of death itself, but also an inclination to turn away from activities or pursuits that foster healthy growth and expansion of the self and growth in others. He sometimes refers to these dimensions as love of death and love of life. From the perspective of death orientation, "force" (p. 36) is the power to transform a man from a living thing into a corpse. What Fromm characterizes as a "necrophilous" person is a person "who loves all that does not grow, all that is mechanical" (p. 37). Having is more important than being and emphasis is placed upon control as a means of compromising aliveness. Such a person "is in love with the killers and despises those who were killed" (p. 36). Necrophilous people "deal with murder, blood, corpses, skulls, feces; sometimes also with men transformed into machines or acting like machines" (p. 38). They are also people who strangle the joy out of life. At one point, Fromm reflects that "good is reverence for life" while evil "is all that stifles life, narrows it down, cuts it into pieces" (p. 43).

It is clear from reading Fromm that he accords love of life – love of death as a separate dimension and separate force within the human psyche even though many of the characteristics of love of death can be seen to overlap those of malignant narcissism. Fromm related his conception of love of life – love of death to some of Freud's original conceptions of a life instinct and a death instinct. Unlike Freud, Fromm considered that "the death instinct represents psychopathology and not ... a part of normal biology" (p. 46). Life instinct or what he would refer to as love of life represented "the primary potentiality in man..." (p. 46). Fromm admitted that he was at a loss to provide a "full answer" to the question, what induces a man to adopt one orientation in preference to the other? As he thought about modern life, however, he observed that:

> In giant centers of production, giant cities, giant countries, men are administered as if they were things; men and their administrators are

transformed into things, and they obey the law of things. But man is not meant to be a thing; he is destroyed if he becomes a thing; before that is accomplished, he becomes desperate and wants to kill all life.

(p. 53)

The third process or dimension that Fromm identified as making its contribution to the syndrome of decay was a variable he referred to as "incestuous symbiosis" (p. 91). It, too, very much represented a separate third force that was possessed of the potentiality to render human nature evil.

Fromm also related incestuous symbiosis to the pre-Oedipal phase of attachment that both sexes must experience, though in this instance emphasis was placed upon the seductive allure of unification with an all-powerful other as opposed to the desire to over-invest in one's importance and shut out the rest of the world. He believed "that the boy's or girl's pre-Oedipus attachment to mother is one of the central phenomena in the evolutionary process and one of the main causes of neurosis or psychosis" (p. 93). He explained that

this incestuous striving, in the pre-genital sense, is one of the most fundamental passions in men and women, comprising the human being's desire for protection, the satisfaction of his narcissism; his craving to be freed from the risks of responsibility, of freedom, of awareness; his longing for unconditional love, which is offered without any expectation of his loving response.

(p. 93)

Such craving, Fromm thought, also infected mature men and women who, although in a different fashion than an infant might be, were also subject to terrible life uncertainties and to forces that they could not control. Awareness of the profound vulnerabilities attending the human condition produced deep yearning for protection, for safety, and for an enveloping symbiosis that man could rely on to weather the many storms that beset him, Fromm thought. Such cravings, however, rendered mankind susceptible to symbiotic yearning that affiliation with clan, nation, race, religion, or God could offer. And, one could add, to the enticement to surrender to malignant narcissistic leadership.

Fromm was also careful to point out that the desire for symbiotic unification was a fraught process, one imbued with promise of ecstasy and with threat of annihilation to the self. Symbiosis could mean that one was larger, possessed of a sense of power and authority that far exceeded normal human prerogative, or it could expose one to an annihilation of sorts, a death of self that unfolded as one gave up the self to the symbiotic other.

As he had when he conceptualized narcissism and love of life – love of death, he framed incestuous symbiosis as a spectrum that extended from more benign forms to more malignant ones. In its most malignant form, incestuous symbiosis could be expected to subvert reason and rationality;

symbiotic embrace demanded that one surrender independent judgement and thought to the realities that the symbiotic entity clove to. Turning towards reason meant exposing oneself to the painful aloneness that one was attempting to avoid through unification with a powerful other. Malignant forms of incestuous symbiosis also prevented one from experiencing other human beings as fully human. Fromm reflected that "only those who share the same blood or soil are thought and felt to be human; the 'stranger' is a barbarian" (p. 104). The final manifestation of malignant symbiosis was the compromise of independence and integrity. The symbiotically bound person was not free to have a conviction of his own.

Fromm believed that the more malignant one's orientation on any one of the three major dimensions of human experience that he described (love of life – love of death, narcissism, and incestuous symbiosis), the more likely one was to demonstrate malignancy on the remaining two. As he would put it, malignancy on one meant that malignancy on all three began to converge, producing a syndrome of decay that was deeply toxic and that fatally compromised human potentiality to move towards independence, growth of selfhood, and respect for other identities. Man's ability to exercise freedom of choice diminished the more malignant he became; the more he moved towards life, towards separateness, towards engagement with others, the more he maximized the possibility of choice and of free will. He also imagined, somewhat paradoxically, that as humankind became deeply life-affirming, it would be increasingly difficult for mankind to make self-destructive choices. His discussion of free will in the latter part of his book is, for me, one of the most thoughtful and nuanced reflections on this very complex and challenging theme that I've had the pleasure to read.

Fromm's formulation of evil and of malignant narcissism, in particular, will strike one, as the reader moves through this literature review, as more intricate, more elaborate, and in some ways more nuanced than the work of many other authors. In my estimate, it is an extraordinary piece of work that attests not only to his humanity, but to the passion that informed his efforts to grasp who we really are, including our best parts and our darkest and most lethal parts.

Although he did not specifically name malignant narcissism in his 1971 article focusing on the psychoanalytic concept of the life-and-death instinct, Herbert Rosenfeld appeared to be referring to a similar concept when he alluded to a form of narcissism typified by a "psychotic structure organization" (p. 175). He explained that this psychotic structure was "like a delusional world or object" that "appears to be dominated by an omnipotent or omniscient extremely ruthless part of the self" free to indulge itself in sadistic behavior (p. 175). This psychotic organization, Rosenfeld believed, was utterly committed to "narcissistic self-sufficiency" (p. 175) and, as such, could be expected to resist healthy dependency and recognition of another's value. The destructive impulses embodied in this psychotic structure could be "overwhelmingly cruel"

(p. 175). Such a patient, however, might experience his harrowing (to others) omnipotence as promising "quick, ideal solutions to all his problems" (p. 175). In such a manner, the patient was seduced into surrendering that part of him which yearned for connection and the sustenance that benevolent others could provide, replacing it with ever-growing commitment to unfettered narcissistic grandiosity and cruelty. As Rosenfeld said, it was as if the sanest part of the individual's personality was "persuaded to turn away from the external world and give itself up entirely to the dominion of the psychotic delusional structure" (p. 175). Losing the "sane, dependent" parts of himself meant that the patient also compromised his "capacity for thinking" (p. 175).

In his reflections on the life-and-death instinct, he also somewhat famously alluded to destructive narcissism as being highly organized, as if one were dealing with "a powerful gang dominated by a leader who controls all the members of the gang to see that they support one another in making the criminal destructive work more effective and powerful" (p. 174). It was less clear, however, when he made this statement whether he was referring to the psychotic narcissistic structure he delineated towards the end of his paper.

In a 1964 paper, which served as a precursor to his 1971 paper on life-and-death instinct, Rosenfeld focused on the crucial role that omnipotence plays in narcissistic structures as well as identifying core defensive operations of narcissistic personality, including introjection, projection, and projective identification. His discussion of narcissistic dynamics made it clear that splitting was among the signature defenses manifest in narcissism. He also commented that

> in severe narcissistic disturbances we can invariably see maintenance of a rigid defense against any awareness of psychic reality, since any anxiety which is aroused by conflicts between parts of the self or between self and reality is immediately evacuated.
>
> (p. 333)

He added that "the anxiety which is ... defended against is mainly of a paranoid nature ..." Later in this article, he reflected that "the ideal self-image of the narcissistic patient may be thought of as a highly pathological structure based on the patient's omnipotence and denial of reality" (p. 336). One did not know whether these comments might have reflected a premonitory allusion to the psychotic narcissistic structure he was to describe in his 1971 paper.

Edith Weigert (1970, pp. 119–136) appeared to conceive of malignant narcissism within the framework of an ego psychology orientation. Benign narcissism unfolded in response to adequate synthesis and integration of the ego's abilities and skill sets, producing an individual who had trust and confidence in their ability to manage the challenges that life presented them. Malignant narcissism, in contrast, was a consequence of a "weak" ego, one in which consolidation of successfully sublimated ego strengths was relatively impaired, leaving the individual beset by emotions like "anxiety, doubt, anger, rage, hatred, shame, and guilt..." (p. 123). In response, the ego's diminished means of dealing with reality meant that it was subject to "disorganized fight and flight reactions" (p. 123) in the face of a perceived emergency. She elaborated, while reflecting upon psychotic states, that:

> Instead of realistic appraisal of the ego, the emotional self-assessment escapes into hypochondriac or self condemning orgies of frustration rage, or this rage is compensatorily denied in fantasies of grandiosity and omnipotence that set up the false self of a more or less malignant narcissism that denies the defeat of the ego....
>
> (p. 130)

Her conception of malignant narcissism is obviously much more limited in its scope then other formulations contained in this review; it does not attempt to address the breadth of destructiveness to the human community other clinicians found to be a prominent part of their versions of malignant narcissism, instead largely restricting itself to the implications of a developmentally weak ego structure. She did go on to comment, however, that this "negative narcissism is at the core of neurotic and psychotic maladjustments" (p. 127), thereby establishing the foundational role her construct of malignant narcissism could play in human suffering.

Psychiatrist Otto Kernberg conceptualized malignant narcissism as the intersection of what he variously referred to as pathological narcissism and Narcissistic Personality Disorder with severe antisocial behavior, significant paranoid trends, and ego syntonic aggression that could be directed towards either self or others (1984). His conception of pathological narcissism was first articulated at length in his 1970 paper, "Factors in the Psychoanalytic Treatment of Narcissistic Personalities." He said of this group of people that their main characteristics are "grandiosity, extreme self-centeredness, and a remarkable absence of interest in and empathy for others in spite of the fact that they are still very eager to obtain admiration and approval from other people" (p. 52). Contempt, exploitation of others, intense pervasive envy, boredom side-by-side diminished capacity to eke lasting psychic sustenance from their lives, and an impoverished inner life devoid of "good objects" (internal representations of rewarding, fulfilling relationships) all typified the malignant narcissist's enduring state of being. Kernberg believed that their inability to experience sadness, mournful longing, and depression were "a basic feature of their personalities" (p. 53). Such people had endured a "fusion of ideal self, ideal object, and actual self-image as a defense against an intolerable reality in the interpersonal realm..." (p. 55). They were complete and flawless unto themselves. Having thus assured themselves of their own grandiosity and perfection, they could protect themselves against ever having to acknowledge their need for other people.

Kernberg described pathological narcissists as "orally fixated," by which he meant that they were voraciously, unsustainably hungry for the psychic and material supplies that they craved; frustration of such needs could be expected to produce rage. In his original paper, he also conceptualized antisocial personality as a subgroup of narcissistic personality because both groups were typified by similar characteristics. In his article, "Malignant Narcissism: Concealed Side of Psychopathy" (2019). Saeed Shafti argued that the similarity between the "core structure of primary sociopathy and morbid narcissism is more than a minor overlap." He felt that commonality between the two diagnostic categories was "based on an identical deficit, which may be indicated as a lack or shortfall of superego" (p. 16314).

In his remarkable 1970 paper, Kernberg pointed out structural similarities between pathological narcissism and borderline personality organization. Each was felt to demonstrate reliance on primitive defenses, including splitting, denial, projective identification, omnipotence, and primitive idealization. Both groups were also seen to instigate conflict fueled by oral rage.

He further elaborated his appreciation of what the inner life of people presenting pathological narcissism was like in this seminal work. The interior of the pathological narcissist was largely devoid of good objects – representations of sustaining and rewarding relationships – instead filled with idealized representations of the self, "shadows" of the people the narcissist exploited whose only value lay in their ability to feed him, and dreaded enemies. Underpinning the pathological narcissist's blighted interior was the "image of a hungry, enraged, empty self, full of impotent anger at being frustrated, and fearful of the world which seems as hateful and revengeful as the patient himself" (p. 57). He elaborated that psychotherapeutic endeavor revealed "a picture of a worthless, poverty-stricken, empty person who feels always left 'outside,' devoured by envy of those who have food, happiness, and fame" (p. 58). Narcissistic defenses primarily served the function of protecting this emaciated core.

Finally, I shall mention one other important facet of Kernberg's foundational work. He focused attention upon the potential etiology of pathological narcissism. He speculated that

> it is hard to evaluate to what extent (the development of pathological narcissism) represents a constitutionally determined strong aggressive drive, a constitutionally determined lack of anxiety tolerance in regard to aggressive impulses, or severe frustration in their first years of life.
>
> (p. 58)

With respect to the latter possibility, it struck him that chronically cold parental figures possessed of intense covert aggression could often be identified in the history of the pathological narcissist. Usually, the pivotal parental figure was a mother who appeared to function well, but who was possessed of "a degree of callousness, indifference, and nonverbalized spiteful aggression" (p. 59) that produced intense oral frustration, resentment, and aggression in the affected child. The child's deprivation set the stage, Kernberg thought, for a need to "defend against extreme envy and hatred" (p. 59). Kernberg added that in his experience such children often demonstrated unusual character- istics that earmarked them as especially attractive or talented. The mother's narcissistic exploitation of such qualities invited the child to feel "special," thereby setting the stage for the child to pursue "compensatory admiration and greatness..." (p. 59). The presence of such recognizable, exploitable talent helped divert the child towards pathological narcissism rather than borderline personality organization.

Most of Kernberg's ideas in his 1970 paper were replicated in Chapter 8 in his 1975 book, *Borderline Conditions and Pathological Narcissism*. In Chapter 9 of this same book, he elaborated upon the differences between narcissistic person- ality structure and borderline personality organization. The former, he felt, was typified by "an integrated, although highly pathological grandiose self" (p. 265). The inherently fragmented, emaciated self representations that characterized pathological narcissism, in other words, were bound together by the grandiose self; in this way the pathological narcissist could protect himself against the mea- sure of identity diffusion and compromised function reflected in a borderline state.

In his paper on the almost untreatable narcissistic patient (2007), Kernberg cautioned that pathological narcissism which assumed the form of malignant narcissism was "at the very limit of what we can reach (psychother- apeutically)" (p. 527). He also warned about the inherent risks therapists can find themselves exposed to with such patients – risks that included litigious- ness, potentiality of harm to the therapist, the relative ease with which thera- pists could be drawn into sadomasochistic exchanges with patients, and the therapist's fear of and discomfort with sadistic imagery, which work with such patients could readily evoke. The presence of these risks could significantly compromise the sense of safety a therapist required in order to do his or her work with this group of people.

In his 1989 paper on "The Temptation of Conventionality," Kernberg called attention to the danger of malignant narcissistic leadership, stating that

> under conditions of social upheaval, turmoil or stress and in the presence of a powerful paranoid leadership, the group (can shift) into the opposite extreme of endorsing a primitive, powerful, sadistic leader who will assure the group that, by identifying collectively with the threatening primitive aggression he incorporates, they will be safe from persecution by becoming persecutors themselves.
>
> (p. 202)

Kernberg further elaborated many of these ideas in his 2003 papers on sanc- tioned social violence: part 1 and part 2. In part 1, he warned about the inherent narcissistic and paranoid, regressive pull in group process that could lead to the expression of both tyranny and violence. Surrender of self to group identity entailed movement back towards latency age functioning character-ized by concrete distinctions between good and bad, diminished tolerance for ambivalence and ambiguity, reduction of relationships to idealized and per-secutory figures, assumption of a "primitive morality in which the bad are punished and the good always triumph" (p. 689), profound repression of the linkage between eroticism and tenderness in sexuality, analization of sexuality linking sex with excretory functions, an inability to tolerate emotional depth, and a desire to consolidate autonomy and, by implication, identity by embracing the mores and values that group membership offers.

Kernberg believed that the nature and extent of the group's regressive pull dictated its choice of leader; when a group was significantly distressed by a chaotic or confused social context, a narcissistic leader could be expected to be sought out, and when a group felt itself beset by significant threat, a paranoid leader was likely to be chosen. The existence of a paranoid ideology that "explains to a mass its origin and sense, its purpose and future, may contribute to the severe paranoid regression of an entire community or an entire nation" (p. 690). Leaders who demonstrated a "pathological con-densation of narcissistic and paranoid features in the syndrome of malignant narcissism" (p. 693) represented the worst case but often typical scenario of autocratic leadership. Hitler and Stalin were two such examples. Post (2008) offered a similar diagnostic impression of Kim Jong il.

From Kernberg's perspective,

> the leader characterized by malignant narcissism experiences and expresses an inordinate grandiosity, needs to be loved, admired, feared, and submitted to at the same time, cannot accept submission from others except when it is accompanied by intense idealizing loyalty and abandonment of all inde-pendent judgement, and experiences any manifestation contrary to his wishes as a sadistic, wilful, grave attack against himself.
>
> (p. 693 of part 1)

Terror was the inevitable byproduct of such leadership. A community led by the malignant narcissist combined "totally subservient, idolizing subjects, with totally corrupt and ruthless antisocial characters whose pretense of loving and submitting to the leader permits their parasitic enjoyment of his power" (p. 693). Kernberg identified several factors that might create vulnerability to pathologi-cal leadership, including defeat in war, persecution of a religious minority, brutal suppression by an alternative racial group, historical trauma associated with transgenerational effects, and breakdown or disorganization of a "traditional, powerfully structured and socially stable system of government…" (p. 695). As various targeted groups of people suffer grievous injury, the stage is set for them to identify themselves as aggressors in the future, turning the tables on those who have persecuted them, in the process extending conflict and brutality in endless cycles. Kernberg reiterated many of the ideas contained in part 1 in his later 2020 article, "Malignant Narcissism and Large Group Regression."

In part 2 of his paper on sanctioned social violence, Kernberg attempts to further delineate the internal world of the torturer and the terrorist. He cautioned that immersion in a social structure defined by totalitarian ideology that promises opportunities for the exercise of absolute power provides individuals who can be described as malignant narcissists with unfettered means to express their sadism. At first possibly taking pleasure in sadistic acts, their aggression may no longer yield sadistic gratification, instead becoming "mechanized and totally devoid of relationship to an object" (2003, p. 954). Kernberg posited that "eventually the extent of power exerted may compensate for the meaninglessness of murder with the intoxicating conviction of total dominance over the world, and freedom from essential fears of pain or death" (p. 954). The world that he was describing, he felt, was consistent with the intrapsychic world that Chasseguet-Smirgel (1984) had attributed to personalities Kernberg recognized as being malignant narcissists. It was a world that was characterized by an inability to appreciate boundaries or differentiation between objects and that was heavily infiltrated with anal sadistic imagery. None of the "objects" in this world were imbued with humanity or value; all of them were reducible to feces and could be treated accordingly. Poignantly and somewhat chillingly Kernberg commented that in this psychological space "human beings may be treated as inanimate objects, with a thoughtless, even bored dispensation of death" (p. 953).

Interestingly, Kernberg referenced Dicks' 1972 study of concentration camp prison guards, noting that Dicks discovered that guards presented severe personality disorders Kernberg found to be consistent with his appreciation of malignant narcissism. Dicks also reported that guards had emerged from traumatic backgrounds marked by extremely sadistic and controlling fathers and unloving or unavailable mothers. Dicks observed that once prison guards were not operating within the universe of unconstrained power the camp represented, they no longer seemed violent or dangerous.

Turning to Sofsky's 1997 sociological analysis, Kernberg reiterated Sofsky's assertion that absolute power effectively deconstructs virtually all "ordinary" human values. Later in his paper, Kernberg emphasized that "democracy as an ideology cannot aspire to the dynamic force of totalitarian fundamentalism" (2003, p. 959). Totalitarian fundamentalism, in turn, is most dangerously impelled by paranoid vision with its mistrust of otherness. It was his appreciation that

> the problem of alien cultures has become an urgently pressing one, as major migrations of population from one country to another and, particularly, from different ethnic, religious, linguistic, racial, and cultural groups, have been taking place all over the world.
>
> (p. 962)

I think these comments are profoundly important and profoundly prophetic.

Kernberg cautioned that his appreciation of the kind of personalities he referenced in his paper that were drawn to engagement with terrorism and violence, not all of which I have articulated, represented only a limited vista of possibilities that was most reflective of the psychoanalytic viewpoint. Emerging understanding deriving from a number of different social science disciplines would eventually flesh out the important questions he was attempting to address.

Psychoanalyst Heinz Kohut, like Kernberg, devoted a substantial part of his professional life to developing an understanding of narcissism.

In contrast to Kernberg's structural approach (id, ego, superego) and investment in drive theory, Kohut (1975d) posited the possibility of a "rudimentary self" (p. 756) at the very beginning of life and a complementary drive to take pleasure in aloneness and separateness. He added that "The self... does not seek pleasure through stimulation and tension discharge; it strives for fulfilment through the realization of its nuclear ambitions and ideals" (p. 757). The self that Kohut envisioned was informed by two fundamental fears: fear of annihilation/ disintegration and fear of the despair that failure to consummate the potentialities of the authentic self could generate (his so-called "Tragic Man"). His concept of self was at the very heart of his understanding of narcissism.

Kohut's conception of the analytic process required to treat NPD successfully was at odds with Kernberg's model of treatment; in a lengthy section in his book, *Severe Personality Disorders*, Kernberg outlined his objections to the Kohutian approach, detailing, from his perception, its various shortfalls. In an act of what can fairly be perceived as frustration, Kohut expressed his exasperation with the misperceptions and misattributions others had relegated to his treatment process. His comments (1981, 2010) were made only several days before his death:

'These idiots, they don't read what I write!' But again I should have listened... They will claim that empathy cures. They will claim that one has to be just 'empathic' with one's patients and they'll be doing fine. I don't believe that at all! What do I believe?... I submit that the most important point that I made was that analysis cures by giving explanations – interventions on the level of interpretation; not only by 'understanding,' not by repeating and confirming what the patient feels and says, that's only the first step; but then (the analyst has) to move (on) and give interpretation. In analysis an interpretation means an explanation of what is going on in genetic, dynamic and psycho economic terms... A good analyst reconstructs the childhood past in the dynamics of the current transference with warmth, with understanding for the intensity of the feelings, and with the fine understanding of the various secondary conflicts that intervene as far as the expression of these (childhood wishes and needs) are concerned.

(1969–1970, p. 124 and 128)

How surprising, then, to discover, through the agency of two articles Kohut wrote that Daniel Shaw had identified in the bibliography of his book, *Traumatic Narcissism*, that not only had Kohut written about a form of malignant narcissism (I erroneously didn't think that he had), but that his formulation of the same was in many respects very similar to Kernberg's (and in some regards, to Fromm's as well). As Kohut talked about his appreciation of his version of this variant of narcissism, one very much had the sense that he meant to distinguish it from other forms of NPD that he attempted to work with and conceptualize.

Kohut (1976) made reference to "certain types of narcissistically fixated persons (even bordering on the paranoid) ..." (p. 825). He identified his group of narcissists as charismatic and messianic narcissists, writing that neither was "likely to become willing subjects of the psychoanalyst's clinical scrutiny" (p. 830). Feeling that his clinical experience at least allowed him to draw tentative conclusions about these types of personalities, he went on to suggest that:

> These persons appear to have no dynamically effective guilt feelings and never suffer any pangs of conscience about what they are doing. They are sensitive to injustices done to them, quick to accuse others – and very persuasive in the expression of their accusations – and thus are able to evoke guilt feelings in others, who tend to respond by becoming submissive to them and by allowing themselves to be treated tyrannically by them.
>
> (p. 830)

In the same paragraph he made reference to the "evilness" that such people enacted.

He added that:

> The dynamic essence of their current behaviour appears to me to lie in a stunting of their empathic capacity: they understand neither the wishes nor the frustrations and disappointments of other people. At the same time, their sense of legitimacy of their own wishes and their sensitivity to their own frustrations are intense.
>
> (p. 830)

It struck him that such people "assert their own perfection, and they demand full control over the other person... without regard for his rights as an independent person" (p. 831). Such messianic and charismatic narcissists were felt to "fully identify themselves with either their grandiose self (here Kohut seemed to be referring to the charismatic narcissist) or their idealized superego (Kohut's reference to messianic narcissism)." Reliance on the grandiose self or the idealized superego as a means of protecting self-esteem, however, deprived such personalities of elasticity.

He characterized charismatic and messianic narcissists as living in an "archaic world" (p. 831), one that had inflicted devastating narcissistic injury on them by having withdrawn empathic response after teasing them with a modicum of security and delight very early in their lives. Narcissistic injury could take the form of withdrawal or absence of mirroring responses (mother's warm smile confirming value and competence) or through failure on the adult caretaker's part to offer merger experiences (hugging or holding, for example) necessary for a sense of security. The abrupt, damaging withdrawal of narcissistic sustenance "and what the world judges to be their present misdeeds is to them the expression of justified narcissistic demands" (p. 832). They become "super empathic with themselves and with their own needs and they have remained enraged about a world that has tried to take from them something they consider to be rightfully their own..." (p. 832). Kohut felt that the child with unusual congenital gifts would be in a position to assume "prematurely and in toto the function that the archaic self objects should still have performed for him" (p. 832).

Kohut was clearly deeply concerned about the damage that such people could inflict on broader society should they occupy positions of leadership. He drew his reader's attention to what he felt were two critical questions: "How do the characteristic psychological features of the messianic and charismatic person dovetail with widespread yearning for archaic omnipotent figures? And what are the specific historical circumstances that tend to increase this yearning?"

He proposed a concept of a "group self" (p. 837) whose dynamics would unfold in much the same way that was analogous to the self of the individual. He also suggested that group pressure diminishes individuality; "it leads to a primitivization of the mental processes" (p. 839) that could potentiate "cathartic expression of archaic... impulses, emotions, and ideation..." (p. 839). Awareness of all the dynamics that govern an individual self meant that one could "observe the group self as it is formed, as it is held together, as it oscillates between fragmentation and reintegration, as it shows regressive behaviour when it moves toward fragmentation..." (p. 838). He believed that in applying psychoanalytic knowledge it might be possible to make "a contribution to the explanation of historical events, of the course... of history" (p. 836). His aim was no less than "man's mastery over his historical destiny" (p. 836). It is significant, I believe, that his expressed need for a psycho-historian emerged in the context of his discussion of charismatic and messianic narcissism. He clearly understood the dangers that each posed to our survival.

Kohut's essay "On Leadership," written in the late 1960s but not first published until after his death in 1985, extends and elaborates his concerns about pathological forms of narcissistic leadership. He warned that:

> Narcissistic leader figures of this type experience the social surroundings as part of themselves. The mere fact that other groups, nationalities, or

races are different from themselves, do not react as they expect them to react is a deep personal affront, the frightening, inimical disturbance of their solipsistic universe. The situation can only be remedied by wiping out those who dare to be different.

(p. 107)

The narcissistic leader imbued with paranoia was particularly dangerous because "They are principally united by their sharing of an archaic narcissistic conception of the world that must destroy those who are different and by the identity of their grandiose fantasies embodied in their leader" (p. 107).

He foresaw that the individual who had endured narcissistic injury themselves might "seek to melt into the body of a powerful nation (as symbolized by a grandiose leader) to cure their shame and provide them with the feeling of enormous strength, to which they react with relief and triumph" (p. 110). He later contended that "The most malignant human propensities are mobilized in support of nationalistic narcissistic rage" (p. 117). Ideals that a pathologically narcissistic leader proposed were nothing more than a "delinquent ego's attempts to justify its misdeeds" (page 122).

As he considered his formulation of pathological leadership in the context of what he understood about the way in which healthy change unfolds in individual therapy, he seemed at times to despair about humankind's ability to successfully reflect upon its potentiality for destructiveness. One can feel him struggling to find answers that might offer hope for a better future.

Frederick Burkle (2015) conceived of the destructive personalities that typified tyrannical leaders as an intersection between Antisocial Personality Disorder (ASPD) and pathological narcissism. Initially presenting themselves as "saviors," such personalities inevitably proved themselves to be despots. Hitler, Mussolini, and Stalin were cited as examples. He reflected that

while my experience and that of others would suggest that in practice the degree of narcissistic behaviour in Narcissistic Personality Disorder remains somewhat stable over time, the potential for an abrupt worsening of narcissistically driven behaviour is always present and may shift along the spectrum to Antisocial Personality Disorder.

(p. 9)

He added that the terms "ASPD, sociopathy, and psychopathy are often used interchangeably in the peer-reviewed literature" (p. 9). He also noted that there was considerable overlap between the characteristics of Narcissistic Personality Disorder and psychopathy. He argued that among the array of personal deficits presented, "Those with ASPD have no personal or social conscience" (p. 11). Indeed, as one read Burkle, the distinctions he was drawing between NPD and psychopathy/ASPD remained somewhat unclear for me. As his article developed itself, he made more references to ASPD and tyrannical leadership than he did to the narcissistic elements of such person-alities. 21st-century examples of tyrants included Kim Jong-il, Milosevic, Saddam Hussain, and Putin, among others. He warned that "ASPD leader-ship needs to be managed as both a global security and strategic priority" (p. 30). He considered various steps that could be taken to identify, deal with, and mitigate ASPD leadership.

Psychoanalyst Daniel Shaw expressed his preference for the use of the term traumatizing narcissism to either malignant or pathological narcissism, feel-ing that the former clearly differentiated the narcissistic form he wanted to explore from other conceptions of narcissism, such as Bach's deflated narcis-sist, Kohut's shame-prone narcissist, and Rosenfeld's thin-skinned narcissist. He explained:

> The term 'pathological narcissist,' often used to describe this set of char-acter structures, is also used, problematically, to label and describe the people he typically exploits and victimizes, whose sense of self-esteem he has traumatically destabilized.
>
> (Shaw, 2014, p. 11)

He also expressed another reservation about using the terms pathological narcissism and malignant narcissism, commenting that he was "frustrated with the pejorative description of these patients as pathological, destructive narcissists," feeling that these terms belied "the gravity and the extent of developmental trauma they have suffered" (p. 17).

As he mentioned at various points in his book, traumatizing narcissists were unlikely to present themselves for treatment and, even when they did, were unlikely to transcend their pain or their mode of relating to others. Usually, they presented themselves in treatment because they hoped to estab-lish an alliance with the therapist to further support their self-justification, their presentation as victim, or to establish the legitimacy of their position, not to change and grow.

Shaw went on to describe the traumatizing narcissist as the "predominantly overinflated, entitled, grandiose narcissist" (p. 12) who attacks, shatters, and suppresses others' subjectivity, displacing the legitimacy and authority of the other person's inner experience with the feelings and perceptions that the traumatizing narcissist imposes through acts of domination, typically to satisfy needs to control and exploit. Traumatizing narcissists demonstrated intractable investment in their own grandiosity, delusional infallibility and entitlement, and in externalization of shame. Shame was so poorly tolerated, Shaw argued, that unless the traumatizing narcissist could protect himself from self-loathing by diminishing others, "literally, mortification, or (psychic) death by shame" could occur (p. 35). The other in a relationship with the traumatizing narcissist could "either kneel at the throne or be banished, dis-inherited" (p. 104). Shaw distinguished the traumatizing narcissist from the psychopath by suggesting that the former creates harm through a "delusional conviction of righteousness" while the latter's efforts to inflict harm are "thoroughly deliberate" (p. 149).

While discussing Fromm, Shaw referred to the trauma that the traumatizing narcissist inflicts as a "rape" of personhood and subjectivity (p. 58). To further emphasize the devastation that compromised subjectivity created, later in his book Shaw referenced Shengold's (1989) characterization of such "interior violence as 'soul murder'," reiterating the poignancy and the devastating nature of the injury that is inflicted (p. 71).

Shaw explained that:

> Narcissism that is traumatic describes a kind of relationship, in which the traumatizing narcissist relates in particular ways towards others for particular purposes.
>
> (p. 12)

Shaw identified what he felt the potential precursors of traumatizing narcissism might be, citing "cumulative relational trauma throughout the developmental years in the form of chronic shaming at the hands of parents and/or other significant caregivers who are severely narcissistically disturbed," thereby identifying narcissistic disorder as potentially self-perpetuating. He added that

> the traumatizing narcissistic parent envies and resents the child's right to dependency, and demands, covertly or overtly, that the child recognizes the exclusive validity of the parent's needs and wishes – which means of course that the child is to be ashamed of her own needs and desires and view them as the parent does – as irrelevant, or as contemptible; i.e., greedy, selfish, weak, morally abhorrent.
>
> (p. 34)

Such a child learns that dependency is worthy of contempt and shame, in response possibly adopting "rigid, manic defenses" that disavow susceptibility to dependence. Shaw deemed that an individual who chose such a course was now primed to become a traumatizing narcissist him or herself.

Unlike other psychoanalytic theorists who focused on distortions unfolding at critical developmental phases in the child's early experience, Shaw emphasized destructive systems of relatedness as setting the stage for human pain. At the core of people's vulnerability and their potentiality was their need both to feel loved and to feel that their love mattered to the person that they cared about. Moreover, these twin needs were felt to be an inherent part of the human condition, manifesting themselves in the very earliest part of life experience in the child's relationship with his or her caretakers. In his view, appreciation of the foundational part love plays in human development and in psychotherapy as a healing endeavor had frequently been an awkward topic that could evoke discomfort and censure amongst many psychoanalytic thinkers, some of whom placed greater emphasis on libidinal and aggressive drives as determinants of both human suffering and creativity. Only by according the desire to both give and receive love the importance that it deserved, Shaw believed, could one hope to appreciate the complex relational patterns that characterized the human experience. Love, in turn, represented a willingness to respect and enhance the other's uniqueness and subjectivity. This "relational turn" in psychoanalytic thinking most closely approximates my orientation to the work that I undertake as a clinician and as a theorist.

Numerous clinician authors who contributed to *The Dangerous Case of Donald Trump* attempted to make diagnostic sense of the dangerous personality they believed Trump possessed. Their efforts are instructive, reflecting diversities of viewpoint that continue to characterize our grasp of how a dangerous personality like Trump's is organized. Keep in mind that all of them are focusing their diagnostic acumen on a single individual whose behavior is now well documented and has become a part of the public domain for all of us to consider. Each practitioner makes cogent arguments, but no clear consensus emerges about what diagnosis is most appropriate or even whether diagnosis, as opposed to dangerousness, is relevant. The lack of consensus that emerges is generally reflective of the state of our knowledge about pathological leadership; there is a great deal that we can agree upon and a great deal that we cannot, largely because we haven't satisfied ourselves that we fully understand what we're seeing. Malignant narcissism is certainly one – but only one – of the constructs practitioners rely upon to try to understand who Trump is and why he operates as he does.

Craig Malkin (2017), a clinical psychologist who wrote a chapter in *Dangerous Case*, references malignant narcissism, which he sees as the intersection between psychopathy and pathological narcissism. Pathological narcissism manifests itself as a variant on the extreme end of the narcissism spectrum that he believed would earn a diagnosis of Narcissistic Personality Disorder (NPD). Briefly, he typified NPD patients as manifesting three prominent characteristics: entitlement, exploitation, and empathy impairment. Paranoia was considered to be an inherent or native feature of pathological narcissism.

In contrast to NPD, he saw psychopathy as marked "not by impaired or blocked empathy but a complete absence of it" (2017, p. 53), He considered that absence of empathy may be a consequence of brain dysfunction evident on neuroimaging that suggests "psychopaths don't experience emotions the same way non-psychopaths do" (p. 53). Malkin cautioned that malignant narcissism was not a formal diagnosis, but a "term coined by psychoanalyst Eric Fromm and elaborated on by personality disorder expert, Otto Kernberg, to describe people so driven by feeling special that they essentially see other people as pawns in the game of kill or be killed ..." (p. 53). In his view, people like Hitler, Kim Jong un, and Vladimir Putin all presented personality organizations consistent with the construct malignant narcissism.

Malkin took care to emphasize that mental illness in and of itself is not enough to establish incapacity to do an important job; what matters instead is our appreciation of the danger that a given personality represents to self and/or to others.

In his description of malignant narcissism, Malkin implicates both sadistic and paranoid components. He also anticipated that should a personality that might be characterized as malignantly narcissistic face significant challenge in its drive to establish and protect its status as inordinately special, a "psychotic spiral" (p. 56) could ensue marked by intensifying paranoia, projection, increasing lapses of judgement, escalating need to impress others, volatile decision-making, and gas lighting.

Psychotherapist Harper West (2017) reiterated the broad range of diagnoses/constructs various mental health professionals had assigned to Trump, including "Narcissistic Personality Disorder, Antisocial Personality Disorder, Paranoid Personality Disorder, Delusional Disorder, malignant narcissism, and some form of dementia" (p. 238). She argued that the most parsimonious way to understand Trump's behavior was to focus on the character flaw that is at the core of such personalities: other blaming.

Within her formulation, low self-worth is the cornerstone experience that sets the stage for poor shame tolerance and an associated consequence, an inability to tolerate blame or accountability. She maintained that "poor shame tolerance causes ... vindictive anger, lack of insight and accountability, dishonesty, impulsivity, entitlement, paranoia, lack of remorse and empathy, self-importance, and attention seeking" (p. 239). Moreover, other blamers "may adopt an aggressive dominating persona to protect themselves" (p. 239). Vulnerability in such personalities was poorly tolerated and self-awareness was experienced as shaming. Intolerance of self-awareness meant that such personalities avoided therapy.

She went on to speculate that people she called other-blamers were "likely exposed to developmental or attachment trauma, such as abusive, shaming, rejecting, or neglectful parenting" (p. 240). She felt that children exposed to trauma endured chronic fight or flight reactions and chronic exposure to fear response, leading to anxiety-based behaviors such as impulsivity, hyper-activity, irrationality, volatility, impetuousness, poor frustration tolerance, and poor concentration.

She believed that other blaming compromises compassion and empathy, leading to objectification and depersonalization of others. She cited Bancroft's (2002) comment that while objectification of others could protect the other blamer against guilt and empathy, it was the "critical reason" an abuser tends to get worse over time (p. 246).

Depersonalization and avoidance of accountability was thought to enhance entitlement. She suggested that other blamers could be expected to place a premium on loyalty, on isolating their partners, on a commitment to power and the right to misuse it, and on efforts to promote an image of success. She warned that other blamers who occupy positions of leadership could be expected to produce a loss of stability and empathy in the societies that they lead.

Psychoanalyst and psychologist Howard Covitz (2017) distanced himself from discussion of specific diagnoses, choosing instead to focus on Trump as suffering from an unspecified personality disorder.

In their prologue to the first edition of *Dangerous Case*, psychiatrists Judith Herman and Bandy Lee also sidestepped diagnosis of Trump, preferring instead to reference mental instability and evil:

> A man can be both evil and mentally compromised – which is a more frightening proposition. Power not only corrupts but also magnifies existing psychopathologies, even as it creates new ones… a political leader's grandiosity may morph into grotesque delusions of grandeur. Sociopathic traits may be amplified as a leader discovers that he can violate the norms of civil society and even commit crimes with impunity. And the leader who rules through fear, lies, and betrayal may become increasingly isolated and paranoid, as the loyalty of even his closest confidants must forever be suspect.
>
> (2017, p. lix)

Both Herman and Lee argued that assessment of dangerousness could be undertaken through appraisal of mental state and of actions. They concluded that "delusional levels of grandiosity, impulsivity, and the compulsions of mental impairment, when combined with an authoritative cult of personality and contempt for the rule of law, are a toxic mix," warning that "anyone as mentally unstable as Mr. Trump simply should not be entrusted with the life-and-death powers of the presidency" (p. lx).

My sense was that they avoided directing attention to a specific diagnosis both because they had not had direct opportunity to assess the president and perhaps because they felt it was more appropriate and more telling to focus on observable behaviors connoting risk than to tie risk to diagnosis.

Psychoanalyst Lance Dodes focused upon sociopathy as the construct that best captured Trump's clinical realities. He felt that the primary deficit in sociopathy was impairment in empathy. He noted that sociopathy was also marked by an absence of guilt, intentional manipulation, and controlling or even sadistically harming others for personal power or gratification. He saw sociopaths as lacking in those qualities that essentially render people human. He emphasized that successful sociopaths are able to generate an appearance of success because of their ability to cheat, to simulate caring, and to disguise their intentions, making it harder for others to recognize their craziness.

He brushed up against the term malignant narcissism, suggesting that sociopathy is a "major aspect" of that construct without providing further clarification. He appeared to imply, without saying so explicitly, that malignant narcissism could be construed as an intersection between narcissism and sociopathy.

Dodes linked the development of sociopathy to early, primitive emotional problems manifest in rage reactions in response to disappointments and an adherence to alternate realities as a means of protecting the self from actualities that the child did not like. He also cited research connecting sociopathy with disorders of the prefrontal cortex and the amygdala.

Dodes identified prominent defenses manifest in sociopathic personality, including projective identification and splitting. Projective identification, in contrast to projection, was seen to be a process in which the impulses or attributes one projected into another person were experienced as so dangerous and so threatening that they had the potential to incite the sociopath to attack others. Splitting that the sociopath relied upon was conceived as being an unstable process that divided the world into a shifting landscape of good and bad people who were variably experienced as presenting threat of attack, depending upon how they were perceived at any given point in time. The sociopath was viewed as feeling justified in rage reactions he or she developed towards scapegoated groups. Sociopaths could also be expected to demonstrate rage reactions to imagined slights, producing reckless, destructive behavior that compromised impulse control. Efforts to protect the self against challenges to the sociopath's interpretation of reality occasioned rationalization and outright lying. In Dode's view, the inability to accurately appraise the world and maintain genuine, reciprocal emotional relationships led to more paranoia.

One important defensive attribute of the sociopath was his or her ability to employ a predatory form of empathy, allowing the sociopath to identify vulnerabilities in a target personality. Sociopaths were said to engage in an endless quest for power and admiration, unmitigated by basic empathy or guilt.

Clinical Psychologist Dr. John Gartner (2017) directed his attention to malignant narcissism in his appraisal of Trump's personality. He began his chapter by drawing attention to Eric Fromm's depiction of malignant narcissism as the quintessence of evil. He noted that Otto Kernberg considered malignant narcissism as possessing four salient propensities: Narcissistic Personality Disorder; antisocial behavior; paranoid traits; and sadism. He referenced Kernberg's comment (Goode 2003) that malignantly narcissistic leaders like Hitler and Stalin had been "able to take control because their inordinate narcissism is expressed in grandiosity, a confidence in themselves, and the assurance that they know what the world needs." Both leaders expressed "their aggression in cruel and sadistic behaviour against their enemies: whoever does not submit to them or love them" (pp. 89–90). He also cited Pollock's (1978) observation that "the malignant narcissist is pathologically grandiose, lacking in conscience and behavioral regulation, with characteristic demonstrations of joyful cruelty and sadism" (Gartner, 2017, p. 90).

Gartner went on to systematically review each of the four components of malignant narcissism that Kernberg had included in his formulation. The combination of disorders that Gartner described as falling under the rubric of malignant narcissism could be expected to produce a leader who feels "omnipotent, omniscient, and entitled to total power; and who rages at being persecuted by imaginary enemies, including vulnerable minority groups..." (p. 92). Malignant narcissists could "harm others and enjoy doing so, showing little empathy or regret for the damage they have caused" (p. 93).

The confluence of psychological realities contributing to malignant narcissism meant, for Gartner, that narcissism and malignant narcissism "have about as much in common as a benign and malignant tumor" (p. 90). He reminded his readers that Fromm (1964) had asserted that malignant narcissism is "a psychiatric disorder that makes you evil" (p. 93). He warned that success emboldens the malignant narcissist to become even more grandiose, reckless, and aggressive. He also seemed to share Fromm's view that the malignant narcissist lives on the border of psychosis. Gardner suggested that it would be challenging to differentiate between lies the malignant narcissist told for political advantage versus lies that grew out of a genuine delusional disorder.

Whether as a component part of malignant narcissism or as a quality that had emerged in Trump as a genetically based predilection, Gardner observed that Trump appeared to be possessed of a hypomanic temperament compatible with dispositions early psychiatrists like Bleuler, Kraepelin, and Kretchmer had described (Bleuler, 1924; Kraepelin, 1908, 1921; Kretchmer 1925). He expressed concern that Trump's hypomanic bursts of activity often culminated in recklessness and poor judgement.

Gardner appears to agree with Fromm that malignant narcissism is a madness that tends to grow in the life of the affected person.

Clinical psychologist Michael J. Tansey took the position that Donald Trump's behavior could best be described by the "exceedingly rare diagnosis of delusional disorder..." (p. 104) Delusional disorder, he underscored, is "far more severe than what has widely been proposed as merely Narcissistic Personality Disorder, merely Antisocial Personality Disorder, or merely pathological lying" (p. 104). Besides being shrewd, calculating, and convinced that the truth is spoken only when it happens to coincide with his purposes – what Tansey referred to as being "crazy like a fox" – he also believed that Trump possessed a well-hidden, core grandiose and paranoid set of delusions that are disconnected from factual reality – or what he referred to as "crazy like a crazy" (p. 115).

Delusional disorder, he noted, was a psychotic disorder that compromised a given individual's appreciation of reality. He explained that delusions are beliefs "that exist despite indisputable, factual evidence to the contrary" (p. 105); that they are held with absolute certainty; that they can be built around a variety of themes, "including grandeur and persecution" (p. 105); that they are not manifestly bizarre; that deluded people tend to be extremely thin-skinned and humorless, particularly when others questioned the validity of their delusions; that delusional beliefs are central to the person's existence;

and, finally, that delusional disorder is "chronic, even lifelong, and tends to worsen in adulthood, middle-age, and beyond" (p. 106). People burdened with a delusional disorder elaborated delusional beliefs in a consistent and logical way. Tansey thought that the general logical reasoning and behavior of such people was unaffected "unless they are very specifically related to the delusion" (p. 106). He also explained that people with delusional disorders typically possessed a heightened sense of self reference, over investing trivial events with undeserved importance and meaning, especially if they contravened delusional premises. He warned that unlike schizophrenia, "delusional disorder is neither bizarre nor is it readily apparent to the outside observer" (p. 105).

For Tansey, delusional disorder captured an essential truth about Trump: that he was at times psychotic and incapable, in spite of the great responsibility he carried, of differentiating what was real from what was not.

Like Tansey, psychiatrist Henry J. Friedman (2017) focused upon the paranoid elements in Trump's presentation, suggesting that Trump appeared to demonstrate paranoid character structure. Individuals possessed of paranoid character structure could be expected to consistently produce ideas and responses that find exaggerated danger of malevolent intent in others and in the situations they encounter. He warned that the major totalitarian leaders of the 20th century manifested paranoid thinking and, moreover, that their destructive acts represented an enactment of their disturbed ideation. Friedman attributed the deaths of millions of people to such a dynamic, arguing that "pure paranoid based ruthlessness" rendered targeted groups of people enemies of the state (p. 156). Paranoid ideation effectively mobilizes both fear and hate, particularly in less well-educated segments of a given population; he expected that paranoid characters need to be able to identify an enemy against whom the paranoid character's hatred can be directed.

Somewhat like Tansey, Friedman felt that the focus on Trump's "so-called narcissism" (p. 157) minimized the significance of his paranoid beliefs, inducing others to overestimate the level of functioning of which he was truly capable. Friedman also echoed Tansey's caution that it would be easy for people to see Trump's behavior as an extension of political maneuvering as opposed to a reflection of the severe pathology inherent in his paranoid character structure. He considered that the interplay of forces inherent in leadership a paranoid character offered meant that there was likely an overlap of the paranoid leader's personal hatreds and those of his followers.

In his experience, treating people possessed of paranoid character was "always arduous and rarely effective" (p. 160). He added, significantly, that "any attempt to 'understand' Trump from the perspective of his childhood or of what he is re-enacting from his past is, in all probability, a hopeless and unnecessary task" (p. 161). He added that "character formation of the paranoid typology becomes so autonomous that, once it is solidified, it is practically meaningless to try to find an explanation for its existence in a particular individual" (p. 161).

Reflecting the wide diversity of opinion about legitimacy of diagnosis/formulation, psychiatrist James Gilligan (2017) redirected his reader's attention towards dangerousness. Feeling, in part, that diagnosis potentially carried with it the implication that insanity and violence are somehow inevitably confounded with one another, he asked his audience to consider that dangerousness was a more useful construct because, at least in Trump's case, incitement to violence and threats of violence were manifestly apparent, particularly towards perceived enemies. In this respect, he saw Trump's behavior as consistent with the dangerous behavior that dictators and autocrats manifested towards the people subjected to their power. He believed that judgements about unprecedented and abnormal dangerousness are necessary if societies are to protect themselves.

Psychotherapist Diane Jhueck re-framed Gilligan's emphasis on dangerousness. Noting that nearly half of all US presidents could be seen to have been struggling with mental illness (a percentage that would have been higher, she said, if mental illness diagnosis included personality disorders), she concluded that the important question to ask was whether the specific form of mental illness a given president manifested was a cause for concern about dangerousness. She wished to underscore that mental illness was not synonymous with either an inability to fulfil duties as a president or with destructive behavior.

Citing personal characteristics that she felt were consistent with narcissism and psychopathy (or possibly psychopathic tendencies), Jhueck identified a variety of behaviors she saw as manifestations of these forms of mental illness that constituted clear danger, not just to the citizens of the United States, but to the world at large. Mental health symptoms that implied dangerousness included, as a partial list, impulsive blame shifting, claims of unearned superiority, delusional levels of grandiosity, inability to tolerate criticism and perceived threats to his ego, an obsessive need to be admired, and a lack of insight and confirmation seeking that make certain mental disorders particularly dangerous in a position of power. Early in her chapter in *Dangerous Case* she referenced a study by Monahan in 2001 that potentially established high scores on the Hare Psychopathy Checklist as "more strongly associated with violence than any other risk factor we studied" (p. 176)

Psychotherapist Elizabeth Mika began her chapter by noting that "tyrannies are three-legged beasts (consisting of) three wobbly legs... the tyrant, his supporters (the people), and the society at large that provides a ripe ground for the collusion between them" (p. 289). Referencing Dr. Ian Hughes' work, she conveyed that political scientists call this three-legged beast "the toxic triangle" (p. 289). In her conception, the force binding all three legs of the toxic triangle was narcissism. Narcissism was also the force that rendered the insidious encroachment of tyranny so difficult to recognize. In such a fashion, she felt, tyrannical forces could reassert themselves successfully throughout the long course of human history.

Mika maintained that all tyrants "are predominantly men with a specific character defect, narcissistic psychopathy (a.k.a. malignant narcissism)" (p. 290). Included among the characteristics of malignant narcissism were severely impaired or absent conscience; an insatiable drive for power and adulation; the ability to use manipulative charm and a pretense of human ideals to pursue distinctly primitive goals; and a compulsion to treat other people as objects of need fulfilment and wish fulfilment. Malignant narcissism served the tyrant well in his quest for power, for adulation, and the right to exploit as well as containing the seeds of its own destruction. Unimpeded as they are by inhibition or scruples, tyrants were free to lie, cheat, manipulate, destroy and kill, but, notwithstanding the extraordinary power they accrued, they were fated to deconstruct themselves precisely because of the way they were organized as personalities.

Unlike many authors, Mika speculated about early precursors of malignant narcissism. Citing biographies of tyrants (Fromm 1973; Miller 1990; Newell 2016), she identified early manifestations of vanity, sensation seeking and impulsivity often accompanied by poor self-control, aggression, callousness, a strong competitive drive and a desire to dominate as prominent developmental characteristics of such people. She emphasized that

> it is impossible to rule out narcissistic upbringing as being involved in raising a future tyrant – creating a narcissistic injury that shaped the child's life and set him on a path of 'repairing' it through a ruthless and often sadistic pursuit of power and adulation – *even when there is no evidence of overt abuse and/or neglect in his biographical data*.
>
> (pp. 291–292, italics mine)

The point that she makes is reminiscent of Daniel Shaw's contention that traumatizing narcissism may be self-perpetuating primarily because it destroys the subjectivity of the other – a catastrophic yet perhaps largely invisible injury that would escape the biographer's eyes. She further speculated that narcissistic psychopaths/malignant narcissists might possibly arise from an impairment in the development of object constancy in affected children. Her comments were intriguing and hopefully will be the focus of further consideration she directs towards this subject in the future. Lastly, she wondered whether lack of empathy could emerge from an inborn cause or a narcissistic/authoritarian upbringing.

Somewhat like Hannah Arendt (1963) whose purveyors of evil could not think and feel, Mika was reminded of Burkle's (2015) appraisal that people possessed of impairments characteristic of malignant narcissism could be "smart but not bright" (p. 292). Referencing a passage in a paper that Dabrowski wrote in 1986 and that Mika translated for her chapter in *Dangerous Case*, she noted that intelligence is "subsumed under the primitive drives (for power, sex, and adulation)" (p. 292).

Mika considered different levels at which a malignant narcissist might function, varying from serial killers to tyrants. Tyrants possessed the right combination of manipulativeness, self-control and intelligence that allowed them to seduce others long enough to put their grandiose ideas to work on a large scale. The charisma that characterized tyrants was, simply, "the ability to tell others what they want to hear" (p. 292). Once in power, tyrants could fully unleash their sadism "under the cloak of perverted ideals, which they peddle as a cover for their primitive drives" (p. 292). Strong sadistic drives compelled the malignant narcissist to ruthlessly pit people against one another as a means of dominating and consolidating power.

The tyrant's followers could be expected to project their hopes and dreams onto him, finding that the more grandiose his sense of his own self and his promises are, the greater their attraction and the stronger their support. The tyrant's self-aggrandizement "heals the followers' narcissistic wounds, but also tends to shut down" rational process (pp. 295–296).

Mika asserted that the tyrant consolidated his bond with his followers by promising to address aggrieved entitlement deriving from either real or imagined injury. She thought that the tyrant had little interest in the well-being of his followers, essentially holding them in contempt. Narcissistic rage was felt to grow out of the narcissist compulsion "to purge, psychically and physically, all that is weak and undesirable from the narcissist's inner and external world" (p. 299).

Mika paid particular attention to societal conditions creating receptivity to malignant narcissistic leadership. Among the vulnerabilities identified were a growing and unbearably oppressive economic and social inequality that privileged members of society ignored, a breakdown of social norms, and "a growing disregard for the humanity of a large part of the population and for higher values" (pp. 300–301). Such societies demonstrate "an inevitable split in their grandiose and their devalued parts and denial of the shadow, which is projected outward on Others" (p. 301). She underscored that "the narcissism of the elites make them blind to the encroaching tyranny" (p. 302).

Like numbers of other clinicians, Dr. Ian Hughes believed that pronounced dangerousness in a personality was a result of a coalescence of three crucial dimensions of disordered personalities: psychopathy, narcissism, and paranoia. People who possessed all three simultaneously were people who were more likely to behave destructively towards the rest of humanity, particularly if they came to occupy significant positions of leadership. Personalities like Stalin's, Mao's, and Pol Pot's provided disturbing examples of the terrifying cruelty and callousness that such people were capable of enacting, resulting in the deaths of millions that they governed or attempted to dominate. Hughes articulated his position in his book *Disordered Minds – How Dangerous Personalities Are Destroying Democracy* (2018) as well as in *Dangerous Case* (2019).

People whose personalities were organized in a way that maximized their dangerousness were also people who were likely to assume positions of oppressive authority at those points in history when the governed had absorbed unendurable narcissistic wounds, often in the form of wealth inequality, profound humiliation, or the social degradation of being dispossessed of dignity, security, and respect. The sense of certainty that the dangerous personality possessed side-by-side his ability to act decisively in an unfettered way offered an oft-times irresistible invitation to identify with tyrannical power that followers believed they could harness to redress their own wounds. Hughes warned that the tyrannical leaders he was describing were ultimately always self-interested; their appeal was to others' alienation, but it was never infiltrated by concern for their followers' well-being. Hughes' appreciation of the process that eventuated in tyranny was captured by the construct 'toxic triangle' that Padilla, Hogan, and Kaiser conceived in 2007. The toxic triangle encompassed destructive leaders, susceptible followers, and conducive environments.

Hughes argued persuasively that democracy was probably unconsciously conceived as a way of protecting society from the devastating effects of pathological leadership long before anyone could articulate some of the psychological realities/dynamics that attend potentially lethal personality disorders. He observed that after making only intermittent appearances in human history, democracy began to assert itself with increasing insistence at the end of the 18th and beginning of the 19th centuries. Seven of the core principles that defined democracy appeared to serve the function, Hughes thought, of ensuring that tyranny was unlikely to become the dominant form of government. These seven "pillars" of defense against pathological leadership included the rule of law; electoral democracy; separation of church and state; social democracy; protection for human rights; pooled sovereignty; and cultures of tolerance.

Hughes did not specify particular etiologies that led to triangulation of the dangerous personality disorders he was describing, but he did feel that early life experience likely had a profound impact on unfolding brain development and on the shape (including the neural networking) that defined one's internal representation of relationships and of life experience. Broadly speaking, early environments that fostered love and fun enhanced humanity; those marked by hate, fear, and abuse broadly undercut potential for humanity and decency. He asserted that his emphasis on the quality of early life experience as an important determinant of adjustment was a core psychoanalytic principle.

Finally, I would like to briefly mention Michael Stone's (2018) paper that considers where psychopathy falls along a spectrum of negative personality types, including destructive personalities that embody paranoia, narcissism, and sadism. Drawing on extraordinary clinical experience extending across the lifetime of his career, Stone makes the case that at the end of the spectrum he proposes are "persons who embody the attributes of narcissistic, psychopathic, and sadistic (traits)" (p. 178). He concludes that evil, like Shengold (1989), represents an act of "soul murder," which could be described as the "nullification of another human being" (p. 178) through the destruction of their subjectivity, whether through acts of violence and physical torture or psychological control and degradation.

In considering the literature just reviewed, one sees that there is only limited appreciation of the etiological factors arising from nurture experiences that can be seen to contribute to malignant narcissism and to related conceptions, like paranoid disorder and psychopathy. Heinz Kohut provides a blueprint of the kinds of early narcissistic injuries that may help prepare the ground for the formation of what he calls charismatic and messianic narcissism. These injuries were said to take the form of specific kinds of empathic failures. He also took note of constitutional factors that may contribute to the establishment of a grandiose self. Otto Kernberg offers us a relatively extended description of possible psychodynamic causalities underlying malignant narcissism, but his appreciation appears to be a somewhat limited one compared to the particularity he realizes in his characterization of malignant narcissistic realities. Both West and Shaw focused on the formative impact that shaming experiences had upon a developing psyche. West also called attention to abusive, rejecting, or neglectful parenting while Shaw highlighted damaging patterns of relating that undercut subjectivity and people's need to both love and be loved. From his perspective, exposure to parental narcissism could potentiate traumatizing narcissism in children. In his attempts to grasp the origins of sociopathy, Dodes queried whether disproportionate early rage reactions to disappointments and evidence of adherence to alternate realities that a child relied upon to protect the self represented important precursors of a sociopathic personality organization. Like Hughes, explanations also potentially implicated brain function. In his conception, disorders of the prefrontal cortex and amygdala assumed potential prominence; for Hughes, the impact of environmental experience on the development of healthy neural networking was compelling. Hughes was also mindful that nurturance experiences that failed to expose the child to enough love and fun or to too much hate and fear during important developmental phases represented a potential source of compromise, but he spent limited time identifying the formative part disrupted nurturance might play in the development of pathological narcissism. Relying on biographical literature describing tyrants' early life experience, Mika identified a number of markers that seemed to typify their psychological profiles. She also raised questions about disturbances in object constancy, about the impact of an authoritarian upbringing, and about unspecified brain impairment limiting empathic response. And Friedman was adamant that the foundational forces contributing to paranoid character structure were unlikely to ever be found.

The literature review also makes it apparent that many practitioners identified the same elements of disturbed personality organization making their contribution to a toxically destructive personality, but they differed – sometimes significantly – about which of these elements played the most important role. For Tansey, it was delusional disorder; for Friedman, it was paranoid character structure; for Dodes, it was sociopathy; for West, it was other blaming; for Kohut, it was the interface between what he referred to as charismatic and/or messianic narcissism, on the one hand, and paranoia, on the other; and for others, like Hughes, Malkin, Gartner, Stone, and Kernberg, it was a combination or an intersection of pathological narcissism, psychopathy, predilection to cruelty, and paranoid personality disorder. Burkle thought the destructive personalities he was describing represented a regression from pathological narcissism to ASPD. Even Fromm, who first introduced the identifier malignant narcissism, conceived of malignant narcissism as a triad consisting of pathological narcissism, death instinct, and catastrophic symbiotic yearning. Only Mika and Shaw appeared to view malignant narcissism as a unitary construct.

In what I consider to be an important paper, Colleen Covington, using Hannah Arendt's concept of banality of evil (1963), comprehensively reviewed psychoanalytic literature that bears on susceptibility to malignant leadership. A lengthy 2012 paper called "Dabrowski: The Dynamics of Concepts" (author unspecified) appeared to suggest that Dabrowski, much like Arendt, believed that for many people, if not the majority in any given society, it was easier to be bound by social context, relying on dictates of conventionality that defined normative thinking, modes of feeling, and morality rather than drawing on a well-articulated sense of self and individuality to direct their choices.

For those interested in doing so, two wonderful articles about the nature of evil are worth reading in the context of any consideration of malignant narcissism. The first is Anna Aragno's 2014 paper called "The Roots of Evil: A Psychoanalytic Inquiry." The second is Gavin Ivey's 2005 paper entitled "'And What Rough Beast...?' Psychoanalytic Thoughts on Evil States of Mind."

On a personal note, I want to express appreciation to Otto Kernberg for his enduring courage in confronting the most daunting parts of the human heart and attempting to make sense of what he saw. His work has extended over decades and has surely exposed him to punishing, disconcerting experiences in therapy and to a view of his own soul that might well have been too frightening for many another practitioner to endure. While very different than the work of Daniel Shaw, who understood what he called traumatizing narcissism through its relational implications and whose work also strikes me as remarkably brave, Kernberg's decades-long effort was anchored in drive theory and object relations. It is his belief that the dynamic interrelationship of one's internal objects mirrors itself in the way that one deals with external reality.

I also want to pay homage to Heinz Kohut for his conception of self. The construct of a self, as the reader will soon see, is very much a cornerstone in my conception of malignant narcissism as well as offering me the means through which I could better articulate my own phenomenology.

Now I must ask the reader to indulge my conception of malignant narcissism. I do so in a context, as the reader can see, that is characterized both by a multiplicity of competing diagnostic constructs and, simultaneously, by significant commonalities between different groups of practitioners in the way that they view what I have called malignant narcissism. As Daniel Shaw (2014) has pointed out, ferreting out science is a bit akin to blind men exploring an elephant. I can only hope that the piece of elephant I think I have laid my hands on will enhance our understanding of what is perhaps the most destructive form of human personality.

I think it can fairly be said that the literature review the reader has now moved through offers nothing less than an appreciation, albeit a still preliminary one, of our attempts to better understand potentiality for a particularly virulent form of human evil.

References

Aragno, A. (2014). The roots of evil: A psychoanalytic inquiry. *The Psychoanalytic Review*, 101 (2), 249–288.

Arendt, H. (1963). *Eichmann in Jerusalem: A report on the banality of evil*. New York, N.Y.: Penguin.

Bancroft, L. (2002). *Why does he do that? Inside the minds of angry and controlling men*. New York, N.Y.: Berkley Books.

Bleuler, E. (1924). *Textbook of psychiatry*. New York, N.Y.: Macmillan.

Burkle, F.M. (2015). Antisocial personality disorder and pathological narcissism in prolonged conflicts and wars of the 21st century. *Disaster Medicine*, 1 (October), 1–11.

Chasseguet-Smirgel, J. (1984). *Creativity and perversion*. New York, N.Y: Norton.

Covington, C. (2012). Hannah Arendt, evil, and the eradication of thought. *The International Journal of Psychoanalysis*, 93 (5), 1215–1236.

Covitz, H.H. (2017). Health, risk, and the duty to protect the community. In B., Lee (Ed.). *The dangerous case of Donald Trump*. (2nd ed., pp. 191–202). New York, N.Y.: Thomas Dunne Books.

(2012). Dabrowski: The dynamics of concepts.

Dicks, H.V. (1972). *Licensed mass murder: A socio-psychological study of some SS killers*. London, U.K.: Heinemann.

Dodes, L. (2017). Sociopathy. In B., Lee (Ed.). *The dangerous case of Donald Trump*. (2nd ed., pp. 78–87). New York, N.Y.: Thomas Dunne Books.

Friedman, H.J. (2017). On seeing what you see and saying what you know: A psychiatrist's responsibility. In B., Lee (Ed.). *The dangerous case of Donald Trump*. (2nd ed., pp. 154–162). New York, N.Y.: Thomas Dunne Books.

Fromm, E. (1964). *The heart of man*. New York, N.Y.: Harper & Row.

Fromm, E. (1973). *The anatomy of human destructiveness*. New York, N.Y.: Holt, Reinhart, and Winston.

Gartner, J.D. (2017). Donald Trump is: (A) bad, (B) mad, (C) all of the above. In B., Lee (Ed.). *The dangerous Case of Donald Trump*. (2nd ed., pp. 88–103). New York, N.Y.: Thomas Dunne Books.

Gilligan, J. (2017). The issue is dangerousness, not mental illness. In B., Lee (Ed.). *The dangerous case of Donald Trump.* (2nd ed., pp. 163–173). New York, N.Y.: Thomas Dunne Books.

Goode, Erica. (2003). The world: Stalin to Saddam: So much for the madman theory. *New York Times,* May 4.

Herman, J., & Lee, B. (2017) Professions and politics. In B., Lee (Ed.). *The dangerous case of Donald Trump.* (2nd ed., pp. liii–lxi). New York, N.Y.: Thomas Dunne Books.

Hughes, I. (2018). *Disordered minds: How dangerous personalities are destroying democracy.* Winchester, U.K. & Washington, U.S.A: Zero Books.

Hughes, I. (2019). Disordered minds: Democracy as a defense against dangerous personalities. In B., Lee (Ed.). *The dangerous case of Donald Trump.* (2nd ed. pp. 446–457). New York, N.Y.: Thomas Dunne Books.

Ivey, G. (2005). 'And what rough beast …?': Psychoanalytic thoughts on evil states of mind. *British Journal of Psychotherapy,* 22 (2), 199–215.

Jhueck, D. (2017). A clinical case for the dangerousness of Donald J. Trump. In B., Lee (Ed.). *The dangerous case of Donald Trump.* (2nd ed., pp. 174–190). New York, N.Y.: Thomas Dunne Books.

Kernberg, O. (1970). Factors in the psychoanalytic treatment of narcissistic personalities. *Journal of the American Psychoanalytic Association,* 18, 51–85.

Kernberg, O. (1975). *Borderline conditions and pathological narcissism.* Lanham, Maryland: Rowman and Littlefield, Inc.

Kernberg, O. (1984). *Severe personality disorders.* New Haven, Conn.: Yale University Press.

Kernberg, O. (1989). The temptations of conventionality. *The International Review of Psychoanalysis,* 18, 191–204.

Kernberg, O. (2003). Sanctioned social violence: Part I. *The International Journal of Psychoanalysis,* 84 (3), 693–698.

Kernberg, O. (2003). Sanctioned social violence: Part II. *The International Journal of Psychoanalysis,* 84 (4), 953–968.

Kernberg, O. (2007). The almost untreatable narcissistic patient. *Journal of the American Psychoanalytic Association,* 55 (2), 503–539.

Kernberg, O. (2020). Malignant Narcissism and Large Group Regression. *The Psychoanalytic Quarterly,* 89 (1), 1–24.

Kohut, H. (1969–1970). On leadership. In P. H, Ornstein (ed.). *The search for the self* (volume 3, pp. 103–128). New York, N.Y.:Routledge.

Kohut, H. (1975d). Remarks about the formation of the self. In P. H, Ornstein (ed.). *The search for the self* (volume 2, pp. 737–770). New York, N.Y.: International Universities Press, Inc.

Kohut, H. (1976). Creativeness, charisma, group psychology: Reflections on the self-analysis of Freud. In P. H, Ornstein (ed.). *The search for the self* (volume 2, pp. 743–843). New York, N.Y.: International Universities Press, Inc.

Kohut, H. (2010). On empathy: Heinz Kohut (1981). *International Journal of Self Psychology,* 5 (2), 122–131.

Kraepelin, E. (1908). *Lectures in clinical psychiatry.* Bristol: Thoemmes.

Kraepelin, E. (1921). *Manic depressive insanity and paranoia.* Edinburgh: Livingstone.

Kretschmer, E. (1925). *Physique and character.* New York, N.Y.: Harcourt and Brace.

Malkin, C. (2017). Pathological narcissism and politics: A lethal mix. In B., Lee (Ed.). *The dangerous case of Donald Trump*. (2nd ed., pp. 46–53). New York, N.Y.: Thomas Dunne Books.

Mika, E. (2017). Who goes Trump? Tyranny as a triumph of narcissism. In B., Lee (Ed.). *The dangerous case of Donald Trump* (2nd ed., pp. 289–308). New York, N.Y.: Thomas Dunne Books.

Miller, A. (1990). *For your own good: Hidden cruelty in child- rearing and the roots of violence*. New York, N.Y.: Noonday Press.

Newell, W.R. (2016). *Tyrants: A history of power, injustice, and terror*. New York, N.Y.: Cambridge University Press.

Padilla, A., Hogan, R., & Kaiser, R.B. (2007). The toxic triangle: Destructive leaders, susceptible followers, and conducive followers. *Leadership Quarterly*, 18, 176–194.

Pollock, G.H. (1978). Process and affect. *International Journal of Psychoanalysis*, 59, 255–276.

Post, J. (2008). Kim Jung-II of North Korea: In the shadow of his father. *International Journal of Applied Psychoanalytic Studies*, 5 (3), 191–210.

Rosenfeld, H. (1964). On the psychopathology of narcissism: A clinical approach. *The International Journal of Psychoanalysis*, 45, 332–337.

Rosenfeld, H. (1971). A clinical approach to the psychoanalytic theory of the life and death instincts: An investigation into the aggressive aspects of narcissism. *The International Journal of Psychoanalysis*, 52, 169–178.

Shaw, D. (2014). *Traumatic narcissism*. New York, N.Y. & London, U.K: Routledge.

Shafti, S.S. (2019). Malignant narcissism: Concealed side of psychopathy. *Biomedical Journal of Scientific and Technical Research*, 22 (1), 16310–16315.

Shengold, L. (1989). *Soul murder: The effects of childhood abuse and deprivation*. New York, N.Y: Fawcett.

Sofsky, W. (1997). *The order of terror: The concentration camp*. New Jersey, N.J.: Princeton University Press.

Stone, M.H. (2018). The place of psychopathy along the spectrum of negative personality types. *Contemporary Psychoanalysis*, 54 (1), 161–182.

Tansey, M.J. (2017). Why "crazy like a fox" versus crazy like a crazy" really matters. In B. Lee (Ed.). *The dangerous case of Donald Trump* (2nd ed., pp. 88–103). New York, N.Y.: Thomas Dunne Books.

Weigert, E. (1970). *The courage to love: Selected papers of Edith Weigert, M.D.* New Haven, Conn. & London, U.K: Yale University Press.

West, H. (2017). In relationship with an abusive president. In B., Lee (Ed.). *The dangerous case of Donald Trump*. (2nd ed., pp. 237–253). New York, N.Y.: Thomas Dunne Books.

Chapter 3

Mother

As far back as my subjective memory extends, I recall feeling frightened and utterly perplexed by the two people charged with my care. Fright was the predominant emotion up to the point that I was able to stand back and – privately, for to do it in my parents' presence would have been dangerous – ask questions about what was taking place in my world. Fright now had two new companions, the ability to question and the ability to observe and remember, however inadequately, what was taking place around me and inside me. No longer was I just overwhelmed by bewildering and suffocating fear; I began to be able to think about what was happening to me, starting a lifelong journey defined by a search for patterns that I hoped could help me make sense of my world. This shift probably took place earlier than I can appreciate that it did, but my recollection is that I was around eight or nine when I began to make a very earnest and consuming commitment to investigation. Asking myself lots of impossible questions I couldn't answer was scary, but at the same time it was somehow comforting to have these solitary conversations with myself. They provided me with a private refuge where I could retreat from a world that mostly felt threatening and dangerous, bereft of much support or warmth from other people.

Of course, very little did make sense to me at that point in time. There was so much of me that was incomplete and so much of me, as I was all too aware, that was badly compromised, it was probably harder for me to stand back and successfully observe self and others than it might have been for someone who was healthier. I suppose, however, that in the long run it was the conviction that everything that was happening within me and around me could make sense that sustained me and allowed me to endure the terrifying inner world endemic fear helped create.

I think my parents must have intuitively recognized what was going on in my head, though only in a very rudimentary way. Paradoxically denying me a voice or an opinion of my own, they now simultaneously sought me out as someone who must know something about the human condition, expecting, hoping that, somehow, I could save them from the storms and addictions which beset them that they were unable to deal with themselves. I was, at one

DOI: 10.4324/9781003246923-3

and the same time, seemingly both larger than they were and smaller, a conduit for their thoughts and feelings that was to have little mind of its own. It was now my task to say what each needed to hear in the conflict they experienced with one another, but to do so in a way that didn't offend their antagonist.

Perhaps an example would be helpful. Each night before my mother went to bed, she spent approximately an hour to an hour and a half in the bathroom preparing herself while my father waited. The transformation at the end of this process was both tragic and hilarious. What had at the outset been a stunningly beautiful woman whose appearance approximated Ava Gardner's now had become something that looked like a Gila monster with small garbage cans strapped on its scalp. Topping it off, she slathered on blue grey facial cream thick enough for one to be able to write one's name on the side of her cheek. Very much like something out of a B grade 1950s sci-fi horror flick. Zontar the Thing from Venus, but adorned in a transparent baby doll nighty. She capped off her preparations with 6 ExLax and two Carter's little liver pills (also laxatives) which produced predictable and sometimes devastating results in the morning as she struggled to get to the toilet in time.

Inevitably, shortly after reintroducing herself to my father, she would call me into her bedroom complaining he was uninterested in her sexually. She would want my advice. I think I was 10 or maybe 11 at the time that these scenarios unfolded (and they could do so several times weekly, at the worst of times). Tragically and hilariously, I didn't have a very clear idea what sex was (this was the mid-1950s, after all), but I could feel that the stakes were high. What was I to say to her? Of course, he was uninterested in her. She had gone to great lengths to render herself not only unattractive, but bizarre and strange looking for reasons that I could not begin to understand in that frame of my life.

And what did I say to him when he complained that my mother had done the very thing I couldn't talk to her about? That of course she was terribly messed about because he brutalized her verbally much of the time they spent together? I was tasked with forging a reply that would somehow convey a measure of support to each without generating offence in a context in which each was already hurt and in a context in which I largely possessed gross misinformation about the subject matter.

The reader has probably already perceived my objectification of my mother in this context. Objectification undoubtedly reflected disassociation (emotional numbing) born of considerable fear. I had to transform my mother into a "thing" that I could stand back from and privately treat as an absurdity. A taste for the outrageous and the grotesque in my humour has remained with me throughout much of my life. It has undoubtedly served self-protective functions. How gratifying and how relieving to discover later in my life that others (like the Monty Python troop) occupied my sensibility. I somehow found the means to share my own black humour with others. Their laughter was confirming.

I do appreciate that the example just given of my parents' sexual interaction is raw and probably disturbing to read. I offer it because it captures the improbable, otherworldly quality that infected much of my early experience.

To survive the impossible conundrum which my inadvertent "wisdom" had created for me, I began to construct models, however crudely and intuitively, of what each parent was like and how each operated. I relied on such models to help me anticipate what I could say to soothe one parent without inciting the other. The whole project was born of fear. Fear infected every word I said in this peculiar, surreal context. The disturbing and very dangerous sense of the power I was enacting also frightened me. Hovering above all of this was a private self, one that weighed, watched, appraised – seeking to protect "me" from the actualization of threat. And as I watched that self-operate, I had confirmation that an "I" existed, tethered, as it was, to find a way to survive another moment, another encounter, more impossible paradoxes.

Because so much of parental behavior was seemingly arbitrary, unpredictable, and, to me, irrational, vigilance was my constant companion, though I could not have named it. It weighed on me and exhausted me, teaching me to contrive much of what I showed the outside world. There were moments when I seemed to be able to free myself from vigilance and contrivance, experiencing transient or sometimes modestly extended occasions when joy, playfulness, and spontaneity defined me. I can remember embracing such moments, desperate to hang onto them and to find a way to expand them. Perhaps there was more to me than the unrelenting contrivance and vigilance I knew all too well. Perhaps there was a real self, unfettered by pain and fear that might find the means to express itself, one that was genuinely me. Tantalizing, fleeting glimpses, but enough to suggest there might be more beyond the starvation of spirit that I knew. I also gradually became aware that at times I seemed to be capable of a kind of creativity that my friends appeared not to possess, at least not to a similar degree; it, too, seemed to promise substance, but its presence, like my other gifts, was maddeningly ephemeral, very much resistant to my attempts to replicate it. Increasingly, vigilance and contrivance appeared to be winning with the passage of years, displacing the glimmers of aliveness that I sometimes experienced. I felt increasingly hollowed out, confronted by an interior that looked to be barren.

As obviously crazy and chaotic as my mother was (like my father, she, too, was addicted to alcohol), and in spite of the cruelty she episodically enacted, she could also access emotion in a way that he could not, responding to a broad array of feelings that informed her actions and her presence. One could feel an aliveness in her she was struggling to sustain, perhaps much as I was. Though I could not have articulated it at the time, I realize in retrospect that what I saw in my mother represented fragments of a self trying to come together to form a cohesive whole. This struggle was quite palpable, which rendered it both very poignant and rather disturbing to watch. I think I can remember reflecting at the time that none of the pieces seemed to fit together.

I couldn't figure out where my mother's centre was. It felt like she was trying to paste together disparate and oft times fundamentally incompatible parts into a single picture that was mostly at odds with itself, perhaps like one of Picasso's portraits of his mistresses. I could feel her desperation as she tried to make it work, casting about for unity and coherence she never seemed to be able to manage.

She drifted into reveries and dreaminess she invited one to share with her, perhaps as a means of establishing connectedness. Heaven knows I wanted connection, but as much as I wanted to participate in what looked like a gratifying experience for her (and, potentially, I imagined for me), I never found any substance to her dreaminess I could latch onto. The content she provided was vague, woolly, sometimes conspiratorial, and relatively inarticulate or, alternatively, it embraced idealizations of me that struck me as utterly implausible, as if she had no sense of who I really was or what my pain was like. I simply didn't know what to do with the terrible fictions that infused and defined her at these times, but I also didn't want to offend her by turning away from her when it appeared she so badly needed to come together with me.

At still other times my mother could be wickedly funny and irreverent, often as a means of neutering my father, which I secretly applauded. Sometimes her pushback in the face of his contempt was articulate and appropriate (mockingly deriding his ideas either publicly or privately with withering, irresistible intelligence). At other times her efforts to oppose him could be disjointed, shocking, or frankly bizarre (conspiring to trap my father with her homosexual friends on a boat trip and watching him squirm; jumping up on my father during a gathering of his executives and their wives, wrapping her legs around his middle, and declaring herself a Cherokee Jew). Her acts of defiance, which I suppose were meant to affirm selfhood, seldom remained triumphant in the face of the inevitable counterattack which ensued, but, in spite of promised obliteration, she continued to fight back in whatever manner she could in a given situation. These acts struck me as very courageous at the time and I had admired her for them, but I also recognized she was gradually losing her battle and losing herself. That recognition was profoundly unsettling. Not only would I lose the ineffective and sometime protector I had; I had growing evidence that the self could be destroyed, which was one of the two things I feared most.

Other parts of my mother were devastatingly self-critical and perfectionistic which, dangerously, I knew could infect her assessment of anything I did. At other times she could be utterly compelled by her need for order and by a measure of cleanliness punishing for anyone around her. These strictures helped contribute to an impression of craziness because they were so outlandishly drawn. The vastly inappropriate seductiveness that she directed towards me, sometimes couched in the frame of humour, but just as often not, further contributed to a sense of an unstable, out-of-control dangerous personality seemingly unaware of the damage she was inflicting. Sometimes my mother's seductiveness was laced with a conspiratorial tone that invited me to join with her in our mutual fear/loathing of my father. On still other occasions she could engage in either deliberate or, possibly, unintentional acts of cruelty quite devastating to endure, typically inciting my father to direct his rage towards me. And (this is not meant to be an inclusive list) there was also a mother who episodically showed herself to be warm, who could appraise reality accurately, and who could be empathic.

While we all move back and forth between different facets of our personalities, sometimes wearing one face and then another, my mother's transitions between her different faces struck me (and still do) as abrupt and arbitrary, one reality utterly and completely displacing the other within the passage of a moment. Sudden, incongruous transitions I could not understand most of the time. Undoubtedly these experiences further contributed to my sense of a fragmented person.

Because I so desperately needed an ally in order to be able to survive the devastation which my father visited upon me, I had to turn aside the many forms of threat that she manifested, instead idealizing the better parts of her so that I could feel safer. It was of course an impossible undertaking and one that was fated to fail. The shared world we sometimes tenuously established always fell apart as other pieces of her dominated our interaction. When she left my father the first time, I understood. I saw her desperation to survive as being much like my own. When she separated from him the second time (after remarriage), I went with her, only – perhaps one should say inevitably – to discover she was barely able to parent, too skeletal and too devastated spiritually to effectively look after someone else. Her ongoing anorexia, prominently and noisily displayed after each meal, served as a reminder of what could happen in the face of my father's relentless assaults. The visage she presented was frightening: at 5 foot 7 inches, she was well under 100 pounds and at her worst, in the very last years of her life, she was barely 85.

As I got older, I began to rely on my increasingly irreverent sense of humour to convey to others (and possibly myself) what I had experienced with her. So much of her behavior had been so outrageous and so bizarre it was easy to get other people to laugh as I caricatured her. It felt like a relief to be able to do so. It was an acceptable way both to disguise my rage (sometimes from myself) and to express it.

In spite of the perceptiveness that my humor implied I possessed, there remained much that I did not acknowledge about the experience I had with her, particularly the sexual abuse she had introduced into our relationship. Once my mother left my father for the second time and I became part of her household, I found myself sharing a bed with her (I was 15–16 at the time). Night-time preparation included the transparent baby doll nighty. I was only half aware that what she was doing felt wrong. Next to the profound uneasiness I was unable to fully define for myself was also a feeling that somehow what she was doing must be okay. To have fully acknowledged the sense of threat her behavior provoked would have meant admitting to myself that I couldn't be safe with her either, that I was living in an out of control, damaging world dominated by other people's toxic impulses.

My own sexuality, of course, was pushing me very hard while all of these events were unfolding with my mother. I was being invited to respond to my mother's seductiveness, but never to admit or confirm that I found her body arousing. I was not capable of recognizing she was feeding off the confirmation which my emerging (and certainly distorted) sexuality was providing her. In an adult context I can see that in toying with me sexually she transformed the fear which sexuality engendered in her (and which she had so prominently played out in her night-time rituals with my father) into a sense of power. No longer was it necessary for her to feel compelled by insatiable need to move herself towards sexual exchange she was afraid could murder her spirit. Instead, she could identify herself as an aggressor who possessed prerogatives of choice not accessible to her in a relationship with an adult male. "Toying" is a good word to describe what I felt at the time. She could play with me and with the effect her sexuality had upon me. Her sexual instigation, however, was as often as not chaotic, demonstrating itself in front of my friends and hers in a manner that was certainly uncomfortable for everyone involved (checking to see if I was erect when I came in from a date, playfully placing her foot in my crotch when I walked into a room). People responded to these surreal encounters with her by attempting to reconstruct them, often with humour, attributing benign or acceptable motives to her troubled behavior. The effect was disconcerting for me, making it harder for me to appreciate what was happening to me in my relationship with her. I imagined, in response, that my discomfort and my embarrassment must be overblown or overstated, that my mother's behavior, was, in some way, a variant of normal parenting. As already alluded to, I very much needed to believe that, because without her, there was only the abyss that I faced with my father. Even harder to put into words for myself was the sadistic triumph her sexual provocation sometimes seemed to create for her. It required decades for me to see that cruelty further consolidated power and authority for her as well as imbuing her sexuality with a measure of aliveness.

In what ended up, on balance, being a half unintended act of compassion, my mother sought to extend her intrusion into my sexuality by arranging for me to sleep with a prostitute so that I might discover what sex was (I was still 16 at the time). It had been her plan that this act would take place in the bed that she and I shared. She would oblige me by leaving the apartment for the afternoon. I somehow had enough self-preservation to resist her, insisting that I see the prostitute, who occupied a different apartment in the complex where we lived, on my own. This woman proved to be gentle and kind and generous, taking a great deal of time with me and seeming to demonstrate what appeared to be genuine concern for my emotional well-being. My mother naturally wanted a blow-by-blow description of my experience. I pleased her and myself by sharing only some of it. Shortly thereafter I began a relationship with my first serious girlfriend which, although stormy, was immensely important to me.

As damaging as my mother was, she still offered me fleeting anchors of perception and empathy I could rely on to support an illusion that she was caring. As previously referenced, it was an illusion in constant need of repair. It constantly fell apart and I continuously tried to fix it. In spite of the ramshackle, frighteningly inadequate security umbrella she offered, I did see she could also sometimes tolerate my anger, which was confirming for me. I can remember thinking that I was often unfair to her, knowingly directing anger towards her that I couldn't take to my father. While she sometimes joined with me in my appraisal of my father, both allowing me to give voice to my pain and sharing common cause with me, I was very much aware that our alliance was an uneasy one – and one that could fall apart all too quickly if she became offended, often for reasons I could not begin to anticipate. As noted, I could also see and certainly feel that there was a part of her that took delight in the cruelty she intermittently inflicted on me. Whether she was setting me up as fodder for my father (dressing me up in clothes she knew he would attack me for wearing, for instance) or turning on me abruptly with scathing appraisals, I could see the look of apparent satisfaction that her sadistic acts had generated for her. It is hard to capture with words the mixture of desolation, outrage, and betrayal that such moments created for me. Certainly a sense, as was true of our "shared" sexuality, that she delighted in "playing" with me. I struggled to discern why, probably partly because I so badly needed to find human reasons – and therefore redeeming ones – that could mitigate her toxicity. I told myself that her cruelty was a reflection of my father's, an echo of all the pain and helplessness he had caused her that was now being directed towards me. As I look back, I think I can also recall feeling that something else, something bigger, possibly something more malignant, was lurking inside her, something that escaped my understanding but not my visceral response to her. I think I also tried to turn aside this appraisal of her, finding it too dangerous and too impenetrable to deal with at the time.

Improbably, notwithstanding these contradictions and insoluble paradoxes, I could feel relatively safer with her than I did with my father. As risky and as uncertain the business of soliciting support from her was, she did intermittently offer what looked and felt like a safe harbor, however imperfect and impermanent. At times, then, I could hide myself in her, however brutish and punishing her personal dynamics were. Of course, my desperation for safety and for confirmation drove me towards her in spite of the terrible damage her unpredictable behavior could inflict. It was sometimes at least something, somewhere I could pretend there was comfort.

My mother did eventually lose her battle with herself. The shards of self that remained to her were not enough to sustain her. Her presence was increasingly infected with conspiracy theories and paranoia (through which she meant to confirm her intelligence and her identity) and by out-of-control drinking she needed to sustain herself hour by hour. Multiple marriages to a number of narcissistic men made their contribution to the terminal erosion of her spirit. By the time she was 63, her liver no longer worked. Throughout my adult life, she continued to turn to me to help heal her. I could not. My own wounds and my own confusion about what had happened to me limited my efforts as did the increasingly toxic nature of her behavior. She could not bear to let anyone get too close to her and I was not sufficiently self-possessed at the time to endure the various forms of verbal assault she directed towards me. I simply did not know enough about myself or about her to provide her with the comforting presence she needed. I do have to acknowledge that, even had I been able to offer her something better, she might not have been able to accept it, save only for brief periods of time. It took some considerable time for me to accept that someone can be too broken to fix. To save myself, I had to leave her behind. Her aloneness still haunts me and saddens me.

Throughout all of my experience with my mother, my observing self kept me company, prodding me, asking questions, trying (usually without success) to synthesize, to construct order where so little seemed to exist and attempting, also often without success, to find ways I could reassure myself and soothe myself with meaningful insights. My efforts so often felt futile, birthing desolation I thought must bury me. But as I have already implied, my observing self was not just friend and companion, but assassin as well, sometimes unceasingly echoing the disdainful, accusatory voices of my parents, particularly my father's. One of my patients described this part of his own process as being like having a murder squad in his head.

So, observing self was both friend and foe, companion and unwelcome intruder. It did affirm identity, but it was hard to feel after its incessant attacks that I wanted to be the "me" it kept reminding me I was. I also noticed, where my mother was concerned, that my ability to observe and to integrate ideas was far more compromised than it was when I made effort to understand my father. Although I was acutely aware of her craziness, seeing my mother with any clarity up through my middle adulthood was probably too threatening for me to bear, whereas seeing my father as he was, was necessary for survival.

My relationship with my mother was certainly profoundly disturbing, reverberating throughout my life in a variety of expected and unanticipated ways I was left to disentangle, as best I could, through my own work and through the help of various therapists, mentors, and friends who enabled me to at least partially find my way through a bewildering landscape. To say that the journey was variably an unnerving and disconcerting experience that evoked cacophonies of painful emotion as well as episodic triumphs and insights probably doesn't do it justice. And this work remains imperfect and incomplete, as it must, though it is fair to say that after a lifetime of effort I have been able, increasingly, to realize a kind of peace – one in which a measure of understanding and compassion begin to displace some, maybe much, of the pain this relationship occasioned.

I am very much aware that had I had the opportunity to learn more about my mother's early life, I might plausibly have understood even more about her, but she never allowed herself to tell us a great deal about what had actually transpired. Her portrait of her parents and of one of her siblings, in particular, struck me as rigidly idealized, inaccessible on a meaningful human level beyond the caricatures which were proffered. Given her choice of men over the course of six marriages (two to my father) and the fragmentation that was such a prominent part of her, I could at least guess what might have transpired in her relationship with her parents. Her sister also seemed to have made a similar choice in a partner. I speculated that her sense of self had been subjected to shattering blows long before she met my father and that she chose him because he reiterated lethal combat she had faced in her own family. The walls she built around her early experience, I assumed, were necessary for her, protecting her from unbearable truths her disconnected self could not effectively process. Increasingly, I saw her as someone who needed to hide herself from the world, afraid that her own devastation and craziness was all too easy for others to see. On only a handful of occasions during the course of my entire relationship with her did she ever allude to profound early pain. When she did, her characterizations of events that she referenced struck one as outlandish, improbable, and bizarrely hyperbolized. Moreover, her description of important parts of her life varied wildly from one retelling to the next, leading me to wonder whether my memory must repeatedly have failed me. My relationship with her throughout much of my life was defined by elusive, shifting realities that seemed to defy rationality. It became part of my life's work to piece together narratives that allowed me glimpses of the human being shrouded by all the chaos that had obscured my view of her.

It is important to mention, albeit seemingly in the form of a footnote, that among my mother's causalities was a benign pituitary tumor requiring radio-surgery around the time I was in grade school. I can't recall now whether my mother's anorexia had preceded it or unfolded as a dreadful side effect of the radiation itself. I remember researching her condition and her surgery, discovering that some authors, at least, believed that an anorexia like syndrome could sometimes ensue following radiological intervention. It was somewhat comforting to me. It argued that my mother's physical withering might not be a consequence of my father's depredations, but, possibly the result of a dispassionate physical illness. The deeply disturbing and deeply compelling image her anorexia created, however, remained riveting for me nonetheless, echoing, again and again, virtually every time I saw her, my dread about what was happening to me. Almost as if some part of her understood, she obsessively saved some portion of her meagre allotment of food for me, insisting that I take it. And as much as I was frightened that in doing so I was contributing to her inevitable starvation, I was too frightened of my own spiritual withering to refuse her. No doubt she fed me at the time, at least in part, because doing so allowed her to participate vicariously in my satiation. I think as a consequence of this part of my experience with her, I came to view food, without realizing that I had done so, as the means to offset the psychic depletion that so terrified me.

Chapter 4

The Face of Narcissism – Father

Foundational Ideas

Where my father was concerned, there was rarely anyplace to hide. If my mother's walls were fragmented, his were monolithic and imposing. Formidable, relentless and implacable are the three words which come to mind. One could feel the immensity of his force. It was voracious and unstoppable. The menace he projected through rage that always felt dangerously close to the surface was paired with abruptly abusive verbal outbursts that might suddenly and arbitrarily punctuate an exchange with him. These aspects of him made him feel much more threatening than my mother ever had. His rage could bury you, suffocating you with debilitating fear and shame.

I think I was in grade 1 when he asked me to spell my name. I made an error. And then another. The screaming commenced. It feels challenging to capture the intensity of his rage with words. He was beside himself with fury. I was asked again and again to spell my name. I had no idea what mistake I was making. But with each mistake, I could feel his rage escalating. I can recall feeling afraid that he wanted to murder me. At the very least, it was proof that I was utterly despicable in his eyes. My mother tried to intervene. She became tearful and desperate, unable to dissuade him to back away. She began to scream at him and she physically interjected herself between him and me. I was confined to my bed for the entire weekend, periodically subjected to the kind of interrogation I have just described. Just as I thought the storm might subside, it fell upon me again. My mother remained unable to stop him, in spite of repeated intercessions attended by more crying and screaming of her own. Incensing him further, I proved able to spell my name correctly when my mother asked, but not when he did. Somehow, after two-and-a-half days, his rage abated. I never knew why. There was no attempt to apologize or to repair, so I can remember assuming that he continued to feel extraordinary distaste for me.

I was in grade 9 and had just won my letter in varsity wrestling. We were at his country club, in a crowded room. He began to attack my mother, as he often did. I tried to protect her verbally. This infuriated him. His verbal assault became even more ferocious and demeaning. I told him to stop, trying to reciprocate some of the courage she had demonstrated towards me when I

DOI: 10.4324/9781003246923-4

found myself in similar circumstances. To little avail. I threatened to throw a glass of water in his face if he didn't stop. Now rage was turned towards me. Using an even louder voice than that which supported his assault on my mother, he conveyed to the entirety of the dining hall that I was despicable, that he had never liked me, and that I was a source of great shame to him. He was screaming. He moved closer to me to press home his attack. His fury seemed to feed itself. I eventually broke down, sobbing uncontrollably, further intensifying my sense of diminishment. I tried to escape to the washroom. He followed me, continuing to scream, continuing to express his outrage that I was his son. Somehow, thankfully, his outrage with me retreated into a kind of heavy silence that accompanied the drive home. The next morning, in response to my mother's insistence, he made a subdued apology. It was one of only two apologies he ever made to me in my lifetime.

His rages were quite terrifying. They transfixed and overwhelmed. Rage could sweep him and fill him seemingly with little warning, though with the advantage of adult perspective I can make more sense of them now. In the midst of his rage, you could feel his hatred. I came to believe that must be the real measure of his feeling for me. Kindnesses were relatively short-lived and struck me as condescension or forbearance concealing deep revulsion.

In my late 30s, I came to understand that my father was struggling with Narcissistic Personality Disorder. Other than a list of symptoms, it felt very poorly defined as a psychiatric construct. I couldn't find explanations for the origins of his pain or for the dynamics that repeatedly played themselves out in his relationships with himself and others – at least not explanations that made enough sense to me. Sorting through who he was and what drove him was, in various parts, an act of self-preservation, of desperation, and, I suppose, of love. His pain was so manifestly, crushingly present, it felt inescapable. My journey gradually evolved from a position in which I appraised him as an essentially malignant being to one in which I felt I was better able to appreciate the terrible costs which his affliction created for him. Recognizing what he had become and why produced a mixture of compassion for his agony side-by-side outrage for my own losses. My struggle with him felt like the focal point of my life. Unless I could begin to see who and what he was and how he had come to be, it felt like I would never be able to free myself, even partially, from the destructive impact that he had upon me. Towards the end of my life, I have felt grateful for the kind of experience that I had with him, believing that it allowed me glimpses of the human experience I might never otherwise have been afforded. But it was a harrowing journey and one I am very much aware I very nearly did not survive. I would not willingly repeat it, but, with distance, I can say it created an opportunity for me to learn a great deal.

If my mother was able to evince some aliveness from amongst the fragmentation, from the collection of pieces that she seemed to be, my father appeared to be largely incapable of spontaneity, playfulness, and genuine warmth and engagement, though he could feign those qualities. To my eye, when he did so, it never felt real. Rather, it appeared to be an intentioned or constructed act meant to serve some end, but often an end that eluded my powers of apprehension. Dancing meant counting and it meant placing your feet exactly where they were meant to be as determined by the dancing lessons he'd taken. Acts of affection mostly appeared to be stilted, though sometimes one could feel, momentarily, a measure of connection. Humor as an act of generosity and an affirmation of humanity seemed out of his reach. Humor didn't extend affability for him; on the contrary, he appeared not to know how to touch other people or move them by appealing to the defining aspects of the human condition which characterized him and them. Instead, his humor tended to focus on the "funny" aspects of a sadistic or cruel interchange between people that caught his eye. Other forms of humor did not appear to engage him. The awkward, absurd, or preposterous nature of either human or animal suffering was the common currency he relied upon to build his bridges to others.

As I watched him socially, much of the time he appeared to be playacting, going through the motions and feigning human responses so that he could pass. When people told jokes, particularly ones that played upon their short-falls or their foibles, he appeared to be genuinely confused, as if the joke made no sense to him, but he would pretend that it did. Jokes that were obviously self-effacing seemed to horrify him, often provoking scathing verbal attacks, usually in the form of obvious, crude sarcasm or attempts to humiliate.

It gradually dawned on me that he was unable to use humor to touch other people and deepen his bonds with them. Indeed, he appeared to be repelled by that prospect. Watching him, actually, was a bit chilling. A marionette on his own strings. For me, unconvincing form in the absence of much substance. It was painful and confusing to watch his artifice. His smiles were tight lipped and forced. So was his laugh. His manner rarely seemed to convey what felt like genuine kindness or regard. I eventually noticed that the orchestration of self I found so disconcerting was especially prominent when social interaction focused upon communion meant to convey affection, generosity, or warmth. He simply didn't know what to do in such circumstances – as if he was facing a language and a series of transactions that not only baffled him, but wrong-footed him, evoking guardedness, awkwardness, and, oddly it seemed to me, detachment. I could not imagine that he was struggling with the same kind of evisceration of spirit that I was. He felt so big inside me and like such a powerful presence, it was bewildering to watch him act as if the simple language of affiliation and of genuine, mutually satisfying acts of caring required him to back away from people and to curate himself in the peculiar way that he did. What was he protecting himself against, I wondered? What did all of this mean? I remember thinking, "am I supposed to be like this?" That thought filled me with despair. If I acted as he did, I could never free myself from my own contrivance. I would only be escalating my own playacting. I imagined that there must be some underlying music that informed his behavior. I kept trying to hear it, believing that if I did, I might find points of resonance between the two of us that could offer us a means of moving towards one another. Perhaps then I could become more acceptable to him. But I never found anything that sounded like music. Or much that appealed to me as attractive and human. Instead, I heard an endless succession of jarring, discordant notes in the absence of any discernible melody. How I wished that my father could sing, but he never did.

It confused and frightened me I couldn't find the human parts of him, just as I couldn't with my mother. How could I construct an identity with his discordancy and her fragments? Was I fundamentally too defective to experience whatever it was that moved the two people at the very center of my life? It all felt very surreal – as if I was an outsider looking in at a series of jagged, disconnected exchanges that made no sense to me. As was true of my relationship with my mother, only occasionally did I allow myself to see that something was terribly wrong with him. That was both a frightening thought and a comforting one. For the most part, however, I was much more deeply absorbed by all of the deficiencies and absences that seemed to define me.

The question that I'd begun to formulate for myself – what made him feel so uneasy about warmth, connection, and the kind of openness necessary for spontaneity and play – proved, for me, to be one of the cornerstone pieces in my understanding of narcissism. If I make it sound like I was able to distill this question early in life, I should take care to emphasize that I didn't. My response to the quality of contrivance that I experienced in him comprised a series of disjointed impressions and uncomfortable feelings that gradually, with the passage of two to three decades, began to consolidate into more sharply focused perception.

Coexisting with his contrivance was enormously draining. I could feel myself tighten up when I was around him, as if his guardedness was somehow infectious, invading me with reciprocal response. The tighter I felt, the more I found myself trying to replicate his rigidities, as if in doing so I might have imagined I was making myself safer. I could feel my inner life contract in response, probably mimicking what he was enduring without recognizing that might have been so. The invidious comparisons that more or less continuously unfolded in his presence compelled me to believe that his artifice was somehow possessed of more substance than my own and that my deficits of personhood were therefore grotesquely greater than his. He was, after all, as he kept reminding me, a person of extraordinary parts, someone who had transcended crushing poverty through acts of will and bravery to become, as he had me believe, a mythically successful retail executive and visionary.

There was, in fact, compelling reason for me to respond to his contrivance with contrivance of my own. One was acutely aware of the appraising eye he cast over everyone around him, very much attuned to any slight or injury that might be directed towards him. I particularly had the sense when I was with him, both publicly and privately, that I was regarded as a potential source of embarrassment who could cause him compromise.

When I did so, my action was mostly inadvertent. Much of my conscious effort around him was directed towards avoiding the corrosive, seemingly ruthless ascriptions he imposed on me. Open defiance, like my mother's, was almost impossible for me. The emaciation of self that I lived with meant that a risk like that was too great; it felt possible to me that he could utterly annihilate my secretly decimated spirit. This was very much a conscious fear that declared itself evermore emphatically as the years with my father unfolded. It manifested itself as a sense that I could be crushed or obliterated, not only by my father, but by anyone who struck me as resembling him or, indeed, by anyone who was at all forceful or aggressive.

The wariness that one felt around him was suffocating, but his needs dictated that one present oneself as personable and competent, not as afraid. Doing this also demanded a measure of contrivance and orchestration of self that further contributed to the feeling that one was dying inside. Acutely felt vulnerability was so exquisitely experienced it eventually became impossible to hide, resulting in a prolonged period in primary school of devastating bullying. In retrospect, I came to understand as a psychologist that my relative inability to effectively defend myself was all too apparent, readily targeting me for the bullying which took place. At the time, I was convinced that my inability to protect myself confirmed the deep and abiding inadequacy my incompleteness created for me, further exacerbating shame. My father, acutely aware of the bullying and feeling very much diminished by what was happening to his son, escalated his distaste for me. Bullying played itself out over the course of two–three years in early primary school. It meant being terrified to go to school, being terrified at recess, and being terrified at the bus stop both before and after school. It was as relentless as my father's disgust with me. I still live with its effects.

A change of school offered the possibility of resurrection which, miraculously, I was able to effect, becoming, for a period of years, all that I thought my father would have wanted (president of my class, president of the student council, captain of most of the major sports teams, academic honors) only to discover I was still regarded with disdain and contempt. "Stupe" was a favored moniker for me. I could only conclude that my father's judgement must be accurate, that I was fundamentally distasteful and weak, which was unforgivable. There seemed to be nothing I could do to turn away the repugnance that my father felt for me. I concluded that my defect was my endemic fear, which I thought, horrifyingly, was becoming all too transparent again and was certainly repellent to him. I further believed that because I contrived so much of myself, anybody who attempted to get close to me would soon discover that, like my mother, I was skeletal and incomplete. This latter concern was very sharply felt, prompting me to retreat further and further from the people around me. Absence of substance was a mortal sin.

Long after I had finished graduate school, it finally began to occur to me that my father's contempt was ubiquitous and, in a perverse way, democratic. It was his dominant interface with the world. At one point I had concluded that he was misogynistic. Then I recognized that he had contempt for virtually everyone. No relationship was immune to it. The spics, wops, mics, kikes, chinks, and niggers he derided were not exceptions to an otherwise genial humanity. His contempt for them was the measure of him. Very much a relief for me to recognize that it was so, but bonds of shame about my own incompleteness and my fearfulness, though loosened, still held me unbearably tight. It remained for me to puzzle out why contempt was so important to him. As I matured as a psychologist, I could ask myself what function it served and what it reflected about his own internal realities. The more I looked and the more I experienced him, the more I could recognize that he was truly misanthropic. Finally understanding this facet of him played a key role in helping me conceptualize what I came to believe were core dynamics of narcissism. I will return to this theme as different threads in the unfolding narrative wind their way together in this and in subsequent chapters.

Comments made thus far about contrivance and my father's extraordinary sensitivity to injury or slight might seem to imply that he carefully and assiduously impression-managed his own behavior so that particular effects, each of which was painstakingly arranged, could be realized. To be on the receiving end of the vigilance which he imposed, particularly in the company of his self-aggrandizement, certainly made it feel as if such must be the case: a grand master manipulating his every move all knowingly and flawlessly. But as one kept close acquaintance with him over the years and then decades, his mask of infallibility fell away, tentatively at first and then very decisively. Two realizations presented themselves.

First, I began to recognize that the vigilance he so prominently exhibited, while undoubtedly reflective of his own consuming guardedness, also helped him incite vigilance in others around him, which appeared to be quite important for him. Why, I wondered, was it so compelling for him to provoke fear in the people that he dealt with? Or, put another way, what did that tell me about him? Then I began to notice that fear incitement, like contempt, was nearly ubiquitous, or, perhaps expressed more accurately, eventually surfaced in a very prominent and a very tenacious way in virtually every relationship that he had. Sometimes it took the form of an explicit attack or acts of bullying carried out in the company of other people, causing either muted or tangible discomfort in everyone in attendance.

I watched people's responses, hopeful that their reactions could help me better understand my own. Some attendees seemed to convey tacit acceptance or even approval of his acts; others even joined in the bullying themselves. Some few might object, framing their objection with humor, while some small number might take him on, letting him know that his behavior was not acceptable and that they would not participate in it. This latter group of people, as already implied, were exceptions, but they were important exceptions for me to watch. Some of them were clearly furious with my father while others couched their distaste for his behavior in a very elegant, self-possessed, and articulate fashion. How wonderful, I thought, to be able to do either. His attacks and bullying certainly caused me to be afraid. Could I be next? And if this possibility frightened me, were other people in the room, or at least some of them, feeling the same way? If my feelings somehow served as a measure of what other people might be feeling, was it then also possible that others shared what I regarded as base and shameful reactions on my part – palpable relief that if he was attacking others I was safe for a while?

It took some time for me to appreciate that people I thought of as powerful adults might withhold confrontation because they were afraid of being attacked themselves. As I looked back from a perspective of adult conviction, I finally established for myself, I also remembered that in many of these gatherings (certainly not all) my father was surrounded by people who worked for him. It was easy to assume as a youngster, particularly the kind of youngster I was, that they and he were both of one mind – that is, his mind, the boss's mind. At the same time part of my reality as a youngster in these situations also included profound feelings of discomfort infused with my own guilt, by concern for the suffering of the targeted party, and by outrage that I was helpless, compelled to watch yet another humiliation drama unfold.

One summer evening my father was entertaining a number of his subordinates at a barbecue he was holding. He was the chef. I was his assistant. He had a barbecue with a bellows one could operate with a crank. Men and women together were assembled at the barbecue listening to my father expound in hyperbolized fashion on the meat that he was cooking. Conspiratorially, he whispered to me, in an aside, that I was to get two large four-inch firecrackers and surreptitiously slip them into his hand. I did so. Loudly proclaiming and pointing, "Look at that bear over there!" (This was an elegant suburban enclave not far from downtown Minneapolis), he tossed the two firecrackers into the grill with his free hand. It would be a great understatement to say that the ensuing explosions, which occurred almost instantaneously, were loud. Women screamed. Some men did too, though they immediately tried to suppress it. Drinks and hors d'oeuvres were spilled on clothing. But nobody said anything. Nervous laughter. Some strange looks. Finally, some appreciative remarks reflecting the boss's great sense of humor.

Another summer evening and probably another barbecue. I was invited to demonstrate my marksmanship in front of guests (subordinates again). The direction given was to shoot at a large gourd hanging from a tree that served as a birdhouse. I did as I was told. The ricocheted BB shattered the cocktail glass of the woman standing next to me. I remember feeling appalled, ashamed, detached (maybe surreal is a better word), and somehow blameworthy. The assembled guests provided the anxious laughter I had come to expect in such circumstances, but no remonstrations.

With the maturity that my profession provided me, I was able to recognize, in retrospect, that the dynamics and the feelings that I was starting to disentangle had provided me with an intimate look at a very formidable and powerful phenomenon which has played, to my mind, such an important part in human history: identification with the aggressor. As I read Eric Larson's wonderful book, *Garden of Beasts*, I had only to look at my own childhood to understand why the physical and psychological coercion of that particular chapter of human history (Germany 1933) could be so irresistible for so many people. One particularly disturbing memory from childhood assailed me during that reading experience: my chief bully during my childhood years laughingly hanging my pet dachshund by the leash from an elevated porch attached to our house some 15 feet off the ground. I laughed with him. I was sick with fear and loss, but too frightened to oppose him. That impression is indelible. To an outsider, I would have looked like a collaborator. Inside, the sense of personal betrayal that I demonstrated towards my dog, Ginger, still unsettles me.

Another thought occurred to me about the function of my father's vigilance as I reflected, at various points in my life, upon countless examples like the ones provided above. It was a thought that was very hard for me to acquire because I assumed that I was fundamentally different than the "normal" other and certainly different from the adults who attended the events I have described. Could it be possible that the fear my father instigated in others had the same impact on them that it had on me: to shut down spontaneity and creativity and freeze inner life? Did it serve him in some way, in other words, to do that to all of us?

The second realization that presented itself to me also helped open vistas of insight. I started to recognize how imperfect my father's attempts to curate himself and others were. Simply and perhaps somewhat misleadingly put, I began to acknowledge both how out of control he was and how unaware he was of why he was behaving as he did. I didn't have any answers I could give myself at the time and, if I had, it really would have been too dangerous to share them with him, particularly if they were perceptive. Even remotely insightful thinking was not welcome. But there it was. His behavior was enormously impulse ridden, or seemed to be so. I continued to guess that there must be order and coherence somewhere under the surface informing his impulsivity, but I would have to wait a long time for those explanations to occur to me. Recognizing his need to generate fear and vigilance in others, though, eventually proved to be one part of the puzzle.

Impulsivity and addictive behavior constantly derailed the staged presence he appeared to work so hard to construct for himself. The bullying, shaming, and intimidation which I have just referred to abruptly punctuated much of his behavior in an erratic, uneven, out-of-control way. While I had come to see that "nice" didn't typically last very long and that the urge to invoke vigilance and fright would eventually prove itself to be irresistible, I became less and less certain that he was capable of choosing the time and place of his aggressivity. Rather than creating the impression of a master manipulator who planned and directed such behavior, one was left with a sense that he was oftentimes a passenger on a runaway train he was not in any position to restrain. It was a curious thing to notice about him and an important paradigm shift for me. I could anticipate his sadism, but I often couldn't predict when it would visit itself on me or someone else in the circle – and I don't think he could much of the time either. For the most part, it looked like something that was happening to him, though, when it did, he wholeheartedly participated in the urge to hurt and to diminish.

Interestingly, he never seemed to ask himself what was happening to him during these moments. He simply appeared to consummate them without reflection. He didn't consider, at least so far as I could see, how he might be harming himself or others. I puzzled and puzzled over this question. How could he not see? And how could he not feel? My guts were churning with the unfolding of each of these episodes. He looked to be blind to the effect he was having on himself and the people around him. For a while I wondered if this is what he expected me to become. That this was what he believed a man was supposed to be – swaggering, dominating, indifferent to the people around him. While this prospect horrified me, I was deeply confused. If it was good to be a man and if this was what a man was, how was I to find my way? Should I try to be like him? Or should I pull away from him and try to find some other path to manhood? These were very overwhelming and very unsettling questions to have to consider and they permeated a significant part of my life. He unselfconsciously portrayed his behavior as an attractive asset to be prized. His aggression and impulsivity were couched as a strength. There was never an admission that he had gotten himself in over his head in a given instance. His behavior was so tenaciously pursued that at times I remember thinking he was casting himself in a ridiculous light, an outlandish caricature of toughness that was transparently absurd. He didn't seem to be able to possess the discretion to stop himself. The train just seemed to career onwards, escalating wreckage, on its way to the inevitable washed-out railway culvert.

His addictive drinking and his out-of-control sexual appetites were treated in much the same way. Assets to be prized. Testaments to his masculinity and his prowess. Aspects of character to be admired. "Adult" cocktails begin as soon as he arrived home. The drinking essentially never stopped until he went to bed. Restraint, it seemed to me, was only ever tentatively expressed, all too readily displaced by the desire for another drink. Pride accompanied a belief that he could hold his liquor well. That, too, was manly and grown-up. His perception of his drinking suggested that he felt it set him apart, establishing a kind of ascendancy over others who couldn't drink as successfully or as much as he could. And drinking, like his bullying, was supported by entitlement, an unquestioned right he could act upon, seemingly without conscience or consideration for others. If pushed by some unseen internal accuser, he might offer that drinking was the just desserts of someone who worked as hard as he did (he was unquestionably an extremely focused professional who demanded a great deal of himself). There was no acknowledgement, however, of the pain or misgivings about self that informed his drinking. Virtually no self-examination. No attempt to investigate the internal realities that drove the addiction. Never an admission of vulnerability, of error, or of misstep.

Sexual exchange was framed similarly. Hyperbolized masculinity. Desirable prowess. Confirmation of attractiveness. And cause for conspiratorial exchange with other men that, to my young eye, seemed to consolidate admission to a very special fraternity, one that any fellow must want to be a part of if they were solidly male. There were largely whispers of my father's sexual adventures when I was younger and he was variably still married to my mother, but the whispers were loud enough and frequent enough that I soon began to understand that he, like my mother, was not remotely faithful. In my later teens he openly bragged about the various women he knew. Sometimes the language used – probably characteristically – was crude and visceral and it made me feel uncomfortable, though I was loath to show it. Because it was obvious that I was, after all, supposed to view sexuality in the way that he did, I could not tell him that I was uneasy with his manner and his words. I imagined something must be wrong with me. Part of me very much wanted to share in this collaboration, to find some means of coming together with him and consolidating sexuality in a way that he might approve of. I could push myself to try to replicate his version of sexuality, but I always came back to the same place of discomfort. Worse, I had no words of my own to articulate my reticence. That, too, would take some time.

As I was older still, my father's relationships with his girlfriends became even more transparent, largely because he not only told me about them but sought my advice. I even found myself, on one occasion, counselling a woman who had become suicidal after he broke up with her. I can recall being astonished by his indifference to her pain. And in what struck me as a surprisingly casual and glib way, he handed the phone to me to deal with her distress. In the same way that I had not understood sexuality at age 10 when my counselling was solicited, I certainly was at a loss to make sense of the intricacies of relationships at age 19. Shortly after my phone call with this woman began, my father cheerfully absented himself to go out for the evening on another date.

Certainly, in part what made it difficult for me to discern the obviously impulsive character of much of his behavior when I was younger was the air of self-righteousness and seemingly deep conviction appearing to inform his attacks on the people around him. I assumed that he was responding to great wrongs others had committed that had incited moral outrage in him I wasn't in a position to appreciate. Perhaps also contributing to my confusion was the deliberate, methodical way he acted out much of his cruelty. He seized upon people's vulnerability and used it, systematically, to deconstruct them, in the process filling some need of his I could not discern.

My uncle was visiting our family over one of the holidays. He had lost his job some months before and was quite desperate, having been unable to find anything new for himself. My father raised the subject of my uncle's jobless-ness at a gathering of family and friends, including, I think, some of his work colleagues. He talked extensively about some of the big projects that he was working on and did so in a way that struck me as an attempt to impress the people around him. He then began to hint that there might be a place in his organization for my uncle. He implied opportunity and then withdrew it, doing so repeatedly. My uncle's attempts to maintain a professional façade that might support his attractiveness as a potential new executive started to break down, exposing the desperation that his joblessness was causing for him. My father played with him. Soliciting interest and hope, talking about possible functions my uncle might fulfil, and then disqualifying him. This whole process seemed to me to extend interminably, possibly over an hour or more. All played out very publicly. By the end of it, my uncle was nearly in tears. Probably con-fused, probably aware that he was being played with, but simultaneously despe-rately trying to hang onto his composure to keep a job opportunity alive. My father strung him out for months after this conversation, periodically soliciting letters and phone calls that predictably led nowhere. My mother, very much aware of what he was doing – having seen him operate in this fashion countless times before – confronted him repeatedly with his cruelty. In the face of her objection and her pressure, he would seem to back off a bit, only to reinitiate the ugliness. He utterly tyrannized my uncle, exploiting vulnerability, helplessness, and fear until he finally tired of the game.

There is one final aspect of my father's difficulty exerting control over himself which now becomes important to mention: the seemingly irresistible urge to counterpunch whenever others were perceived to have attacked him. His sense of being attacked might reflect an intuitive feeling that others meant to undercut, wound, or embarrass or it might represent reaction to a clear, intentioned attack that someone else directed towards him. In the case of the former, intuition might be based upon an accurate appraisal of the potential threat another person was likely to mount or, alternatively, it might also grow out of what struck one as exquisite sensitivity to injury that facilitated elabo-rate paranoid constructions, or conspiracies, that identified other people as risks. His many bigotries illustrated this vividly. Each group targeted with hatred seemed to be perceived as wanting to use, exploit, or manipulate him; each was also regarded as morally inferior and therefore as worthy of pun-ishment. He always seemed to find justification, in other words, for his con-tempt and his mistrust of the other guy. In so doing he cleared a path for rage that seemed to continuously press him to express itself. Rage that took the form of counter punching was no less resistible and no more containable than other forms of rage that also seemed to dominate him.

So I observed, again and again as a child, that any perceived or actual slight could produce – did produce – storms of retribution he seemed unable to contain. Once the ugliness of a counterattack began, he was caught in its grip. A single counter stroke could endure throughout an evening's social proceedings and sometimes long afterwards, culminating in a vendetta against a given individual he might never surrender. Any mention of that person or any indirect reminder of them could re-incite his fury and his condemnation. Sometimes he might be momentarily dissuaded from his invective, but, once started, it eventually seemed to reinstate itself, involuntarily bringing everyone back to his sense of injury and to his unquenchable indignation.

It was really quite difficult to make any sense of these intimidating displays throughout most of my growing up years. The conceptualization I provided above only emerged after years of personal work. What stood out for me as a youngster was the terrible risk that you faced if you identified yourself as an adversary. Doing so meant having to bear unending and probably escalating excoriation that promised to deny any reinstatement into his good books. At first I concluded that he behaved as he did when he directed his vendettas towards me because I was essentially bad – as must be those other people he spoke of in such condemnatory terms. The quality of personal righteousness that attended his rage flooded me, obscuring any capacity for perception or for thought. Only gradually was I capable of recognizing that his out-of-control counter punching bespoke some kind of struggle that he was having with himself. His incitement to join him in his rages and to support his bigotries somehow always felt wrong to me – perhaps because, somewhere inside, I quietly wondered whether his poisonous assessment of others might be flawed in the way that I hoped his assessment of me was. As much as I took his behavior to heart, I also felt its injustice. Besides hating myself, I also hated him for despising me. Was I really as awful and as compromising as he conveyed that I was? And if I wasn't, did it mean that he might be wrong about others?

These are very difficult and challenging issues for a child to resolve. I deliberately tried to support the idea that his endemic hatreds, including his hatred of me, might not be well grounded, but most of the time, for a very long time, I failed to convince myself. I was caught in a terrible dilemma. Hate myself or hate him. Share his pervasive derision and suspicion of others or open myself to the possibility of others' decency.

Hating him gave way to insight. Finding a way to trust and respect others, where he couldn't, granted me the chance to hear other voices. Insight allowed me to eventually recognize how deeply and profoundly wounded he had been – deeply and profoundly enough that he was unable to trust anyone, erecting walls of cynicism, contempt, and vigilance that kept everyone else out, locking himself up in a world that must have been profoundly lonely and that could and did become paranoid and delusional. To a degree, he could hide in the prejudices and culture wide misconceptions of his times. The effect of living life as he did, nonetheless, must have created a kind of slow, devastating erosion of the soul. If contempt and loneliness are your close companions and rage your defining interface with the world, how could you sustain yourself, I wondered.

Exposure to the kind, gentle, mentoring personalities of numerous teachers who took me under their wings (some coaches) helped me start to translate the alternate path I was looking for. I found I wanted to be someone who could make others feel the way that my teachers made me feel. I felt utterly undeserving of their warmth and acceptance, imagining that they, like my father, must respond to me with disgust and alienation. Somehow, I allowed myself to remain close to them in spite of what felt like suffocating fear that I must disappoint them. I never realized a strong subjective conviction of belonging in these relationships, but I could allow them to unfold. The warmth and respect that these people bestowed was partially transformative, coexisting side-by-side all of the worst things that I saw in myself. Father-surrogate relationships continued throughout my schooling, including graduate school, and extended themselves into the first eight years of my professional career. Initially feeling that I couldn't begin to take in the wonderful resources they afforded me in a way that would allow me to mitigate my pain to a meaningful degree, I discovered, as my life unfolded, just how much of an impact they had. I also had, as a result, clear evidence of how tenacious early pain is and of how long might be required to offset it. And, at that, at the end of a lifetime, I can still see and feel the residual effects of my father's version of masculinity in the private discourse that unfolds within me.

Through the example that these men provided, I was increasingly able to articulate some of the discomfort that my father's brand of identity and sexuality had evoked in me. I could decide that I didn't want to hurt other people and make them afraid of me because, through others' mentorships, I now knew how powerful and how sustaining kindness was. This, too, was not an easy journey. As one will see in succeeding chapters, I struggled with profound darkness and a deadness of the soul for quite some time that deeply frightened me. My insides largely felt like a wasteland, populated with devastating imagery and with rage born of cruelty, exquisite vulnerability, and helplessness. It was hard for me to see that I carried anything redeeming within me. But these lovely men helped me see that there was more to me, that I was capable of feeling other things beyond the devastation which my mother and, prominently, my father evoked in me. So now I was in the position to understand that what had made me feel uncomfortable in the way that my father approached women was his need to "thingify" them, to strip them of their humanity and complexity, rendering them objects he could use and then – importantly – discard without feeling anything himself. It occurred to me that maybe that was the point. Beyond the obvious distastefulness of exploiting somebody else or, worse, subjecting them to deliberate acts of cruelty, I could see another intention: the need to sidestep bonds of warmth and mutuality of affection that create belonging and render relationships, as well as life itself, meaningful and fulfilling. This proved to be an essential insight, one that allowed me to penetrate narcissism.

This foundational realization, however, led to more questions. I wanted to understand what had happened to him, what it was about his life experience that made loving and being loved so toxic. These were answers that presented me with the next series of challenges I would have to move through to unravel the puzzle – not only of his life, but of my own. My training and my work experience enabled me to elaborate my questions further. Love, after all, so much as I came to understand it, necessitated safety, trust, mutuality of respect, tolerance of vulnerability, and interdependence. It also seemed to require restraint, judgement, and a well-articulated appreciation of another's feelings as well as of one's own realities.

In iterating a list of qualities as I have just done, I make it sound like it has been easy for the collective us, including members of the mental healthcare professions, to figure all this out. It wasn't. Our conceptions of what was required to establish a successful love relationship have changed dramatically over time. When I was in graduate school, for example, one school of thought maintained that if a relationship was truly intimate, it meant that partners could share unvarnished truth however bluntly they wished to. That didn't work out so well. Another school of thought believed that people could move in and out of fidelity, engaging with multiple partners without generating harm to trust. Some professionals still hold this view (polyamory), but my sense is they would not attempt to impose it on others save for those who wished to make such a choice for themselves. During my early professional years, in contrast, advocates of polyamory would have enthusiastically encouraged couples to experiment with multiple relationships. The consequences of inciting multiple infidelities, in retrospect, now seem predictable and understandable, but they weren't at the time.

As helping professions, we have spent many years groping through choices that seemed appropriate enough or beguiling enough to integrate into psychotherapy practice, only to discover our conceptions were unworkable. The list of "necessities" for love to flourish that I have provided represents, of course, my own distillation of the knowledge that we have painstakingly acquired over literally decades.

All of which is to suggest that we didn't come by our current understanding of love easily. No doubt our conceptions will continue to change, hopefully in increasingly helpful ways, as they have in the past. The qualities that I just identified above, however, would prove to be enormously generative in better enabling me to grasp what my father's life journey had meant to him.

In the context of what I had come to understand about love, I could see that various aspects of my father's behavior – most prominently, within the purview of what has been discussed in this chapter, his punishing vigilance, his explosive rages, his cruelty, and his endemic contempt – subverted the very conditions required to establish a loving relationship. I found myself asking, again, whether these aspects of character represented a kind of byproduct of narcissism or, possibly simultaneously, whether one of narcissism's core functions was to protect the narcissist against love – as if love were an unbearable threat. Love as threat was not a new idea for me. I watched most of the people I worked with struggle with the risks that it posed and intense fear that it could arouse, creating myriad layers of defense to protect themselves in response. Most of these people, however, acted like they wanted to be able to love and were compelled to pursue it, even though imperfectly, showing themselves capable, to greater or lesser degrees, of tolerating it. If the ability to tolerate love represented a kind of continuum, I thought, maybe people with Narcissistic Personality Disorder experienced love, connection, and community as far more aversive than possibly much of the rest of humanity did. My understanding of what love entailed, then, brought me back to the hypothesis that I shared earlier in this chapter – that giving love and being loved was unbearable for the narcissist.

Let me return for the moment to the subject of my father's impulsivity – his ability to act with alacrity, without apparent hesitation or misgiving. Later in life my clinical experience permitted me to see that which would have been inaccessible to me when I was younger. Not looking at the self served my father's unconscious interests well, allowing him to engage and reengage with the damage that he inflicted on others without exposing himself to the empathy that insight would have imposed. If the function of his behavior was to refute loving feelings in himself and others, the absence of insight and of empathy could be seen to be self-protective, enabling him to turn others away in the various ways that he did without being constrained by concern for their feelings or for the pain that he was causing them.

I observed in my practice, over and over and over again, that when the self was threatened in some important manner, people's need for safety often trumped empathy. It was all about protecting the self. Perhaps a couple of simple examples would be helpful. If someone else's accurate assessment of you felt too jeopardizing, you could turn them away with scathing counter criticism. Some people felt remorse in the moment, but couldn't constrain themselves; many others were only able to experience remorse, if at all, once the moment had passed. The subgroup of people who seemed unable to experience remorse appeared to believe the negative attributes (scathing criticism) they attributed to the other party. Deconstructing the other guy and rendering him or her unattractive facilitated use of the defense. Now you could feel justified for treating someone else badly and get to protect yourself at the same time. You could even demand reparations.

The second example I'm about to give reiterates and deepens many of the dynamics of my first example. Suppose you experience giving an apology as diminishing and threatening, perhaps because it occasions unbearable vulnerability for you. You feel terribly small and unprotected when you face accountability, possibly because others in the past have treated you harshly and punitively. You find ways to sidestep the apology required of you by wrong footing the other party ("you're much worse than I am," "I'm tired of you getting hurt all the time," "if you're not happy, maybe you should leave" etc.). Once again, numbers of people would be aware that their defense was hurtful, but couldn't stop themselves from acting as they did; many others, in contrast, only experienced remorse after the event or, if the self was threatened sufficiently, not at all. Once again, believing in the negative attributes you assigned the other guy facilitated this process. In the moment, you literally experience them as being like the punitive other(s) who had so badly hurt you earlier in your life. You could feel justified in presenting a threat of abandonment, for instance, because the other party was "bad" and you had the right to protect yourself.

But sometimes you might not even be aware of the experiences that make giving an apology so painful for you. You act as you do as a means of establishing your authority and your power in a relationship without experiencing the vulnerability that an apology occasions for you. Your "defense" is automatic and reflexive rather than being informed by a measure of self-awareness. Defense short-circuits the vulnerability you find so painful, ensuring that you don't experience it. It is the work of psychotherapy to help people appreciate the automaticity of their defenses and the impact that their defenses have upon others. Even with extensive psychotherapy effort, some patients cannot tolerate insight or the empathy for the other which insight facilitates. Their resistance is formidable, tenacious, and obdurate. Considering the implications of their behavior feels too catastrophic for the self to bear and, importantly, doing so would compromise defenses they experience as essential to their psychic survival.

The examples I have given of abrogated empathy are simple ones. In actuality, many of the defenses that people employ are complex and nuanced, very much embedded in habits of being that have evolved over their lifetime. Habits of arrogance, condescension, impatience, mistrust, irritability, restlessness, feelings of being hard done by, hyper responsibility ("once again I have to do it all myself"), chronic hostility, sense of victimization, habitually talking over others – the list is potentially endless – capture, again in a somewhat simpleminded way, manifestations of defense. Less obviously, positive or seemingly innocuous human qualities can also serve defensive functions: humor, generosity, empathy, acquiescence, diffidence, charm, creativity, self-sacrifice, etc.

Now imagine that many of these postures intertwine with one another to form systems of defense (what I have called complex defenses) that also serve to protect us. Consider, as well, that these systems of defense unfold automatically and largely unconsciously, insinuating themselves into who and what we are on a day-by-day basis. Some of us are variably aware of the complex defenses we employ; many others of us are not. But how could we be? Unless we do a good deal of work with ourselves and are passionate about knowing ourselves, we probably won't understand why we have come to rely on the complex systems of defense that are such an integral part of our lives. Even when people make assiduous efforts to be self-aware, they can still expect to be possessed of blind spots that remain with them throughout their lives. We may remain unaware, in other words, of the complex defenses that can be such a pervasive part of us as well as the painful life experiences that instigate the use of defense. Moreover – and very importantly – many of us would be largely unaware what it would be like for other people to be targeted by the complex defenses we employ. We don't recognize the injury that we are causing them by relying on our defenses. We need our defenses. We need to be able to enact them without the obstructions that oppressive empathy might create.

To be fair, of course there are people who are all too painfully aware that their personalities batter and wound others, without being able to stop themselves from doing so. Empathy and guilt are very prominent parts of their experience, but, poignantly, they lack the means to step away from what they have become. Many people experience addiction in the manner that I have just described.

Getting people to understand that complex, interrelated patterns of behavior and feeling states serve defensive functions is a core and frequently challenging part of psychotherapy work. It is understandably hard for people to initially grasp the importance of defenses because it feels threatening to take a deep look at ourselves (e.g., "what you're telling me about myself makes me feel like a terrible person"). Helping people feel safe enough to look deeply represents a big part of what one does in psychotherapy.

Even after people are able to stand back and observe themselves, the function of defense often didn't declare itself. What makes this next phase of the work especially challenging is the efficiency of defense. Defenses curtailed the threat that people were trying to avoid before they could experience it. I would so often hear, "but I don't feel afraid – so why do I act this way?" It was only as people meaningfully disrupted defense that they began to experience the sense of threat that drove it. Disrupting defense is hard to do. Softening the reflexive arrogance or condescension or impatience that characterizes you is unsettling and disconcerting. It places people in the position of experiencing aversive affects their defenses allow them to sidestep. Feelings like, variously, remorse, shame, guilt, acutely felt vulnerability (for some people, "weakness"), helplessness, rage they would find unacceptable in themselves, personal diminishment, etc. Moreover, disrupting defense sometimes exposed people to a reexperiencing of the original trauma(s) that instigated defense. Reexperiencing aspects of original trauma can be particularly painful and disorganizing. People work very hard to avoid reexperiencing. If it can be tolerated, however, people are in a much better position to see why they feel compelled to handle themselves in the way that they do. Pain associated with reexperiencing is potentially formidable.

My own sense has been that people who have been able repress original trauma experiences may be effectively protecting themselves against Post

Traumatic Stress Disorder, which produces potentially lethal levels of psychic pain. Quite a benefit, actually. Repression is kind of a spooky, otherworldly defense. We literally forget traumatic experience. It remains inaccessible to us. Some clinicians maintain that repressed memory can reliably be recovered through treatment. Most clinicians now would probably agree that the "recovery" process is likely to produce inaccurate, distorted accounts of trauma. The cost of repression is relative personal blindness. People who have used this defense extensively probably have a harder time coming to understand the origins of their behavior.

I believe that our reliance on systems of complex defense is a pervasive and defining part of each of us, the well-adjusted as well as the troubled among us. Everybody. Good people. Really quite decent people. It appears to be something that everybody does (myself included) either in the face of immediate threat to the self or habitually. Sometimes the complex defenses we employ are subtle, nuanced, and highly elaborated and sometimes they are crudely transparent. People's awareness of the defenses they rely upon to protect themselves can vary considerably as does their ability to acknowledge what they are doing once the defense is identified for them, but employment of defenses often seems to require at least some measure of disabled empathy and disabled empathy, in turn, always seemed to amplify the robustness of defense. Disabled empathy, of course, represents another kind of blindness.

Blindness, in my father's case, was complicated. It was clear to me that he knew he was bullying others, that he could taste the harm and the shaming that he was causing them, and that it was obviously gratifying to him to act as he did. He wasn't unaware of his impact on others; on the contrary, he seemed to thrive on others' pain and impotence. Now I had a new question to ask myself about the interaction between empathy, self-awareness, and defense. One puzzle leading to another and then another.

Even defenses that impose significant costs on us and the people around us typically offer us compromises with our pain that allow us to do the best that we can with what we've got. My father's reliance on a tortured, complex system of defense, possibly to protect himself against love, can be seen to represent a particularly damaging compromise that would tragically limit his capacity to lead a fulfilling life. The in-depth investigation of his life that this book provides should serve to offer the reader an example of what a complex system of defense looks like and how it operates.

As a fitting end to this chapter, let me provide a very dramatic and perhaps disturbing example of the easy facility large groups of people – an entire society – can employ to shut down empathy. In his book, Empire of the Summer Moon, S. C. Gynne describes Comanche efforts in the southwestern United States to offset settlers' incursions onto land that the Comanches considered theirs. Comanche counter response to settlers' attempts to appropriate their lands was strikingly ruthless: captives were tortured in front of their families and babies were hoisted on Comanche spears before horrified parents. Once a raid on settlements finished, Comanche warriors returned home to their tribe, where they were said to show themselves to be very committed, caring parents devoted to child-rearing.

How could two such shockingly different realities coexist so casually in the same people? Can we satisfy ourselves by concluding that Comanches were, from our perspective, a primitive tribal entity that lacked the moral structures so carefully constructed by more humane versions of civilization? But if we give ourselves an answer like that, how do we account for the casual juxtaposition of so-called good and evil that seems to have characterized humanity from its recorded inceptions? Isn't this what we do in warfare? Love the people close to us at the same time – at the very same time – that we devastate our enemies, employing instruments of war that are meant to so terrify and cow our opponents they submit to our will? Even if one allows that the Allied position in World War II was, relatively speaking, possessed of greater moral justification and rectitude than the axis nations, does one not have to acknowledge that the war was brutal for all participants and that it brutalized everybody, inciting participants to engage, on a very large scale, in acts of extraordinary cruelty (e.g., carpet bombing) that the imperatives of war justified? And as people on both sides of the war engaged in such cruelty, were they not also, with varying degrees of success, simultaneously conducting personal lives with friends and loved ones defined by expectations of respect, caring, and empathy?

As a footnote to the Comanche story, the seemingly fearless, ruthless Comanche warrior bereft of empathy and humanity rapidly acquiesced to white pressure for a negotiated treaty when their own wives and children became captives as a result of white military action. Their concern for their families' vulnerability quickly induced them to capitulate.

For me, our capacity to embrace both brutality and love at one and the same time is who we are. We mustn't pretend otherwise. In the past, it has been adaptive for us to unleash our ruthlessness on our enemies at the same time we try very hard to love the people most important to us. In this fashion generally more sophisticated forms of civilization marshaled the resolve and the sense of entitlement required to dominate less sophisticated ones, thereby advancing the broader interests of civilization itself – without rupturing a combatant civilization's own cohesiveness. In this way, people could love the state and each other at the same time that they devastated an enemy. Being able to traverse brutality and love in the easy way we do has therefore been adaptive for our species. The potentialities to love and to brutalize coexist in all of us.

Empathy is a precious human commodity. It is readily compromised. We are designed, it seems, so that we can turn it off. If we mean to safeguard it – as I believe we must if we are to survive in a now remarkably interconnected, interdependent world – we must make assiduous, disciplined effort to protect it and enhance it. One of the intentions of this book is to help elucidate some of the means and the causalities that occasion loss of empathy.

Chapter 5

The Face of Narcissism – Father

The Nature of Relationships

The questions I have just raised about my father's blindness and his cruelty naturally led me into consideration of my father's relationships outside the purview of his relationship with me and with my mother.

By childhood, I was aware that my father characterized his friendships and his collegial relationships in exaggerated, larger-than-life terms, just as he did himself. So and so was the greatest or the best or the most extraordinarily talented at what he did. Or impossibly brilliant. Or inconceivably tenacious in overcoming Herculean obstacles. Even identified enemies were similarly formidable, testament to his own heroic status. When I was very young, I unhesitatingly accepted such portrayals. It was exciting to think of my father in mythic terms, though it did make him that much more intimidating as well – someone whose achievements I could never emulate. Indeed, he made it quite clear that I could not hope to do so, that his successes and his gifts of character were so formidable it would be doubtful I could ever approximate his talent. By the same token, I was given to understand that I was expected to replicate the immensities he saw in himself and that failure to do so carried with it disqualifications of shame and disgrace.

His greatness, then, was a mixed bag for me but, increasingly, I found myself feeling that it was too self-congratulatory, too exaggerated, and too self-indulgent for me to comfortably be able to share in the celebration he assigned himself. It just didn't feel real. And believing it carried with it the implication of my own terrible inadequacy. By the time that I was around eight or nine years old, I found myself dreading these soliloquies. I was implicitly expected to join in his self-congratulation, echoing his aggrandized appraisals of himself. Mercifully, sometimes I was only required to listen appreciatively. At their most awkward, his soliloquies could be mawkish or even maudlin in tone (especially if he was drinking). I recollect having the sense that these moments felt very insular, as if I was standing on the outside of his world watching him feast on his own praise. Even if I did all that he wished, or that I imagined he wished, I had no means of touching him nor did I feel I could enhance his celebration by participating in it. Mine was a scripted part and an inauthentic one at that. His celebration was not generous

DOI: 10.4324/9781003246923-5

in the way that human celebration can be; it made no room for me to augment celebratory mood with reciprocal feelings of my own. Layered on top of
all of this was acute awareness that failure to provide him what he wanted, in
the form and to the degree that he wanted it, would result in injury for him
and subsequent wounding for me.

Just as I was held captive – a virtual prop with no dimensions or personhood of his own – so too were his "friends." Indeed, many of them were very
successful themselves. For some, the opportunity to trade testaments to
shared greatness was probably gratifying, but I wonder now if they recognized
how little else there was in their relationship with him to support meaningful
human connection. Listening to some of these sometimes seemingly endless
conversations was disconcerting: giants from Odin patting each other on the
back who never somehow seemed to get around to talking about themselves
in human dimensions. The feeling that most closely approximated my reaction to these conversations was a mixture of intimidation, envy, and loneliness. Much of the interaction felt like caricature.

Sometimes when my father waxed prolific about his own greatness and the
greatness of those in his listening circle, he encountered resistance. People
trying to move past the walls he was erecting so that they could engage their
own humanity and his in a more comfortable, genuine format became impa-
tient with him. Some gently poked fun at the outlandish proportions he
assigned himself and them. Others openly resisted his hyperbole in a frank,
outspoken way. They wanted more from him and they wanted more for
themselves. In such moments he appeared to be utterly defeated, very much at
a loss to understand what was being required of him. I thought his perplexity
in these contexts was painfully evident.

My father was probably most at ease with himself talking to others he
could regard as less accomplished than he was. In the company of such
people, he dialed back his self-importance (though it still appeared to be
present), often adopting what struck me as a deliberately folksy, "I've got
working-class roots, too" kind of delivery. To my eye, he was able to make it
work better sometimes than others. The more performative the presentation
was, the less successful it was; the more he could allow himself to connect
with the realities of their lives, the more tangible and satisfying the connection
appeared to be. The performative elements of his interactions with people,
whether colleagues or the average Joes, were always prominent, at the best of
times fading into the background only to make their presence felt again
before too much time had elapsed.

I can speculate that my father might have felt more comfortable talking to
what he would characterize as average people because they were not felt to
challenge his ascendancy. In the presence of people whose accomplishments
approximated his own, his inflated appraisals of himself and of them became
more dominant parts of the social exchange. His behaviour and sometimes
theirs brought to mind elaborate threat displays that competitors might direct

towards one another. Elaborate and sometimes grotesque pissing contests. These exchanges came to feel dangerous to watch, sometimes eventuating, as they did, in open belligerence as one participant tried to one up and outdo the other. On some few occasions that I witnessed, it had been necessary for onlookers to provide physical restraint to prevent a literal battle from taking place. I can remember my mother commenting to me that any time my father was in the presence of someone whose achievements he felt significantly eclipsed his own, he became obviously ill at ease. It had been her experience that when this happened he was likely to find an excuse to leave whatever event he was attending.

Only in retrospect have I been able to recognize that my father's relationships were largely transactional, often built upon some shared rapacity he and the other party were intent upon pursuing. At various points in his life my father established informal business partnerships. These "partners" enjoyed larger-than-life attributions, much like his corporate colleagues. He was on the lookout for vulnerabilities in the marketplace – people, for example, who might be desperate to sell some land, a business, house etc. He and his partner might follow the property over time, instigating phone calls to take the temperature of the seller and to tease them with the prospect of an offer that never materialized. When the seller's desperation overtook them and an extraordinarily good purchase price could be realized, a purchase was made. The process was typically an elaborate one, extending over months. As I listened to my father tell these stories, his pleasure in dominating these people and winning his deal was unmistakably prominent. There was a pleasure to be had not just in getting a fire sale price, but in humiliating the other. I suppose as I heard him talk about his retailing and merchandising work at large corporations he helped direct, he demonstrated similar pleasure in being able to disguise, lure, and confound store clients. Of course, business is business. But the pleasure he took from manipulation and exploitation of others seemed to be defining for him. It was very much the sum of his parts rather than a part of the whole he could bring to bear on his profession.

Once shared rapacity no longer existed, relationships seemed to dissipate. Or worse, should he sense vulnerability in a partner or a colleague he could profitably exploit, he readily did so – with alacrity. As much as he might express deep injury about perceived disloyalty others demonstrated towards him, he was unapologetically and unhesitatingly ruthless towards them. It was an odd juxtaposition for me to witness as a youngster. Expectations of unswerving and unfaltering loyalty he regularly betrayed in his relationships with others. Relationships were not sustained by depth of understanding of the other's human circumstance, by compassion, or by bonds of attachment and respect: value only existed if others partnered themselves with his voracious, exploitative appetites.

Relationships also appeared to be infused with parsimony. Carefully calculated transactions meant to ensure that my father was the dollar winner. Even something that he was passionate about, his fishing, was informed by parsimony. To all appearances, he looked to be generous in offering to take his friends out on his boat for fishing expeditions. The deal was that they could keep only one fish that they caught. The rest were his to sell. In this way he not only had enough money to pay for his gas, but regular maintenance and dockage for the boat as well. He often bragged about this small act of financial prowess. He had created an impression of generosity and even sociability, but had insured, in the process, that it would cost him nothing. He certainly hadn't needed the money at the time. I came to recognize that the microcosm of fishing reflected the way he approached relationships in the larger context of his life. Meticulous attention to what he was getting versus what he was giving. Rarely letting go and giving more than he got. Calculating to ensure the other party either paid for what they received or vastly overpaid.

I cannot overstate my father's commitment to parsimony. It seemed to invade every aspect of my and my mother's relationship with him as well as his relationship with others. He was mindful of every dollar that he spent. Generosity was only rarely apparent and when it was, he soon retreated from it, recalculating what generous acts had cost him or reminding everyone what was owed to him for gifts or favors given. Gift giving could make him angry, as if the impulse to give was nearly inescapably paired with cynicism and contempt. If cynicism and contempt were defenses, what was it about the urge to give and to be generous that made him feel like he needed to protect himself? What was the threat that he perceived, I kept asking myself? Could it be discomfort and a measure of jeopardy he experienced when his behavior evoked affection from others? Were other's feelings of affection aversive for him because they threatened to engender bonds of obligation in him that reciprocal affection of his own might create? More than any other, this question proved to be pivotal in allowing me to unlock narcissism.

Parsimony was also a metaphor, I came to see, for emotional exchange and for relationships. Building his formidable walls around himself meant that other people could never get close enough to hurt him or, more to the point, to use him. Vulnerability was intolerable. He could affirm his power to protect himself by using others and by exploiting their loyalties. He was constantly on the lookout – literally hypervigilant, as I can see now – for any intimation of disloyalty or rapacity in the people in his sphere, continuously anticipating it and continuously girding himself against it. I could also see that his fear of exploitation was so acutely felt that he experienced the rest of the world as being as ruthless and as self-interested as he was. He was living in a projected world, one replete with the demons populating his inner life he unceasingly imputed to other people. How awful for him, I thought. As I was able to put these ideas together, I felt I had a better measure of what his vigilance meant. He could never feel safe. His existence was defined by unrelenting solitude. Desperate to keep everybody out, he had engaged in continuous and compulsive combat with the rest of the world.

Like many people who had lived through the depression, his preoccupation with parsimony most certainly bespoke his response to the harrowing poverty he had endured during most of his childhood and young adult life. Later I will argue that poverty had a devastating impact on him, playing a significant role in the creation of his narcissism.

More should be said about the projected world my father occupied. It dominated his relationships with others and his relationship with himself. He unceasingly accused others of being possessed of the constellation of destructive impulses that defined him. Others wanted to screw him, or manipulate him, or deceive him. Or they were perceived as intending to inflict harm or humiliation. The world around him was felt to be constantly on the make. People, he would always say, were always out for themselves, in one way or another. There were no acts of authentic generosity; everybody had an angle. But I saw that genuine kindness – kindness that he couldn't unmask or discredit – quite unseated him. He was obviously uncomfortable around people whose decency and genuine concern for others could not be compromised by his cynicism. He retreated visibly into a smaller self, using a tiny, high-pitched voice: "oh, aren't you just so nice" or "aren't you wonderful," vaguely sounding like he was full of incredulity. I noticed that he often retreated from such people altogether, usually fairly quickly. These were not the people he seemed to want to associate with.

But if he succeeded in deconstructing someone's decency, exposing ugly intent of one kind or another under the surface, he stayed and bored in, expanding his advantage and leveraging as much discomfort as he might. His sense of relish and celebration in such situations was terribly transparent. At one point later in my life I came to understand that people's failed humanity offered him some vindication for his own. "You see," he seemed to be saying, "none of you are any better than I am – you deserve my contempt." Contempt was gateway entitlement for him. It justified his rapacity. It substantiated his mistrust. And it allowed him to transform his fear of vulnerability into qualities that confirmed power: the capacity to celebrate others' humiliation and the capacity to negate empathy with a virulently misanthropic perspective. Restated in terms I relied on a couple of paragraphs ago, it allowed him to hold the world at arm's-length, sidestepping the possibilities of harm and "weakness" that meaningful intimacy would have entailed.

Living with someone who more or less constantly attributes the worst of himself to others often made me feel like I was living in an upside-down world. My father generated such stature for himself, particularly when I was younger, it was hard to disbelieve him. I was simultaneously repelled by his dark vision of the world and the people in it. It just felt wrong. Like all the other forms of insight that I eventually acquired, appropriate and proportionate disbelief took some time to present itself to me. The world I shared with him was all odd angles and jagged contradictions. I knew the pieces didn't fit, but I couldn't figure out why. Only gradually did it dawn on me that the attributions he directed towards others were mostly not about them, but about him.

His cynicism did equip him to ferret out moral failings in others with astonishing efficiency. As often as not, however, his appreciation of others' tarnished humanity was simplistic, overblown, and improbably overstated. He tried to support his perceptions with invective and outrage. Evidence was supplied in the form of convoluted undercurrents of malignant intent that only he, with the advantage of his wisdom and his unique life experience, could disentangle. His characterizations of the "badness" he saw in others lacked internal coherence, which didn't seem to bother him (but certainly did me). As I have noted previously, I dared not oppose him – at least not too defiantly when I was very young – but privately I found myself concluding that his constructions didn't seem to make much sense. I suppose, again, I make it sound easier than it was for me. Who was I to question a giant? He must be right. Thankfully, my dear mother kept pulling apart some of his more outrageous assertions, helpfully pointing out that he was being preposterous, that he was assassinating others for the very things that he did himself. As always, being the mixed blessing that she was, she might also, confusingly, endorse some of his outrageous conspiratorial arguments, further elaborating them with oddball embellishments of her own.

World War II with the Japanese was prearranged. Roosevelt and the Japanese were in on it together, agreeing on a timetable and a scenario to start the conflict. Thousands of Japanese workers in the pineapple fields had cut huge arrows out of the cultivation to guide the Japanese bombers. Sinister forces operating in the background had set the carnage in motion to manipulate large-scale forces of manufacturing and productivity for their own gain. Always unnamed sinister forces. Unnamed is significant. That left you no recourse to explore the issue further to determine whether the argument had been possessed of any substance. This particular conspiracy theory, in a variety of similar forms, was quite popular during the 40s and 50s, so it had the glow of popular wisdom, a tradable social commodity one could use to enhance others' perceptions of one's acuity. I suppose I cite this particular example because it demonstrates the easy juxtaposition of personal psychology onto national events and the interpretation of history. An inclination to find the darkest parts of himself in others made it relatively easy for him to accept conspiracy theories; correspondingly, her fragility, paranoid outlook, and fragmentation allowed my mother to uncritically absorb improbable ideas.

Similar principles applied to my father's attitude towards race. My father presented axiomatic racial truths. Blacks were lazy. They were shiftless (shiftless was always used with lazy, though I don't know why). They were childlike and guileless. They were unintelligent compared to the white man, so they quite naturally needed his direction. He knew how to look after their needs and harness their limitations in a way that would work best for society. Blacks couldn't self direct (I should say that the word my father used was nigger, or, in a more benevolent mood, darkie). They had no initiative. They always looked for the easy way out. They were dishonest. But, in contrast to the inertia that typified them in the rest of their lives, they were powerfully, uncontrollably sexually voracious and had to be carefully watched to ensure that the white women around them were safe. And then I heard that blacks were a dangerous and volatile force in the broader sense; give them an inch and they would take the proverbial mile, subverting white rule and hard earned, much-deserved white privileges. Give them guns and these inert childlike other beings would organize themselves, rise up as one, and annihilate their white adversaries.

No room for compassion in this perspective or for an appreciation of the other as a well-defined human being possessed of uniqueness and an interplay of complex feelings and motivations much like any other people. No recognition of dignity or of suffering in the cardboard cutouts he erected for himself as stand ins for an entire culturally diverse race. Perception driven by his own compulsion to exploit, to use, and to objectify.

Of course, it must be recognized that numerous forces, in addition to personal dynamics, support prejudice. I won't attempt to review them here; my primary interest and focus in the narrow confines of this discussion is on the internal dispositions and realities that shape perception, feeling, and behavior. Later in the book there will be opportunity to broaden context and consider other factors that contribute to prejudicial beliefs.

On a personal level, living with my father's unceasing projection of his own dark impulses onto the people around him meant, as I said, living in a topsy-turvy world. I'm being told that such and such a person is selfish or greedy or devious or ruthless, but that's not what I'm feeling at the time. What I'm feeling is my father's powerful, invasive voice. It's too big and it feels malignant, but my attention is being directed towards someone else's malevolence. I'm being asked to feel that they represent threat, but my father's presence feels ever so much more threatening than the threat he attributes to them. To accommodate him, I try to believe what he's telling me about the other, but the most tangible malevolence that I experience mostly seems to come from him – even when I can see that his appraisal of the other is objectively accurate. Mind bending. And then there are the occasions when my view of the maligned other is very much at odds with his. I can't see the danger that he's spotlighting with his emotion-laden indictments. They just don't make sense. They don't fit my grasp of the person. And, heaven knows, I needed to find somebody in whom I could believe in his blighted world (I suppose, half tongue-in-cheek, that's why Santa Claus became so important to me), so I'm aware, from a fairly young age, that my desperation to find redeeming qualities in others might have distorted my capacity to see them accurately. Finally, there are the occasions when my father directs accusatory intent towards others when I can clearly see that it is my father who is being rapacious, disrespectful, self-interested etc. "Wait a minute, you are doing that to him, he's not doing that to you," I might say to myself.

My portrayal of my 8–10-year-old self must sound unlikely to the reader, but remember that my conversations with myself are unfolding in a paternal environment that more or less continuously demanded that I not trust my own perceptions and which more or less continuously foisted upon me either impossibly inflated or impossibly cynical assessments of others.

As a psychologist, I could see that the projected world that so dominated my father's perception, compelling and re-compelling him to assign his own damaged humanity to others, imprisoned him in an unrelenting solitude, one in which he witlessly found himself relating to the aggrandized and misanthropic parts of himself that he imposed on everyone around him. His world, as a consequence, seemed to be populated with cartoonish two-dimensional stereotypes reflecting his own crude appraisal of humanity. Alone in an existence devoid of connection to the real, complex human beings around him. A relentlessly punishing starvation diet.

During the latter two decades of his life, it finally became apparent to me that my father's exaggerated characterizations of his friendships grossly misrepresented his reality. Prior to that, though I wondered what passed between him and other people that rendered his relationships meaningful, part of me still thought that there must be more to his exchange with other people than I could see. I imagined that my appraisals must be wrong or were poorly informed, that maybe the "great" friendships he kept referencing really existed on terms I could not appreciate. His friendships were typified, perhaps not surprisingly, in the same aggrandized terms as other facets of his life. He was so emphatic about the descriptors he used and brought such imposing conviction to the subject matter of his friendships that I ended up – wrongly – questioning my own perceptions rather than his. Eventually I came to recognize that he had probably not enjoyed many enduring friendships and, at that, I wasn't sure how close he had allowed himself to become to the best of the friends he had.

I very much wanted to believe he had more for himself than I think he did. I was aware of people that he had mentored – as improbable as that sounds, in the context of this discussion – and I was also aware of one friend he appeared to have stayed in touch with throughout a substantial part of his adult life. Maybe, I thought, he had allowed himself to be more open and human with them, but other voices inside me reminded me that was improbable. Now, in hindsight, I can see that my father's relationships, or the best of them, generally followed the same pattern: aggrandized idealization which paralleled (and fed) his own exaggerated view of himself followed by a catastrophic sense of betrayal that might either end the relationship or produce a never-ending vendetta. My stepmother (my father's second wife) reflected on the subject of my father's capacity for friendship shortly after his death: "you know, I don't think your father ever had any friends – not real ones – I think he was alone." Her words have stayed with me, echoing indelible confirmation of his antipathy and his mistrust towards humankind. At that time she also made it clear how painful and how punishing her marriage had been, but as the years separated her from my father's death and she was facing her own end, she began to idealize him. To my mind, her altered portrayals of him bore no relationship to the person I knew. Her idealization appeared to be comforting to her.

Once again, I confronted that haunting question: what had happened to him? I knew that understanding this question would help me understand myself. As this narrative unfolds, I will eventually find my way back to this pivotal question. I think I did find some answers, but I have to set more of the stage before I can credibly consider them.

There are other aspects of my father's relationships with others and with himself that need to be discussed.

One aspect or piece was his aggrieved self. A part of the self that openly cried out about the injustice or the insensitivity or the betrayal that others were felt to direct towards him. This piece of him was unselfconscious: no hesitation, no misgiving, and no mitigation in its expression. Deep offence, deep injury, and of course angry indignation. Howls of it. No capacity to observe or to mediate his emotions. Profound injury accompanied by furious righteousness, fearsome in its display. And these were times, as I noted in the second chapter, when my mother was likely to gore the bull. Some of his other girlfriends did, too. Interestingly, as he was challenged, his outcry might become more plaintive and childlike. Sometimes it even began that way. He did sound like a small and defenseless child in great pain, a child who expected, no, demanded that others heed his cry. The effect was both comical and preposterous, particularly for one who had couched himself in such heroic terms. I didn't know what to make of it as a child myself or even as a teenager. It made me enormously uncomfortable and it also made me feel like I wanted to laugh. I had no way to process this. It felt like it was at odds with everything that I had been taught about him. Like so much else, it also felt like a dangerous moment, one in which one misstep could cause real jeopardy. Now as I consider this behavior, I find myself thinking that what I was seeing was his real core, an irreparably injured child seeking solace for damage that no one could fix. The exaggerated, dramatic, and even absurd presentation of this pain belied its immensity.

My father did turn to the women in his life intermittently, as he did me, to talk about the privations of his childhood – and objectively I think they were many and formidable. This was another facet of his aggrieved self. Exposing such pain seemed, simultaneously, to evoke hostility, as if the act of stepping into a dependent or a needy position was unbearable for him. His hostility rendered his pain exclusive and forbidding, a private domain that in the end only he could occupy. Outsiders were only momentarily welcome, if that's the right word, pushed away by angry reflection that conveyed they could not hope to understand the magnitude of such suffering. Talking about his pain also evoked unmistakable envy of the other, which made it risky to share in his lamentation: why had he alone been subjected to so many burdens when the rest of humanity (including, particularly, his listener) had been spared? I'm not sure my father ever felt like others were able to soothe him to the degree that he might have needed them to when he was in the midst of such pain, nor did it ever seem to me he was able to soothe himself. Alcohol was his best source of succorance at such times.

As companion to this part of him, my father's relationship with his own mother stands out. I observed that every time he talked to her, he sounded quite literally like a five or six-year-old trying to appease a parent. His language became primitive and infantile; so, too, did the tone of his voice. She responded to him in a somewhat similar fashion, though she did not sound as childlike as he. This happened virtually every time they spoke.

Like his outcries of pain, these exchanges felt preposterous and odd. I had to suppress the impulse to laugh. My mother, on the other hand, never missed these opportunities, mocking him and belittling him, which made me feel like I needed to get out of that version of Dodge as fast as I could. I do remember thinking, "what on earth can this mean?" I had no idea, but I intuitively knew that it was important and meaningful behavior. I was aware that my mother saw my grandmother as a competitor, as someone who endlessly solicited attention from my father, whether through a phone relationship from her apartment in Philadelphia (we lived in New York) or through the face-to-face relationship she had when she visited my father. My grandmother was unrelentingly hypochondriacal. If thwarted – my mother certainly did her best to see that she was – my grandmother's kindly, suffering, plaintive presence very quickly became suffused with what looked like unadulterated hatred. I don't think I can ever forget the rage I saw in her eyes. They were so much like the darkness I recognized in my father's eyes when he was filled with fury.

I knew only that my grandmother's life had been marked by extreme poverty and deprivation that was especially pronounced during my father's growing up and young adult years. I could also see that she unquestioningly idealized him while he still seemed to experience her as his mom who needed protecting. The infantile voice that he employed, however, suggests to me now that he also yearned for protection himself, perhaps protection that their shared circumstances or her own limitations might have prevented her from providing. They felt like they were joined together in their perpetuities, held fast by suffering and trauma I was not privy to, much like storied World War II orphans who forged bonds of care with one another that the adult others around them found difficult to penetrate even after the rigors of the war had passed.

As I think about my father's relationship with his mother, I can perhaps better understand his pointed antipathy towards women. The childlike yearning that was so evident in his voice and so prominent in his relationship with his mother rendered women a potential source of compromise for him. Facing a woman and facing the need she could elicit in him – particularly the immensity of childhood need long unrequited – likely created threat for the tough guy, bullying persona he so relied on to keep himself safe. Far easier to denigrate the woman and transform her into a two-dimensional sexual object without much of an intellect. That way he could afford himself protection from the frighteningly intense dependent yearning he carried within himself. A woman became a thing he could use and discard without feeling much.

The best of my father was his storytelling. He was a consummate story-teller. His stories were imaginative and creative. And they were filled with a sense of adventure and excitement that made them magical. He clearly loved stories. On reflection, storytelling was the one time I could hear his music, the one time I could hear him sing. And when he told stories, I think it was probably the only time I could let my guard down with him. I knew that so long as he was telling his story, he was immersed in it and immersed in sharing it with me. The depredations that could otherwise expose me to attack were not likely to unfold. I could let go and lose myself in the story and in the marvelous twists and turns of plot that he invented. A very little oasis, but one that meant a great deal to me. It would prove to be my father's storytelling that elaborated itself into some of the answers that I was looking for. I think his love of storytelling led to my love of literature and helped to set the stage for my lifelong fascination with other people's stories.

My father could create momentary magic in his relationships with other people, casting a kind of spell about himself that rendered him charismatic. His wonderful storytelling was certainly part of that. I sometimes think that those bits of him might have reflected what he could have become, but they all too quickly became harnessed by his feral, ruthless instincts on the lookout for advantage and for opportunities to exploit. As much as he was able to sustain it, charisma usually ended up being used to fill some darker motive. It confused people. They kept looking for the lovely guy they thought they had caught a glimpse of. He might tease them by reappearing in a transitory way, but he never stayed. He never could. Nice didn't last. But it did last long enough to tantalize people to keep them coming back to find that other fellow.

Chapter 6

The Face of Narcissism – Father

There Can Only be One God

My father's intransigently angry, aggrieved self was particularly likely to make an appearance when others contradicted or disagreed with him. This facet of his anger, at least, was somewhat predictable, though it might be hard, in any given situation, to understand why he experienced a particular voice as contrary. There was no evidence of softness or vulnerability when such anger overtook him. His mode of attack was invariably intensely personal. He targeted – or invented – personal characteristics in the other that he slandered his opponent with. Humiliation and shame were his weapons of choice. Short, startlingly blunt assaults on the other person's dignity, often taking the form of a single word or three-to-four-word label meant to devastate. He was surprisingly good at it, though sometimes – rarely – his attack was so obviously misplaced that it evoked corrosive laughter from his audience. Attacks were often carried out publicly, which made them that much more likely to feel more intensely shameful, but they could also be undertaken in the privacy of a person-to-person exchange where his revulsion for his target and his anger felt even bigger.

"Little" was a popular adjective, delivered in a mocking tone. So, also, were racial slurs. Attacks on competence or on character were common. If a woman was involved, her appearance was often the target as was her intellect (one neighborhood woman deserved the sobriquet "pig face" when she disagreed with him). These executions seemed to be both remorseless and entitled, carried out with no discernible hesitation. So far as I knew, they were not followed by apology or by any obvious attempt to repair nor did they seem to occasion painful self-reflection. One saw him act this way again and again when others disagreed with him or challenged him, never mind criticized him. He didn't appear to have any choice in the way that he reacted. Divergent opinions were most often experienced as assaults that evoked indignation, righteous injury, and unhesitating effort to obliterate and intimidate the other. A one trick pony. Very little means to mediate differences, to learn from them, or to use them to instigate self-evaluation. If the other pressed their point home successfully, my father's sense of victimhood became very pronounced, sometimes eventuating in the childlike presentation

DOI: 10.4324/9781003246923-6

described in the previous chapter. This transition could be particularly maddening to live with, especially when he alternated rapidly between verbal assault and victimization. Being on the receiving end, for me, meant having to contend with somebody who never pulled his punches, but who expressed outrageously disproportionate injury when even a whiff of criticism was implied. I had two childhood nicknames for my father. The first was the hoary wrath holder (I didn't know what hoary meant at the time, but I think an author had used it to characterize a frightening troll-like creature I found described in something like a Grimm's fairytale). The second was fragile tyrant. These names helped.

As an adult, I could put into words what eluded me as a child: my father was largely unable to make room for other personalities or other voices. His voice had to occupy the biggest space. It had to dominate. As I watched him, I begin to realize that he expected others to "twin" themselves to him, treating themselves as an extension of his wishes, his feelings, his perspectives, and his impulses. Praise ensued if they did so. Shaming followed if they did not. But even when people accommodated him, they could still be rebuked or contradicted, especially (and seemingly paradoxically) when they replicated his voice emphatically. His reaction in these contexts was certainly puzzling. Had they not given him what he wanted, and, at that, in spades? They had, after all, seemingly cloned a version of him in themselves and provided a passionate imitation. But then, I thought, maybe that was the problem. Their passion and their ideological purity were perhaps too much for him. Did he now feel that the depth of conviction they used when they employed his voice threatened to compromise his prerogative of initiative? His need to position himself as a unique visionary? I'm the prophet. I get the boomy voice. Your voice, your presence, your passion has to remain more muted than mine. If it gets too big, you become too dynamic. I'm the shaker and the mover. Don't attempt to appropriate my power. Perhaps an obvious answer, but a tough one for me to sort through. So, acolytes had to color between lines: worshipful, unswervingly loyal imitations of the master but never the master himself. Convincing echoes of him, but NEVER more.

In the discussion that's about to unfold, I will review material I have already explored, but I do so with the intention of focusing more directly on the theme that I am now trying to highlight – my father's efforts to invade and assimilate other people, transforming them into vessels he could fill with himself. I watched my father attempt to do this to the people around him. Some openly resisted him, as I noted in an earlier chapter. In the context of his workplace or even his personal life, they were often other senior executives on approximately the same level as he was. Their accomplishment and their "greatness" enhanced his own sense of aggrandizement, but he often found himself facing intense conflict with them. They got to keep their sense of self, but in the presence of frequent and often intense boundary wars that sometimes took the form of the rutting displays previously described. Subordinates, to varying degrees, were not so lucky. Open disagreement rarely seemed to emerge in his business interactions with them (I was witness to interchanges in the workplace on many occasions over the years when I spent time in my father's office) or in his social interface with them. Because my father was so engaged in storytelling, he provided nearly daily accounts of his encounters with the people around him. What he told me seemed to confirm what I saw: his colleagues either allowed themselves to be subsumed within his personality, accepting reality as he defined it or they faced assassination and expulsion. On some few occasions, however, I can remember my father demonstrating compassion towards people he had discovered lacked the talent to do the job. I kept hoping I would see more of this side of him, but it never became more prominent.

On one occasion my father came home from the office, he was very much pleased with himself. He had installed a full-size traffic light on his desk. If he liked what his people were talking about, the green light was on display. If they wandered into territory he began to disapprove of, up came amber. Red, he said, meant stop talking immediately. He so instructed people working for him when he was conferencing with them. So far as I could see, the ambiance he created around him was straight jacketing; it involved policing people, placing pressure on them to focus on what they thought he wanted rather than giving them the freedom to explore ideas in a more freewheeling, person-centered way. Step away from yourself. Think about me. Think about what I want you to be. Any boss subordinate relationship is possessed of such pressures, of course, but some bosses, by virtue of who they are as people, are keenly aware and very much desirous of the need to enhance and expand a given employee's unique gifts; my father, on the other hand, appeared to want to erase people and replace them with a version of himself.

Most disturbing for me were the people who sounded like my father, as if they had swallowed substantial parts of him holus-bolus, either utterly abandoning their own personhood and replacing it with their imitation of him or disguising it with a facsimile of him so that he might never discern what was really going on inside them. My younger self preferred that they were doing the latter, but I was afraid that many of them were doing the former. Quite a chilling drama to observe. Were they deeply, but privately anguished, as I was, about diminishment of the self and about survival of the self? Oddly, unlike me, some of them seemed to be pleased with their new selves, almost exuberant in the way that they channeled my father. I was quite horrified. These people seemed to have lost themselves, but felt transcendent and even embellished in response. That idea also frightened me. Could people lose themselves and not know it happened? Could you become a ghost or a wraith and be the happier for it? Very, very pressing questions for me to answer.

I felt myself quite consciously struggling against the identity he seemed to want to impose on me, but I had to do so in the context of constant accommodation, constant anticipation of what was safe and what wasn't. I consciously resisted becoming a version of him. He could feel it and he hated me for it. I could feel that. None of this was ever spoken, but it was a very powerful subtext. Head in my own direction and follow my own promptings and face humiliation and shaming that could terminally damage the self. Fail to do so and endure catastrophic and perhaps permanent loss of self, allowing someone who felt like a stranger to replace me. I didn't want the monstrous realities that seemed to occupy my father to become me. That prospect quite terrified me, all the more so because I had compelling reasons to believe I was becoming a monster myself, as will be seen in the next chapter.

As a youngster in grades three and four I used to watch a wonderful art show on television, the John Nagy show. TV wasn't much in those days, but this show was really quite endearing. Nagy was a gentle, lovely guy. It's a shame the show hasn't been replicated for contemporary kids. John Nagy taught kids how to draw. Each week showcased new techniques and interesting new subject matter to try to capture on paper. He put together an art kit replete with instruction manual, chalk and water color, and sundry other interesting things. For a small fee you could send away for it and get one, which I did. When it arrived, I was pretty excited. My parents naturally wanted to know what it was. I could sense apprehension in their initial reactions, particularly my father's. What followed were hushed conversations carried on loudly enough that I could overhear bits and pieces of them. They were uncomfortable I was interested in art. Their whispering suggested this was not something they expected a young boy would want to do. I was confused. My mother was an artist and, for a period of time, my father had even attempted oil painting. The whisperings became explicit parental concern that expressed itself after perhaps a month or so. Real boys didn't want to draw. Real boys were more preoccupied with sports and rough-and-tumble play (I did those things too). I noticed that they seemed to screw up their faces into expressions of concern, in the peculiar way that parents can, whenever they looked at me. Very soon their concern reached unbearable proportions for me.

About this time, they decided to tell me more about what was really wrong. The phrase "real boys," it turned out, meant that they thought something was wrong with my sexuality (I had already discerned that, but hearing them say it, actually say it, was so much more awful). My interests meant that I was different, aberrant in their eyes, clearly not a good difference. My passion for classical music also had a similar effect on them. I didn't know why I liked classical music, but I just did. I didn't seem to be able to enjoy the music that was popular at the time or that became immensely popular once rock 'n' roll got its start, but I could fake it. Pretend to be part of my generation's culture – culture that was supposed to be captivating and immersive, but just wasn't for me. I remember feeling that I wished I got the music that everybody else did. It would mean that I was part of something that I was supposed to be part of rather than being set apart in a bad way. It would also mean that I didn't have to keep secrets about my differences.

From time to time, when I was able to afford them, I would buy classical albums – full-length 33s – rather than the 45 rpm pop songs my friends were purchasing. I hoped they wouldn't notice I didn't have any of the latter. I tried to sneak my classical purchases home unobtrusively under my jacket, but given my size and the size of a classical album, that was a very iffy proposition. Soon after my parents confronted me about the intersection of interest in drawing and sexuality, I gave up John Nagy. I quietly hung on to classical music. I could do so because my mother left my father around this point in my life for months at a time as she attempted, haltingly but with a kind of success, to forge a life apart from him in the US Virgin Islands. That meant she was not around much of the time, nor was my father because of his late work hours, leaving me free to listen to my music without intrusion when I got home from school.

Identity, then, was something that had to be forged with great care and with no small measure of secrecy in the presence of my father's invasiveness. I think it was much the same for his colleagues and friends. Unless you were a giant yourself, you probably had to carefully construct an understated version of yourself or, worse, surrender identity and incorporate him if you were to exist in his world – the caveat being that if you were in his presence, he expected to be able to subject you to his terms. Those terms demanded that there was really only one fully formed voice in the room: his. Others were expected to shut themselves – no, cram themselves – into a small space so that he could claim grotesquely disproportionate space for his own personality.

When I could set the maelstrom of my own emotions aside, I found myself asking why? Why does he need to do this? And later as a psychologist, what function does it serve? How does it protect the self?

I tried to imagine what he was feeling and project myself into the context of his world, as I had come to know it. He was someone who needed to elicit vigilance and threat in other people. That implied that he didn't feel safe himself. Could his need to obliterate others reflect the same concern? To outward appearance, he looked reckless and fearless, but then why go to such trouble to intimidate and negate other people if your own position was already well protected? Perhaps that was the point. Invasion and negation were his protection, a kind of armor. But then, what was he protecting himself from? It looked like he felt jeopardized by people with a well-defined sense of self, people who were equipped to head in their own direction and express divergent points of view. People possessed of independence of thought, initiative, and personhood. From his perspective, voices clambering to be heard, voices who might potentially overpower his own. He desperately wanted to either be the only voice or the biggest voice in any given room, but that meant, quite literally, listening to yourself talk all the time. That brought me back to the word solitude again. And the word starvation. I could not imagine how he fed himself and kept himself company if he could not allow other people in. Quite an extraordinary cost to pay. So, what was the offset?

I played with numbers of ideas. Indulgence of vanity? In and of itself it didn't appear to me to be compelling enough to employ such costly defenses. I concluded it had to be bigger than that or more complex. Perhaps he was afraid that if others had a voice they could bury him. After all, he did live in a projected world, again as I understood him. Did his own abiding rapacity elicit perpetual fear that others would try to dominate him as he did them? This felt like a better answer, but it wasn't entirely satisfying either. It didn't help me understand why he was so rapacious in the first place. Still, I could imagine that his own towering rapacity projected onto the world would make the world a pretty scary place.

Later in this process – perhaps sometime during the third decade of my life – it struck me that accommodating lots of unique voices meant inter-polating one's own needs with the needs of others. I need to speak, now they want to speak, I must make room for them (and possibly validate their ideas or change my own), now I get to speak again. A simple yet multifaceted social interaction that affords intellectual stimulation, opportunity for gen-erativity, connectivity, confirmation of community, intimacy, and a willingness to allow others to enter the self and have an impact on it. I already had reason to believe that some of these things were aversive experiences for my father. Given that he experienced other people as wanting to take a mile if he gave them an inch, maybe he was afraid that others could disrupt his sense of self. Get inside and start wrecking the interior. That made a little more sense. Given his own runaway needs, in the form of out-of-control addictions and out-of-control emotions and impulses pressing for expression, I could see he might feel any endorsement of someone else's needs or their personhood might be dangerous for him. They could swamp him and bury him with their own rampant hungers and with their own malevolence. This seemed a more convincing interpretation than fear of domination, but it still begged the question, "what drove his rapacity?"

That question made me wonder if somehow during my father's formative years he experienced others as having relentlessly exploited him. That might mean that such an early threat was still very vivid and very manifest for him, a threat that he could displace by confirming for himself, again and again, that he was the biggest, baddest bear in the woods, compulsively asserting ascendancy with each conquest, but never, ever feeling safe enough to relin-quish combat. As I considered this dynamic and its compulsive nature (allu-ded to in Chapter 4), it felt like a variation of trauma response. Punishing preoccupation with threat (re-traumatization), arousal that supports hypervi-gilance, hypervigilance that potentiates hair trigger stress (fear) response, repeat. As much as my father tried to hide it, I could feel and hear the fear that resided very close to the surface underneath his posturing. I think his fear and certainly his sense of injury were manifest to me fairly early on in my life, though I didn't know what to do with them save to treat them as warning signs directing me to try and stay away from him.

As I reconsidered a trauma formulation, it struck me that my father's version of trauma response seemed not to include an endlessly preoccupying and debilitating focus on mental rehearsal of counter responses to the inevitable intrusion he expected from other people. This is a core part of trauma experience. It's what renders trauma disorder – what is known as PTSD – so painful and so compromising. People can't stop thinking about all the things that can go wrong and they can't stop thinking about all the things they need to do to protect themselves. The rehearsals are torturous and compulsive. To escape them, people cut themselves, abuse drugs, and take their own lives. This prominent piece of the trauma experience seemed somehow to be short-circuited in him. Did his impulsivity help insulate him from the full effect of PTSD suffering? He was largely a "don't think – just act kind of guy." He appeared to be free to do just that without the burdens of deliberation, hesitation, or conscience. The more that I came to see narcissistic experience as being infiltrated by a significant trauma component, the more I wondered how he had escaped the unbearable agony that compulsive rehearsal (also a form of re-traumatization, in my estimate) typically produced. Impulsivity and compromised empathy appeared to provide me with part answers.

I still felt unsettled. I was sure there were other answers to be found that would help me make better sense of his interminable need to overpower, subjugate, and either materially or spiritually rape the other.

I also remained fascinated (and horrified) by some people's jubilant willingness to refashion themselves in my father's image, happily discarding their own identities as they did so. Identification with the aggressor never fully satisfied me as an explanatory dynamic. A niggling feeling at the back of my head said that maybe there was more. "More" only seemed to declare itself to me with any real conviction during the latter stages of my professional life. Again, because of the necessity of building ideas one upon the another, I will explore these adjunctive ideas later in the book.

Chapter 7

The Dark Side – Father

Cruelty

A taste for cruelty, as will already be apparent to the reader, was a very prominent and disturbing part of my father's character. Cruelty was endemic. He appeared to rely on it to divert himself from the peculiar burdens that his inner life generated for him. Some of his acts of cruelty were relatively benign and others quite frightening. I have already provided some illustrative examples. As a child, I could see that he delighted in hurting and humiliating others; what I couldn't figure out in any given situation was the risk that a particular set of behaviors posed for me. Admitting to myself just how big his cruelty was probably evoked intolerable threat. At times, his urge to wound was so unmistakable that, even had I tried to look away, I couldn't miss it. So, too, was the delight he experienced when he saw he had disrupted or, more satisfyingly, annihilated his target. I can see now in retrospect that I minimized and disguised the meanness of spirit he wove into our daily lives. Sometimes I did so with humor, laughing with him at some of the things that he did. These were just guy activities, I told myself, something that all boys and fathers do. Without realizing it, I also think I laughed to appease him, hopeful that if I did so he would experience me as a pleasing compatriot rather than attuning himself to my vulnerability.

My father would situate himself in an open window on the second floor of our house in Minneapolis. He armed himself variously with a BB gun, a pellet gun, and a 22 capable of shooting shrapnel shells. His choice of prey determined choice of gun. He could sit in the window for hours waiting for his opportunity and often did. Literal hours. His favorite target was male dogs. When they entered the rose garden, his attention quickened. He might call me over in hushed whispers, full of subdued excitement. "Hey, Rich, come over here – now wait, wait – yeah, that son of a bitch is lifting his leg – watch this!" This dialogue might play itself out over a couple of minutes. It was conspiratorial in tone, as if he and I were sharing a special moment. His dénouement fulfilled itself when he had a chance to shoot the dog's exposed balls. Hitting the target – which I thought was improbable, given the distance and reliance on a BB gun – produced a satisfying yelp from the dog, who invariably left the scene with a remarkable burst of speed. "Look at that dawg

DOI: 10.4324/9781003246923-7

skedaddle – I got that som bitch! Did you see that? He's never coming back to my rose garden!" …. as if the rose garden was the point of the exercise rather than the chance to terrify and injure the animal. At such moments my father typically lapsed into good old boy talk, the tough language he ascribed to the hard times in his childhood.

Shrapnel shells and pellets were for squirrels and chipmunks. Victory produced similar exclamations of gratification and excitement. Victory in this case, though, usually resulted in death of the animal, which sometimes could take some time. I don't recall there being a second shot to end suffering. An injured animal's gyrations could also produce an excited running dialogue. "Did you see that little bastard jump when I hit him?" etc. etc.

One weekend afternoon my father found a wasp nest in the attic on the other side of the screened opening venting attic air. I was invited to watch the fun. I think in those days people used DDT or a pesticide like that to deal with insects (this would have been the first half of the 50s). He had me approach the screen with him, insisting that we both stop only inches from it. I dared not flinch or pull away or show hesitation. I understood what was required of me, so I found a way to suppress my panic and create the appearance of composure. The activity on the other side of that screen looked to me like a miniature version of hell: numbers of what looked like the biggest wasps I had ever seen, moving about the outside of the paper nest and the screen itself. No doubt proximity inflated my estimate of their size. The reader may have also already understood that I was acutely aware there may have been wasps on our side of the screen as well. If there was a tiny opening in the framing around the vented space we would be in trouble. We were in a small enclosed attic space with an awkward avenue of escape through a narrow opening that could only accommodate one of us at a time. I was distracted by my father's excited tones, "Watch this – wait till you see what happens to these little bastards now!" I cringed. I had seen the effects of this poison before. I knew that almost instantly the insects would find themselves in frenzies of agony – convulsed bodies, stinging themselves, flying jaggedly in all directions. My panic became suffocating. We were unleashing a firestorm of insect rage and terror. My father was fascinated and obviously gratified. "Look at them little bastards… That'll fix 'em." Their death was both sickening and fascinating. I could not look away. I also wanted to be sure that all of them were dead.

My father had placed me in numerous other situations like this during the course of my childhood, situations fraught with threat. As I think about these experiences, I imagined that at some level he had to be aware of my fear and of the potential harm he was exposing me to. The paradigm was always much the same: a situation possessed of significant manifest threat that unleashed crushing anxiety that I needed to suppress if I was to protect myself from the disgust he would have directed towards me had I not done so. On some of these "play dates," panic could have created substantial injury. During one snorkeling expedition he guided my raft over a particular section of reef, telling me to slide off carefully, only to discover that there were sea urchins – dozens of them – positioned inches from the underside of my body. On another he instructed me to swim off the end of our fishing boat after he had been warned by the captain we were in shark infested waters. I was expected to swim to a buoy about a quarter-mile away and back again. I did as I was instructed. I could feel the depth of his antipathy and his murderous intent even through the heavy veil of my own dissociation.

Frighteningly, sometimes I found myself feeding off his acts of cruelty in the way that I suspected he was. I felt so dead inside, so shrunken, that I welcomed the aliveness and the engagement that a moment of cruelty could create for me. The agony my emptiness caused neutered my feelings. Fear and numbness were two of my three most prominent feelings. As it was, there was very little I could find in myself that didn't feel scripted or embarrassingly deficient. Watching my father engage in sadistic acts seemed to allow me to feel something and I was quite desperate, I can see looking back as an adult, to feel anything at all. A scrap of bread in a devastated landscape. I took the poisoned chalice. Cruelty twinned itself with the other growing reality inside: rage. Each time I drank from this cup, I could sense, sometimes only subliminally, that the gratification cruelty provided felt disturbingly wrong, another awful reality I was compelled to hide from others. But I was riveted by some of the cruelty. I didn't seem to be able to look away from parts of it. It did seductively awaken something in me.

From a very early age the cruelty around me began to seep into me. I remember night times being particularly terrifying because I had to face sleep. I think I can actually recall having terrifying nightmares in kindergarten and grade 1, but it may have been a bit later (I also have to acknowledge that nightmares may have begun earlier than that simply because they exceeded the grasp of my memory). I can still remember some of the multicolored monsters – Caterpillar like things – that pursued me. I think I can also remember trying to escape, but being frozen in slow-motion running that doomed me to whatever annihilation awaited me at the hands of these villainous phantasms. The dreams included repeated outcries to my parents for help; it seemed to me in the dreams that my parents heard me, but remained benevolently indifferent to my pleas.

I do recognize, of course, that dreams recalled 70 years after their occurrence, particularly dreams informed by trauma, are likely to be subject to very considerable distortion. The fact that I still remember these dreams very vividly does not substantiate their accuracy. The terror that they impressed upon me and that seemed to pervade my childhood at bedtime over a course of some years, however, may be more reasonably believed by the reader.

My bedroom was on the third floor of the house and was well isolated from my parents, who remained downstairs until their much later bedtime. I do remember feeling a sense of doom as I climbed those stairs with the parent who was designated to put me to bed. I knew once my parent left my room and it was time for sleep, I didn't dare call out for help. Doing so would only solicit fearsome anger. I was on my own. I had to deal with my own demons somehow. I had to find some way to suppress my fear and contain it. I couldn't tell my parents about it. That would have been dangerous. I would look around the room at various articles of clothing, books, toys, carefully scrutinizing each pile, reminding myself that they were just common objects, not the living, threatening things they seemed to become in a darkened room. No matter how much I tried to reassure myself, the things in my room would always seem to move about before sleep came to me and I always felt that I was in danger, frozen in place, unable to speak or move. Without understanding it then, I was probably in that place between consciousness and sleep that today we would describe as a hypnagogic state. I certainly didn't know that then. I thought I was going crazy.

I was fascinated by the book *Alice in Wonderland* that my mother read me at some points during my childhood. Subsequently, as an adult, I wondered why it had been so important to me. Now I think that it offered me reassurance I could survive my unconscious mind and the nightmares it produced. Falling down that rabbit hole into a surreal world was a lot like falling asleep. I don't know when my mother began to read this story; it may have been around the time that my Caterpillar dreams began. So it may be that the genial world of Alice introduced a monster into my dreams at the same time that it reassured me. One of my favorite adult movies, *Pan's Labyrinth*, struck me as being about the same kind of theme, though with a different twist: a young girl who tries to construct a benevolent imaginary world intended to protect her, only to find it invaded and deformed by the horrors around her.

I remember much later – perhaps around grade 4 and 5 – listening to my parents talk about me in the more proximate bedroom they now occupied in the new house we then lived in. It was again a case of talking behind my back in front of me, in whispers manifestly intended to hide their voices, but conducted loudly enough that I could hear them. I never knew whether that was an effect they meant to achieve or whether this was simply an act of miscalculation. Believing it was a deliberate act made it feel that much more awful. Even as a miscalculation, which I suspected it was, it was still transfixing. I had to just lie there and endure it. I couldn't get up and challenge them or confront them. That would have precipitated an Armageddon I didn't want. So, I pretended to be asleep, but took in every word with the very few exceptions of words I couldn't hear. Lengthy iterations of all the worst that I knew they thought about me. This went on night after night. The act of listening engendered morbid retaliatory fantasies. Elaborate, bloody, vindictive ones that I sated myself on. It was both gratifying and destructive – more evidence that I was bad and that I was disturbed. You weren't supposed to hate your parents, particularly in the 1950s, but I certainly did. So there I was, lying in bed, thinking of the various ways that I could murder them, devising intricate plans to end their lives. I couldn't tell anybody about any of this stuff either. I just carried it. And judged myself.

Eventually, I graduated to committing acts of cruelty myself. I was encouraged to hunt and shoot things, as my father did. Hunting created a broad context of social appropriateness that helped make it easier to cross lines outside a hunting venue. I began to look for things to shoot in the backyard, much like my father did. With my father's full knowledge and implicit sanction, I undertook other acts of cruelty towards animals, often with friends. Surgery on living frogs as preparation for the surgeon I was to become (dropping out of medical school at the beginning of year two, my father wanted me to fulfil the dream denied him). Living animals inserted in model rocket ships as part of an exploration of "science." Before long, I had established a small graveyard in an unused part of our backyard (12 to 13 graves) warehousing the different animals I had killed, some with friends and some on my own.

Doing what I did, particularly when I did it on my own, always felt subliminally dirty, but, most prominently, it was hard for me to feel anything at all for the animals. The moment of death, watching the light go out of the animal's eyes, was both powerful and disturbing. Now as I try to recapture those moments, I can remember wanting to understand what made things alive. I felt so dead in contrast, it was as if I was trying grasp what separated me from other living things. The moment was powerful because I could deny life even though I couldn't feel alive myself. A terrible, brutal kind of envy and a soul-destroying way to try to express my own pain. Each "murder" felt like it was dragging me further into the darkness. I began to become very frightened about what was happening to me, but I had no one to talk to.

I may have had occasion to read about psychopathy around grade 4–6, or perhaps I overheard an adult conversation about this subject. I can't remember which. A holy Trinity of signs indicating psychopathy had been described. I certainly ticked the cruelty to animals box. I was relieved that I wasn't a bed wetter. I wasn't sure I hadn't been a fire setter (I had a hazy memory of being accused along with two friends of setting a fire in a field adjacent to my school, but had/have no recollection of having done so). So, I had to accept that this third sign was a maybe. I felt quite sick to my stomach. Was this who I was? Someone utterly unredeemable, incapable of any genuine feeling for others' suffering, possessed of an indelible and, as I understood it, irresistible urge to visit pain on others that would only escalate as I aged? Someone who could "pass" as normal who would always know that he didn't belong in normal society? Now I was not just empty, but monstrous. I was very much afraid that sooner rather than later, much like the defectiveness my parents had identified in me, the people around me would soon discern that I was fundamentally evil.

I can imagine that reading some of this material must be unsettling. I do appreciate that. I share it because I think it is an essential part of living in a narcissistic surround. It's also my belief that my internal realities help provide clues to what was going on inside my father. My deadness, my inability to feel, my starvation, my reliance on sadism to engender aliveness, and even the mask of normalcy that I wore all captured important aspects of his experience. I did not know that as a child. I only saw the ugliness piling up in my own insides. And with the passage of time, instead of being just dead and empty, my interior was replete with rage, with vindictive impulse, and with frightening, cruel imagery. Increasingly, that's how I managed to fill myself to offset my emptiness. I eventually concluded that this reality, too, was reflective of what my father's interior must be like. I had certainly come to know his rage and his need to obliterate the other as a signature part of his presentation.

I remember seeing Patty McCormick in a movie called *"The Bad Seed."* It was very disquieting. While I wasn't as manifestly evil as she was, it felt like there was a very thin and insubstantial line separating me from her. I was afraid that with much more of a push, my own cruelty would overtake me and the people around me. Being around a narcissistic personality made it feel as though that push was just around the next corner. There was very little opportunity to experience salutary feelings and impulses; most exchanges evoked brutish reactions inside, further consolidating my growing conviction that I was fundamentally incapable of ever being able to eclipse my own darkness.

When I was around 12, a very important experience unfolded in my backyard. I had stabbed a chipmunk with a lawn implement, nearly cutting it in two. The agony I saw in its face flooded me. I was intensely, acutely aware of its suffering. I couldn't look away. Inside, privately, I made a sobbing apology. I don't think I said anything out loud. And then I felt relief. I realized that I was capable of compassion. The measure of compassion that I felt alongside the horror at what I'd done was so big that it felt suffocating. It's bigness and its intensity reassured me. I wasn't just blackness. There was a human part of me.

As I look back now, I can see that there were numbers of other experiences that offered tendentious confirmation of humanity throughout my childhood and adolescent years, but the noise of my own immense deadness and the cruelty that I carried inside obscured my possibilities. The reader may have already discerned them, but I certainly couldn't see them in the midst of my struggle with my father and myself. I needed an "epiphany" big enough and dramatic enough, like my experience with the chipmunk, to turn my head and show me that I could be more than I thought I was. Even with this new evidence, however, I was still subject to several decades of variably intense misgiving about my capacity to love and to give.

Losing my humanity has remained my biggest fear in life. The darkness of my childhood never feels as far away as I would like it to be. Part of my own vigilance – a very substantial part – has directed itself towards trying to anticipate situations that would lead to compromised humanity and re-immersion in the darkness that I knew all too intimately in the early years of my life. In truth, I can see that this fear had been so deeply impressed upon me it could be naught else but a lifetime companion. Will this person or the next unseat me in some unexpected way, being too brutish, too devious, too provoking for me to manage, unleashing ugliness and cruelty within me I've worked so hard to understand and contain? Will I repudiate my hard-earned humanity with a single retaliatory act? These questions have been the stuff of my nightmares.

On a few occasions my father talked about the sadistic paradoxes he cre-ated for people, watching them twist helplessly in his grasp. He revealed that he was aware others backed away from street fighting, as he referred to his own brand of interaction, because they couldn't bear to see and feel the dark things in themselves that he knew he could evoke. That, he said, gave him quite an advantage, because he could act without hesitation, as I well knew. He was admitting that he prized his ruthlessness, that it set him apart from others, granting him powerful means to overpower personalities whose nice-ness and decency prevented them from pushing back. In his upside-down world, ruthlessness and freedom from empathy represented strength and a source of pride. They allowed him to stand back from and above the rest of humanity, affirming a sense that he was both better and more powerful than those he perceived to be "weaker" than he was. I could hear in his words intimations of his own omnipotence and his entitlement. In his upside-down world, inability to feel enhanced rather than diminished him. How, I won-dered, could he tolerate numbness that I found so agonizingly painful, cele-brating it as a prized asset rather than feeling the desolation that it was causing me? What could cause him to make such terrible sacrifices and then not only tolerate them, but embrace them? I didn't know how he had reached a place like this inside himself, but I was certainly afraid I would eventually find myself occupying the same space he did. I at least knew that I didn't want that for myself, but part of me felt, guiltily, that if I loved him, I ought to try to emulate him. This struggle also confronted me with old questions about masculinity I have referred to previously: was this not who I was sup-posed to be if I were truly manly?

My father did not often make admissions of the kind I have just described. Such moments were extraordinarily important for me. Another doorway or window offering me a glimpse of his soul. He knew he was ruthless. He used it. It made him feel bigger. He was taking the measure of everyone who moved into his world, assessing their capacity to resist him or to disrupt his domination. He tested people brutally. And compulsively. Compulsively, I realized, was telling. Maybe it meant that he was not free to do otherwise, not free to let down his guard, not free to be gentle, not safe enough to love or to be vulnerable in other people's presence. That was certainly my experience of him. These are, of course, concerns I have already raised; I reiterate them here as a reminder that my exploration of myself and of my father seemed to keep bringing me back to the same points of reference.

If these questions that kept introducing themselves were possessed of any value, I had further indication that my father experienced love as toxic and as compromising. But then how does one move comfortably through life making a virtue of that absence? It was certainly an absence, as I perceived it in myself, that caused me terrible distress and shame, an unspeakable secret I had to hide. As I came to understand with greater conviction that the capacity to love, to give, to feel empathy and compassion, to make sacrifice for others, to tolerate obligation, and to participate in constructive, fulfilling dependencies appeared to be the essence of humanity, the very best that we have to give each other and the very best that we could aspire to, I could appreciate how precarious my father's position must have felt for him. But he gave no evidence of distress. He was seemingly proud of his damaged humanity. Weakness and compromise were prominently paraded as strengths.

Most of the time – incredibly – he seemed to be able to pull it off. Look at my status. Look at my wealth. Look at my beautiful wife. Feel my power. Remember how effectively I can threaten you and diminish you. Remember my brilliance. My uniqueness as a visionary. You need me. Only I can solve the big problems. Diffuse. Distract. Deflect. Look where I tell you to. Don't look at the hole in my soul. A consummate magician endlessly performing sleight-of-hand tricks meant to turn people away from his terrible deficits while he engaged them with an array of assets and weapons meant to inspire envy and/or wrong foot them. Back up the Batmobile and blow smoke. Again and again and again. It almost looked effortless when he did it, but I can recognize now what extraordinary energy such relentless effort required. It would exhaust and deplete most people, but he seemed to feed off it. Look at my greatness. Look again. Look again. Don't you wish you were me? Don't you wish you had what I have? Think of how small you are in comparison.

What I eventually came to refer to as my father's compensatory self was the aggrandized self I've just described. He relentlessly pushed it into others' view, calling their attention to it. He appeared to be very much enamored with it himself. I suppose the construct of compensatory self captures the familiar narcissistic motif of Narcissus staring lovingly at his own image. The self-congratulation that attended celebration of my father's compensatory self, however, struck me as obviously overinflated, almost to the point of being grotesque at times or, alternatively, absurd. The more I looked – the more I understood what I was seeing – the more tawdry it all felt and the more tragic. My father trotting out the same tasteless configuration of himself, over and over, betraying his infatuation with his own broken humanity. What ought to have been a transparently nightmarish creation seemed instead to mesmerize, transfixing his audience with admiration or, depending upon the effect he wished to achieve, with fear. Were people too afraid of their own darkness to look at his and see it as it was? Did they somehow wish to identify with the "strength" and power he attributed to himself so that they might imbue themselves with similar attributes? A sense, in other words, that we can all be supermen? Or, more subtly, was I seeing evidence that a significant portion of humanity is hungry for structure and direction from malignant leadership that sanctions and authenticates dark, tribal impulses that the tribe needs to call forth to feel safe? A kind of reflexive, innate accommodation creating receptivity to an exploitative leader prepared to decimate perceived competitors.

On still another level, I found myself thinking about how inherently terrifying our inner lives are – replete with monsters and nightmares we project onto the external world and onto each other, rendering our outsides as dangerous as our insides. In the face of such chaos and threat, do we turn to decisive others to tell us how to blend malevolence and generativity in ways that serve our group or our community, making us feel safer with ourselves and with those we have been told to perceive as enemies? My experience with my own nightmares and fantasies underscored very dramatically for me just how disruptive and terrifying the intrapsychic world is. My long experience with patients, with my dearest friends, and with the arts that have so sustained me confirmed that we are, all of us, frightened by what we carry inside. The greater people's fear of their inner world, the more likely they seem to be to build rigid, inflexible structures, including unyielding moral schemas meant to protect them, to define what they can and can't feel, to limit and constrain their thought, and to deny the presence of impulses deemed to be unacceptable. As I look around me, I see those strictures imbued in punitive law, in fascistic governmental structure, and in straight jacketing religious ideologies. If my conception is possessed of any validity, it would seem to imply that humanity carries a terrible vulnerability within it, vulnerability to be led by others we willingly allow to harness (perhaps harvest is a better word?) the best and the worst in us so that our group can survive and so that we can live more comfortably with ourselves. We seem to be willing to give such leaders the power, in other words, to use us as they will, ready to believe that their interest must be synonymous with ours so long as they can create an imprimatur of strength, fear, and feral instinct. We let them tell us when it's acceptable to unleash our own versions of hell that we carry inside us and when we are expected to constrain ourselves, even if only to serve their ends. In the process, we may remain blind to other, more humane possibilities that might serve us, or the collective us, better. Because I think these ideas are so important, I will return to them later in the book.

These conceptualizations helped me better understand the disturbing phenomenon I'd mentioned briefly earlier in this book: people's willingness to swallow my father and reconfigure themselves in his image without feeling a sense of decimation but, instead, demonstrating a sense of completion and celebration with the new self they acquired. This thought led to still another, perhaps more frightening thought: are we inherently set up to move through a series of identities proffered by "stronger," more threatening personalities as the context of our life changes for us?

Many of the ideas that I have just discussed pertinent to the dynamics of an authoritarian personality are not new. In tying them to my personal experience in an intimate way, however, I hope to bring them alive in a fashion that a discursive, academic text could not.

As I watched my father's compulsive, repellent dog and pony show restage itself again and again, I became increasingly aware of just how frantic the entire endeavor was. He was almost never at peace with himself. He was always hustling, sometimes obviously and, to a non-practiced eye, sometimes subtly. Trying to hide a core secret, the inability to love, and transform it somehow into an admirable asset required extraordinary work and interminable shucking and jiving. His only choice, as I have mentioned earlier, when he was around decent people who insisted on their decency and appeared immune to his subversion, was to run away.

By the third or fourth decade of my life I began to recognize that there were cracks in the wall, times when even he felt momentary horror at what he had become. I can remember him turning to me at such times and half telling me, half asking me, "I'm a monster, aren't I?" Sometimes this kind of searingly painful insight arose in the context of a poignant discussion, but most often it seemed to come unbidden, surprising both of us, I think. My appreciation was that his own death was quite terrifying for him, representing, as I think it might have, anticipated confrontation with ugliness and cruelty he kept trying to turn away from in himself. I then understood that the dog and pony show wasn't just for others – it was a means by which he could distract himself from his own terrible realities. Like a Dorian Gray who can convince himself that his outsides looked good but who knows that the portrait awaiting him in the attic will horrify him when he finally has to look at it.

As I put these additional pieces together, I thought I now better understood my father's rage and his incessant attempts to evoke envy in other people. As much as he called attention to his wealth, the reality was that he was devastatingly impoverished. Unable to love and to give, he couldn't get. The wasteland that I felt within me also existed in him, though his landscape must have been far more bereft of hope than mine had ever been. I can see now that his unceasing efforts to evoke envy in others were a reflection of his envy of them. Envy that they were genuinely and deeply connected to the people around them. That they could love and give and therefore sustain themselves. That they were possessed of an internal richness – assets like spontaneity, playfulness, generosity – that he could never possess himself. Though largely unconscious most of the time, the envy he experienced had to enrage him. And the perpetual starvation he endured meant that he was fearsomely voracious, stuffing as much power, money, status, and sadistic pleasure down his gullet as he could endure, only to always end up in the same place, starved and empty. The goodies that he so hungrily pursued could never fill him, but they did distract him from what would have been a disastrous confrontation with the self. The caveat was that he could never stop. He was perpetually on the lookout for more, always more, always pushing himself, always shoving other people out of the way so that he could have a bigger share, and always frantically shoring up the whole rickety structure with relentless predatory energy. It still surprises me that it all worked as well as it did for as long as it did. The costs for him were tragic. As was true of my response to my mother's life, my heart breaks when I think about the kind of life he lived. Compassion is of course co-mingled with a complex brew of the pain and damage that he inflicted, which I still contend with. I feel vaguely guilty, too, about the array of people he hurt, as if somehow being with him implicated collusion.

Chapter 8

The Cost of Narcissism

Clinical Depression and Complex Post-Traumatic Stress Disorder

I would like now to talk more about two particular forms of damage my relationship with my father occasioned: depression and complex post-traumatic stress disorder. I have described at some length the profound and terrifying sense of starvation that defined my experience in a narcissistic surround. I would reiterate a nearly omnipresent fear that my own resources, my substance, was so ethereal and so limited that the self could easily be crushed. Lest the reader think that I am offering an adult perspective, I can very much confirm that as a child of eight or nine years I experienced dread of a psychological – not just physical – but psychological annihilation. I felt as if I would cease to exist if there are any less of me, but in order to survive my father's rage and depredation, I was required to erase myself to a very considerable degree in order to be safe. It was quite a challenging juggling act, as I have already said. At best, a half-life. One in which I felt half alive and half dead. An apparition rather than a person. Being around my father subjectively felt like having one's life force drained away. As an adult, it struck me that vampire mythology may have grown out of an appreciation, however vaguely articulated, of narcissistic predation.

I remember reading one opinion in grad school suggesting that children don't experience full-blown clinical depression. At the time I read it, I was incredulous. I knew very well at that point, looking back, that I had endured significant and often compromising depression during my childhood years. I wasn't aware of what the diagnostic criteria for depression were when I was a child, but I certainly knew that I felt suffocatingly depressed, as if I were at the bottom of a very deep and rather dark hole with very slippery sides from which I could never hope to escape. Importantly, I didn't understand the broad impact that depression has on people and that it was having on me. I used food to offset pain, typically sweet fats like baked goods. Fortunately, I was heavily involved in athletics so I could eat as much as I wanted without worrying about weight gain. Weight did, not surprisingly, become a problem later in life. My sleep was certainly disrupted, often by nightmares, or, alternatively, I overslept, still struggling to get up in the mornings in spite of the excess rest I had enjoyed. I have no doubt that my sleep cycle was badly

DOI: 10.4324/9781003246923-8

compromised. It was extraordinarily difficult for me to enjoy myself, though I was capable of doing so over short bursts of time in my family environment and over substantially longer periods of time in a benevolent context, like summer-long overnight camp. Guilt and self-hatred either assailed me or else felt like they were uncomfortably close to my surface much of the time. Periodically I felt quite suicidal, though I never somehow came to the point of either formulating a plan or attempting to act on it. Now I wonder why I didn't. Where did all that resilience come from? I also faced very significant challenges sustaining concentration and effort which I mistakenly attributed to laziness or to some kind of undefined character flaw.

In the preceding paragraph, I have endorsed a symptom array that would have earned me a diagnosis of clinical depression or, more formally, Major Depressive Disorder (MDD). I qualified for MDD rather than Major Depressive Episode (MDE) because my life was punctuated with multiple episodes of depression. Intensity of clinical depression would have been characterized, variably, as mild to moderate depending on its expression at a given point in time.

I want to take a little bit more time now to direct attention towards a particularly prominent aspect of depressive experience that I have just referred to, disrupted concentration. I would attempt to read a page of text and find that my focus was unseated by intrusive thoughts and preoccupations. Sometimes they reminded me I was too limited to understand the material I was attempting to take in (the "you're probably too stupid" voice). At other times they engaged me with broader worries and concerns I had about myself or my environment. Disruptions could present themselves seven or eight times during the course of trying to get through a single page. They could (and often did) trigger either disturbing or escapist fantasies that elaborated my fears or offered me some surcease, however momentary. Escapist fantasies invariably led to more guilt and self-recrimination as I recognized that I wasn't being productive. At the end of a single page, I would usually feel quite exhausted, but I would demand that I push on. Homework was interminable. It dragged on for me longer by far than it did for my friends, seemingly confirming the intellectual inadequacy I'd always suspected. This process went on literally year after year. With each year's renewal, I felt less and less confident that I could continue to extend myself and win the kind of grades that earned me some protection from my father's caustic censure and disappointment.

At private school, I had the advantage of Masters – many of whom were quite lovely people – who closely supervised everything I did, as they did other students. Once I moved into public school during my last two years of high school, I kind of fell apart. My grades were still more or less acceptable, but my ability to work and to sustain effort really began to deteriorate. I was utterly perplexed and panic stricken. Though I was acutely aware of the terrible struggle I had faced trying to get myself through academic material, finding it harder and harder each year, I still didn't understand what was happening to me. I had expected when I changed schools to be able to maintain the same work ethic, but I couldn't. I knew my work didn't begin to honor whatever ability I had. I remember thinking, is this where I'm going to find myself heading – dissolute, self- indulgent, and too corrupt with problems to ever hope to make a life for myself? I was acutely embarrassed. I already felt like I was faking brightness and now my realities had caught up to me. Soon everyone would be able to see that I lacked the substance to be able to pursue a life, that I was a deeply flawed echo of what I was supposed to be.

I began to notice a pattern. At times I could be productive, but then I would back away, almost involuntarily, retreating from work and effort as I allowed myself to be caught up in escapist fantasies or distracting adventures with my friends. Then scathing self-recrimination began. One substrate that appeared to be driving this pattern, I eventually realized, was depression itself. Through my work with patients, I could see how frightening depression was for people. Severe depressive pain set the stage for people to be afraid of another depressive experience. Sometimes this fear was explicit and sometimes it wasn't, but I learned that I could infer its presence with some confidence even though people weren't aware that fear of depression was compelling for them. They acted out their fear in ways that affirmed its presence. Fear of depression, I discovered, was related to subjective depletion. The more that life or circumstance demanded from people with depressive histories, the more depleted they felt, and the more depleted they felt, the more frightened they became of getting depressed again. They could allow themselves limited periods of productivity, but productivity seemed to be followed by significant compromise and inertia after only relatively short-lived effort. As they started to feel depleted, or, alternatively, as life escalated its demands, they compulsively engaged in escapist tactics that I guessed were meant to give them the opportunity to replenish themselves, but which, inevitably, unleashed self repudiating attacks that further intensified both depletion and depression.

All of us, including those of us who have not been subjected to intense depression, need to replenish ourselves and need to recover from the depletion that substantial, sustained effort brings about. I am describing a process, however, that is marked by very uneven productivity and work capability, a kind of discontinuous, jerky sort of progress marked by fairly sharp contrasts between relative successes and obvious lapses. The overall impression created as such a process unfolds is one of unreliability and irresponsibility.

As an aside, as I worked with people with depression, I came to understand that their primary challenge involved learning to trust their resilience in the face of the threat (sometimes poorly understood) that depletion created for them. I found that people who had been severely depressed did best when they were exposed to escalating responsibility in a graduated way, much like some of the paradigms we rely on to help people mitigate fear. Rushing back into responsibility and the demands of productivity all at once seemed to occasion disastrous outcomes. People angry with themselves for letting themselves or others down who attempted full re-immersion in their life's demands sometimes were able to demonstrate persistent effort over fairly prolonged periods of time (months or even for a couple of years), but they always seemed to crash and burn, facing yet another devastating encounter with depression. Graduated exposure appeared to be effective, but I saw that it took far longer than anyone might imagine it would (in my work with patients, not uncommonly a couple of years, and that was whether or not psychotropic medication was included in their treatment regimen). Clearly, such a prolonged process works best with the support and understanding of educated family members.

I watched my own depression follow a similar course, intimately tied, as it appeared to be, to my own subjective sense of depletion. The bewildering up and down course of my work in the last two years of high school and all of university and graduate school that neither I nor my profs could make sense of, punctuated alternately by acts of brilliance and lapse, now begin to make sense to me. I eventually established a very strong work ethic, but only after years and years of effort and struggle. Depletion and the depression it implicates have always nipped at my heels and still do.

Up to this point in my narrative my internal realities seemed, in many significant ways, to capture important aspects of my father's experience. Not a one-to-one correspondence, by any means, but close enough to be very informative. Where, then, was my father's depression? While depression was oppressive for me, it appeared not to exist for him. I don't think I ever heard him say that he was depressed nor did he ever appear to be, even towards the end of his life when he faced a decade long physical deterioration. I saw outrage, a childlike presence, howls of indignation, grievous betrayal, debilitating and intractable mistrust, hypervigilance, and an engaged raconteur and salesman, but never depression and never self-recrimination. Only once did I see him cry, at least that I can remember. There were occasions when he appeared to be relatively at peace with himself, almost quiescent – usually when he was fishing or working on a project by himself – but for the most part what struck one was his energy and his passion. His passion might often be married to destructive feelings and impulses, but it was there to be felt by anybody who spent any time around him. Not at all a depressive presence. He was certainly anguished, manifest in the many ways that he found the world objectionable. He cried out about various perceived injustices nearly unceasingly. But he never looked or acted like he was depressed. I thought, as I came to understand him better during my adult years, that he certainly had cause to be. Indeed, I could not imagine someone living as he did, becoming the kind of person that he was, without experiencing significant depression. As I knew, his solitude, the absence of stable community in his life, and his formidable, enduring psychic pain all represented very imposing risk factors for depression. How, then, did he manage to sidestep it?

It may be helpful for me to comment now that I never regarded the energy I saw in my father as a manifestation of hypomania. There are several reasons why I believe this was so. Its character never changed; it followed a relentless course; in its own perverse way, it was stable; it was not punctuated by periods when he was obviously depressed nor by periods when he appeared to be inert and listless; and it more or less consistently served predatory ends. As a point of information, hypomania is marked by transitory periods during which people experience a heightened and unreasonable sense of personal well-being and competence side-by-side indications of compromised judgement and impulsivity. It is also associated with elevated levels of energy and irritability. It is felt to be a component of Bipolar Disorder and Cyclothymic Disorder, both of which, like depression, are classified as mood disorders. Of particular importance, its presence is thought to offset depressive experience. I did entertain the idea that my father's remarkable levels of energy, grandiosity, impulsivity, and hostility might represent an aberrant and particularly toxic version of hypomania more or less unrelenting in nature that served as a defense against depression, but it certainly wasn't the classical and therefore more pedestrian version of hypomania I was used to seeing in my practice. My father's version of hypomania seemed to be more consistent with very early psychiatric formulations embracing the concept of a hypomanic personality – a more or less stable personality structure prominently characterized by hypomanic activity.

As I considered my father's relative imperviousness to depression, I wondered if his impulsivity – that is, the readiness and willingness to act without being constrained by concern about consequence – might have helped inoculate my father against depressive experience. Impulsivity, or what is sometimes referred to as disinhibition in psychological literature, is believed to arise from a variety of different causes and, as such, carries different implications in different clinical contexts. Broadly speaking, however, difficulty controlling impulses does not appear to protect people from anxiety and depression; on the contrary, it appears to be associated with a multiplicity of symptoms consistent with both of these broad categories of disorder, including suicidality.

Our discussion now leads us into consideration of the literature on psychopathy. I will restrict myself to outlining major trends and prominent themes that are relevant to the issues I am addressing. Accordingly, many of my comments will reflect generalities I have abstracted from this literature rather than citing individual research findings. My intent is to provide a metaview of this body of work so that my reader has an overview of its findings. I will return to this literature in Chapter 10 and expand the perspectives I am providing in this chapter. For an exhaustive look at this literature, I would recommend the *Handbook of Psychopathy* (2019) edited by Christopher Patrick published by Guilford Press.

The psychopathy literature seems to suggest that if reckless impulsivity (or marked disinhibition) is paired with a trait identified with the label "boldness," then a significant measure of protection against both anxiety and depression is conferred. Boldness is characterized in different ways by different authors, but, again, broadly speaking, it appears to refer to low fear reactivity (fearlessness), venturesomeness (a predilection to take risks), and a need to dominate. I found this conception quite helpful; it suggested where I might look to find some of the answers I was seeking. Understanding how and why traits comprising the construct boldness could enable a narcissistic personality like my father's to largely avoid depression held promise. How was the trait boldness, which was certainly a part of him, interacting with the other parts of him in a manner that mitigated the effects of depression?

I initially discovered myself thinking about my father's sense of omnipotence. Other people could challenge him successfully, but as I think of it, when they did, he would avoid them if he couldn't annihilate or assimilate them first. I guess, in this way, he fiercely defended his dominance and his entitlement to it, refusing to allow people to undercut it for long. The battles were bloody oftentimes, but he held onto his dominance even if it meant ejecting the other party from his life. Being dominant, establishing his right to bully, and affirming his "I'm the only guy who can do it" posture was a matter he was willing to go to war over again and again – whatever it took to confirm ascendancy. To my mind this whole endeavor looked like a very iffy proposition, because you had to win every battle that you fought and either push the other guy off the field or overpower him. Every battle. Oh my gosh. Wouldn't you be afraid you could lose? Wouldn't the whole proposition seem terribly daunting and wouldn't it be very depleting? Within his framework, though, this kind of dominance was something he had to do. As I understood him, in order to feel safe, he had to be the biggest voice, if not the only voice in the room.

Did self-aggrandizement and dominance feed him enough to deflect depression? I couldn't imagine that they would. It did strike me, however, that his intolerance of vulnerability and his poorly understood but nonetheless profoundly imposing fear that others could tear into him or exploit him should he appear to be weak rendered depressive experience intolerable for him. He couldn't ever let go and admit fallibility, not just to others but to himself (that was just as dangerous); he dare not express misgiving or uncertainty; and he rigidly avoided self-reflection, particularly if it called upon him to make room for other people or to empathize with the injury that he caused. The plaintive, childlike and very vocal cries of injury that he issued in the face of someone else who was pressing home a point that they had to make, moreover, didn't appear to bespeak accessible vulnerability so much as they served to leverage an attack and lay groundwork for entitlement.

So was this what was happening? Was his fear of weakness and the imagined consequences it could impose so big and so utterly compelling that depressive experience became impossible for him? His greater need was to feel safe and to feel safe he had to forsake his humanity. Was this terrible sacrifice what rendered him impervious to depression? A kind of massive fear can trump mood sort of explanation? If the defenses that one employs neuter capacity for empathy, compassion, conscience, and self-reflection, does one somehow also inoculate oneself against depression? Are these qualities necessary for depression to occur?

This explanation feels like a part answer to the question I have raised. I can't say that it strikes me as entirely satisfactory. For one thing, it feels almost too poetic and lyrical. Additionally, my own experience with depression in the patients that I have worked with confirmed for me that in many life contexts depression is such an irresistible force it will have its way. Move over. Here it comes. Now you have to deal with it.

Having expressed these caveats, however, I do acknowledge a continued affinity for this idea. If we have to neuter our human parts to render ourselves unassailable and untouchable, maybe our capacity for depression does face compromise. I should note that what I saw in my father – that is, his imperviousness to depression – I felt I saw in all but two of the six narcissistic patients that I treated over a relatively long course of time (nine months or more). I would describe four of the six people who persisted in long-term work as deeply anguished individuals, very much tormented by the kinds of lives they were living. Anguish was either expressed as depression (again, two patients) or as a sense of chronic alienation and anger. All but two of the six construed their problems as arising entirely outside themselves, not from within. Five of them were there (one willingly) because employers or partners or both presented them with ultimatums. Two (including the one who had been prompted to come by an employer and did so willingly) came in response to their own pain, but one of them could not consider his own contribution to it. Only the patient who agreed with his employer that he needed help fully embraced introspection; the remainder were either implacably or variably determined to avoid it. With the exception of the patient who could allow himself to experience depression and who could tolerate extensive self-examination, the rest of this long-term group of six people were markedly impaired in their ability to experience empathy, compassion, and generosity towards others. The course of treatment with these five people was predictably uneven, marked by interruptions as they withdrew from treatment for various periods of time, only to reappear in response to pressure others brought to bear on them or, in one case, because of intractable depression. The work with all of them was hard and bruising.

Had I had opportunity to work with some of the other narcissistic patients I saw on a longer-term basis, I might well have decided that depression was, after all, a prominent part of their clinical presentation. In the long-term patient I saw who was depressed, but intolerant of introspection, little progress could be made. In the second narcissistic patient in whom depression was prominent, accountability was embraced. This person very much wanted to recognize – more than that, feel – how much he had hurt others. Treatment proved to be a successful endeavor.

The greatest number of narcissistic patients that I worked with I only saw over a relatively brief course (several sessions), denying me the opportunity to carefully assess levels of depression. Most typically, narcissistic patients showed up on my doorstep in response to the disruption my work with their family members was perceived as causing them; it felt like I was being checked out, much the way an opponent might check out an adversary, so that my vulnerabilities could be exploited to their advantage. What usually followed was a campaign to discredit my work based on the personal flaws they felt they had identified or, more generically, on flaws that they felt could be attributed to my profession ("he's not really interested in you, he just wants you to keep coming so he has an income"). Should these tactics fail and the family member (sometimes a spouse) persist in their treatment work, my narcissistic opponent typically disappeared, usually not to be heard from again. Occasionally they came back and some few even struggled with self-awareness, attempting to pursue greater self-knowledge, but, in the end, it always seemed to me that it felt too dangerous for them to surrender the rapacity and bullying that essentially defined their relationships.

In my exploration of imperviousness to depression, I am setting aside, of course, complex questions about the biological underpinnings of depression that may arise from intricate interactions between psychological stress and biochemistry. We are, after all, becoming increasingly aware that psychological events impact and change physiological/biochemical realities and vice versa. I should add that in making the comments I have about the relationship between depletion and depression, I do recognize depression may arise from a variety of sources; I see sensitivity to depletion as a particularly prominent way that depression manifests itself, but my clinical experience tells me it can wear other guises. Some of the people with whom I have worked, for instance, seemed to be able to protect themselves from depression by utterly exhausting themselves through over-commitment to work. Slowing down would soon get them into trouble.

My thoughts about this question also led me to genetics. Was there a unique pattern of specific, interacting genes (a so-called emergenic pattern) that helped confer heartiness against depression in my father or in some of my narcissistic patients? Speculation about an emergenic pattern, however, only seems viable when applied to a specific individual, not to a group of unrelated people (save for their diagnosis) whose genetic patterns could be expected to be broadly variable. Typically emergenic patterns only reliably reproduce themselves in monozygotic twins. There is recognition, however, that emergenic patterns do repeat themselves in larger populations. Could they somehow be tied to genetics underlying narcissism? Or could an additive and/or interactive genetic model comprising multiple genes somehow generate heartiness to depression – a pattern that also demonstrates itself to be part of a narcissistic genetic substrate? These ideas feel worthy of exploration to me, but I do not begin to know enough about genetics to make any real sense of them. If one allows that narcissism is a largely genetic disorder, then I suppose one could consider that as part of overall genetic makeup some protection against depression is conferred. To date, there does seem to be growing evidence that various traits comprising psychopathy are shaped, to a degree, by genetic contribution, supported largely by additive genetic effects, but there does not as yet appear to be strong substantiation that the overarching construct we refer to as psychopathy is mediated by an identifiable genetic pattern.

So far as I know, however, there does not seem to be substantive evidence that narcissism is largely a consequence of genetics. The literature on psychopathy notes that one of the three traits composing a triarchic model of psychopathy (disinhibition) does appear to enjoy some heritability, but it is not clear that the other two traits (boldness and meanness, respectively) do. Meanness, however, appears to be closely related to the dimension of coldness and unemotionality (CU); CU, in turn, may be subject to genetic influence, particularly in individuals manifesting a markedly cold and unemotional presentation. I must, again, leave this matter in the hands of geneticists far more knowledgeable than I am. I simply wanted to raise questions about genetics so that the reader might understand, in a very limited way, how challenging and complex they are. As a footnote, I would mention that there may be emerging evidence emergenic patterns and environmental influence (epigenetics) interact with one another. Patience and extended scientific effort will help us figure some of this stuff out. As the reader will see in Chapter 8, I do feel environmental influence played a formidable role in contributing to my father's narcissism. Indeed, some of the genetic research on psychopathic traits simultaneously substantiates, at least to a modest agree, the contribution environment potentially makes to the realization of psychopathic traits in a particular individual.

It is my sense that narcissism represents a subtype of psychopathy, but I am very much aware that some people might disagree with me. I think an argument can also be made that narcissistic personality disorder should be conceived of as a severe anxiety disorder. My reasons for making this comment, if not already apparent, will become even more obvious in later sections of this book.

At the beginning of the chapter, I had said that I wanted to explore two different forms of damage that I can see I sustained in my relationship with my father – damage that appeared to depart from the kind of pain he was struggling with. The second source of injury I am referring to is Post-Traumatic Stress Disorder (PTSD) or what is now informally identified as complex post-traumatic stress disorder. While not yet recognized in DSM-5, the diagnostic and statistical manual mental health professionals rely upon when making diagnoses, complex PTSD represents a very important and useful construct that I hope will eventually enjoy formal recognition.

Complex PTSD refers to PTSD experience arising from early abuse that disrupts and distorts normal developmental processes essential for the construction of a healthy and reasonably well-functioning self. Because essential developmental processes face compromise, the potential damage complex PTSD inflicts is thought to be broader and more encompassing than damage typifying many adult-based trauma experiences.

From the time that I was very young, I can remember rehearsing for anticipated trauma. What would my father say next? What would he do? What crazy thing could I expect from my mother? How would I react? I would obsess endlessly about possible responses. Most of the time there weren't any, prompting me to look harder, to look further, to try to find some option for myself that could insulate or partially insulate me from the sense of intense violation their incursions generated in me. Every time they wounded me, it felt like I had failed myself, that I had betrayed myself by failing to be able to defend myself effectively. Betrayal of self, for me, was and is a powerful phrase. It very much captures what I felt. I both blamed and shamed myself for my inadequacy. I should have been able to fight back, but of course I was also learning that if I fought back, I would incite devastating retaliation. I struck a balance, as best I could, between what I could say and get away with, and what I had to suppress (not unlike a normal parent–child struggle, but, as the reader may appreciate, considerably elevated in its intensity).

It was almost unbearable tolerating the helpless rage piling up inside. I was desperate to create some kind of affirmation of self, some demonstration that confirmed I had the means to push back. Instead, I found myself trapped in a private space dominated by improbable retaliatory fantasies or by endless, tortuous rehearsals of solutions I could never consummate. In spite of all of the rehearsals that seemed to unfold endlessly over interminable periods, when the moment of truth arose and I anticipated I would be able to defend myself, I nearly always failed because I was too terrified to act. I dreaded these inevitable failures because I knew they would give rise to more painful hours of rehearsal that might only abate after a period of two to three days.

I discovered something else that I have alluded to earlier in this book: my terror disorganized me. In the face of it, I literally couldn't think. I was so flooded with terror I couldn't find words. And it disorganized my emotions as well. In that moment of truth when I might have acted to mount resistance to an assailant, I was likely to shake or to cry. Boys were not supposed to cry. My parents seized upon that part of my vulnerability and attacked, variously labeling me "crybaby" or – very typical of the 50s – "you better stop that crying or we'll really give you something to cry about." Following such experiences there were renewed rounds of rehearsal, the search to find the perfect response that would shield me and restore some measure of dignity, rehearsals that always ended badly when the time to act presented itself.

Disturbingly, but perhaps not surprisingly, I found myself unable to act and unable to protect myself when I was faced with either a forceful personality or a bullying personality in the world outside my home. The sense of not being able to defend oneself without incurring fateful risk only amplified preoccupation with my own vulnerability.

There is one other salient aspect of the trauma dynamic that I lived with worthy of mention. I had learned that it was not safe to be too articulate, to fill myself out too much as a personality, or to be successful. Throughout much of my life I did not recognize that I sabotaged potential successes not only because of depression, but because I was afraid that doing well would expose me to attack from malignant, envious others. I could allow myself momentary successes, but then withdrew from them. Doing so made me feel safer, but inflamed depression as I failed to meet my own standards and expectations. During the latter third of my life my fear of being attacked in response to success became painfully prominent; I could literally feel how afraid I was of others' repudiation if I did well. Imagined successes produced punitive, retaliatory fantasies that resulted in my diminishment at the hands of competitors; actual successes yielded significant discomfort and acts of undoing on my part. Maddeningly, I saw that the cognitive style, which I developed in response to the threat my father generated, limited me to think in vague, approximate, impressionistic terms rather than with the precision I wanted to achieve for myself. Say name A when you mean to say name B. Mix up facts that you ought to know well. Find yourself providing a woolly or even inaccurate account of events that you have a good grasp of to ensure that you don't imbue your voice with too much authority. Watching and measuring the people around you, trying to assess whether they can tolerate a strong voice, but mostly expecting that they can't. Consciously sabotaging one's own voice to appease a perceived enemy. And frustratingly, exasperatingly, all of these things would unfold with implacable automaticity very hard to resist. No doubt the disruptive impact of both depression and anxiety on cognitive process, which is well documented in the psychological literature, made their own contribution to some of the difficulties I was having with myself.

My father's cognitive processes, in contrast, seemed to be utterly unfettered, to my envious eye. How wonderful, I thought, to be so free to act. But he wasn't, actually. His cognition had been hijacked as well – by his compulsion to maintain dominance and rapacity. In order to be the guy who knew more than everybody else and who had the biggest voice, he had to be equipped to bludgeon his opponents through argument by affect (overwhelming and subduing the other party with one's own toxic emotional displays) rather than by reason. Argument by affect seemed to be surprisingly effective much of the time. People mostly did back away. Because domination was so important, facts and realities could be swept aside in the service of establishing his ascendancy. And because vulnerability was intolerable, he could never admit fallibilities, even though it might have served him and his relationships well to do so. His interpretations of reality ebbed and flowed, shifting in accordance with his need to suppress other personalities. Although his relationships with others could be defined for a time by a measure of amiability, amiability was always eventually displaced by the compulsion to neuter and subjugate the other. Under these terms, reason was treated as a disposable commodity, readily sacrificed if it stood in the way of that which was most important to him: confirmation that he was the guy who could obliterate the opposition.

We're covering some old ground here. The intent is not to further highlight my own suffering, but rather to elucidate the dynamics of incipient trauma. Trauma yielding pain yielding obsessive rehearsal that occasions endless, compulsive re-traumatization. The voices in your head that you can't stop, that keep going, that keep pushing you, popping up at various points in the day, assaulting you, insisting on hypervigilance, insisting on preparedness, insisting that every possible avenue of insult is anticipated and readied with counter response.

The best depiction of PTSD I have ever seen I encountered in a murder mystery series called "River." The main character finds himself assailed repeatedly by illusory figures hurling insults at him that he desperately and angrily tries to fend off. He knows the figures aren't real (I don't think it was the intention of the series to convey that he was struggling with a hallucinatory experience), but his engagement in these conversations is irresistible and is so vivid affectively (fear, rage, desperation) that he momentarily forgets his surroundings, embarrassing or compromising himself as he finds himself more absorbed by his dialogue with them then he is by real-world events taking place around him. He betrays his engagement with his trauma world with gesticulation and speech directed towards the relentless attackers in his head he can't seem to escape for very long – gesticulation and speech that others can see and hear. He talks out loud to himself when he speaks to his imagined assailants and he sometimes waves his arms at them in exasperation. Immediately recognizing what he has done, because he does appreciate the boundary between the real and the trauma world, he hastily tries to recompose himself, but maddeningly finds himself subject to the same breaches of control over and over as the trauma world becomes too prominent for him to manage. People who know me very well, like my wife, can pick up shifts like this in me, but, hopefully, the cues I expose are less transparent than they were for the main character in River. My wife, however, might say otherwise. I probably do permit myself more unguarded moments with her than I do with others.

Living with PTSD means facing seemingly interminable re-immersion in re-traumatization and hypervigilance. Relax too much, feel too composed, start to feel too safe, and PTSD prompts you to be afraid again, to keep looking over your shoulder, to be ready for the next encounter. Peace and safety are not enduring commodities to be had, but relatively transitory ones to be enjoyed as best they can in those moments when they arise. In my clinical experience, people struggling with complex PTSD arising from severe abuse find it hard to feel safe in the world. A core task of the therapeutic endeavor is to help them feel safe with the therapist. Safety is unquestionably foundational in any therapy, but it assumes critical importance in the treatment of complex PTSD, demanding particularly close and assiduous attention to the patient's experience in the therapeutic relationship.

I have often thought that our brains are organized in such a way that they insist we remember that which has frightened us very deeply. Remember that waterhole, where you nearly got eaten? Don't ever forget. Remain very watchful. Stay wired. Here, I'll remind you what that experience felt like. You'll relive it. And I'll make you relive it if you start to relax in the face of cues that might be construed to imply danger. In fact, if you relax too much, even if you're not in a dangerous situation, I'll remind you that it's not safe to do so.

Profound, repetitively experienced fear has the potentiality of becoming indelible – a kind of fixed presence or unwelcome guest that one carries around inside perpetually trying to compel one to do its bidding. Such is often the case when one grows up in the context that a narcissistic other creates. The consequence is enduring fear, a sense that one is never fully safe in the world. Irresistible re-traumatizing thoughts that are part of the fear or trauma dynamic help ensure that one can never feel adequately insulated against threat. So, too, does the internal representation of the narcissistic other that one carries inside. The specter of narcissistic invasion and deconstruction never feels too far from the surface, even in surroundings that might be expected to induce a measure of security. Even though there are interludes when one can relax – sometimes relatively extended ones that may persist over hours or even a couple of days – fear of violation by an envious, depreciatory other inevitably reasserts itself. That has certainly been the case for me as it has been for many of my patients who evolved in a narcissistic surround.

I look forward to a time when we can understand brain substrate and dynamics better than we do now so that we might do a better job helping people mitigate a condition like complex PTSD. Right now, at least in my experience, complex PTSD occasioned by significant, prolonged early trauma requires prolonged work. There is no single trauma experience, as there may be in an adult trauma event, but multiple points of trauma extending over a course of years, aspects of which can be readily appreciated and others that prove to be subtle and nuanced. Moreover, because complex PTSD significantly distorts or inhibits healthy developmental process, people living with it have to find the means to acquire those parts of themselves they need to live the successful adult lives which trauma has denied them. An appropriate and proportionate sense of personal value, the ability to constructively assert oneself, a capacity to build a sustaining community, a willingness to share internal realities and experiment with one's personality to enhance personal richness and uniqueness, and the capacity to sustain effort and maintain concentration are a very short list of the developmental tasks that have to be addressed. As can be seen from my own experience living with a narcissistic personality, I faced the challenge of piecing together a sense of self from the distorted bits and pieces that my early experience produced. All this has to be done in the face of continuing anxiety and depression. It takes time for people and it is profoundly hard and often discouraging work.

I have struggled with complex PTSD all my life. My mother certainly made her own contribution to it, but the greatest part of it, I would maintain, derived from my experience with my father. I certainly recognized what I have called trauma dynamic in my father and have referred to it in text. I could see, in other words, that his narcissistic behavior looked to be compelled by fear that he could be subjected to the same kind of encroachment and violation he visited on the people around him. I thought I could also see his hypervigilance. He was always ready for battle, sometimes inciting it when it was clearly not necessary to do so. I never saw evidence, as I noted in Chapter 5, that he obsessively replayed trauma in his head as a means of preparing himself to deal with an intrusion. He didn't become distracted by his immersion in his trauma thoughts in the way that I did. He seemed to be spared that component – that agonizing component – of PTSD. I asked myself again, "How was he able to do that?"

When I returned to this question a second time, I found myself re-embracing some of the same answers that I provided in Chapter 5, but this time when I considered the question at hand, it felt like I could do a better job elaborating and articulating my original ideas, possibly because the act of writing offered me more time to play with the material.

My father's greatly diminished capacity for empathy and compassion, his fear of weakness, his vast acquisitive hunger, and his ruthless need to push others aside all facilitated an unrestrained, action oriented, pull no punches style of functioning. He didn't leave himself time to deliberate or to hesitate or to consider other's feelings; he just acted. He didn't have to rehearse responses. They just happened. Usually with alacrity and the appearance of intimidating conviction. He wasn't generally subject to rumination and he certainly couldn't tolerate helplessness for long. Given such a powerful, compulsive drive to act, I could see why he wasn't subjected to the endless rounds re-traumatizing thought that I was. Feel threatened and act. Skip the painful re-traumatization step. It was both attractive and repellent for me to witness. More latterly in my life I could recognize with painful clarity the terrible costs that he had incurred. Broken relationships. Solitude. Failed collaborations. Perpetual fear and restiveness. Add to these a fractured intellect constrained by short brutish sentences lacking nuance and appreciation of complexity that worked well as a means of intimidation in verbal combat, but that significantly undermined his ability to better appreciate the multilayered actualities he was often dealing with.

Chapter 9

Origins of Narcissism – My Father's Autobiographies

In this chapter I will focus on the autobiographical portraits that my father provided me late in his life at my request. I was facing another trip to California to visit him that I anticipated would, in all likelihood, turn out, as other visits had, to be painful experiences for both of us. Even within the format of a very short, two-day trip, I was very much aware how badly and how quickly things might deteriorate between us. I wondered what I could do to render the visit more manageable and, possibly, even enjoyable. It finally occurred to me that I could ask him to create a record or a kind of diary of some of the important events in his life. Throughout my childhood he had repeatedly referenced various parts of his early and young adult years, often telling the same stories again and again. I realized that unless I recorded his stories – or got him to do so – they would be gone forever. He was in his 80s and was struggling with health. It also struck me that having the stories in one place, written down, would provide me with a more meaningful picture of what his life had meant to him than the piecemeal accumulation of oral histories he had shared over the course of our relationship.

When I proposed that he make an autobiographical statement, I had no sense of whether doing so would appeal to him. I did know that he seemed to be compelled to talk about his life – including the most painful parts of it – so I could imagine he might be receptive to my request. I was not at all sure whether doing so might get us into real trouble as he found himself focusing on the formidable sense of injury I knew engagement with his early life could occasion, but, given the risks inherent in any visit with him, I decided it was worth taking a chance. We would either have another terrible get together or his life story might offer both of us an interesting and rewarding focus for the two days we would have with each other. I made my proposal over the phone and he seemed to be modestly interested. When I arrived in California, however, I discovered that he had filled 3 or 4 90-minute tapes and was getting started on still another tape. He had pulled together various pictures and family documents as well. While he certainly talked about numbers of profoundly disturbing experiences, as the reader will soon see, he was obviously gratified to have been given the opportunity I presented him. We actually spent a reasonably enjoyable visit.

DOI: 10.4324/9781003246923-9

Once I got back home, I had my secretary type out all of the tapes. As I reviewed his 64-page autobiographical statement, I could see that the meandering chronology that characterized his narrative made it difficult for one to be sure when some of the important events he was describing had taken place. He made attempts to chronologize, but I think chronology was often hijacked by emotion. Talking about one set of experiences triggered poignant memories of other experiences that sidetracked an ordered narrative, but these diversions also served to help one better appreciate the salient emotional themes that had punctuated his life. I could see that the document he had provided was immensely meaningful. It was, as I had hoped, a collection of many of the different stories he had told me about himself, but all in one place. The totality of this narrative was certainly greater than the sum of its parts. I was also in a position to be able to read between the lines. I had, as additional source material, comments he had made to me throughout the years – often during anomalously unguarded moments – about various important relationships he described in his autobiographical statement. Plus, I had the advantage of actually knowing at least some of the players, which offered me the opportunity to draw upon my own perceptions (however accurate they might be) as a resource.

I decided I would ask him to return to the statement he had given me to see if, together, we could create a more coherent sequence to the storyline. He agreed and enthusiastically provided me with, essentially, another complete autobiography, this time of 40+ pages, double spaced. Chronology was still problematic, but by comparing the two autobiographies, I did feel I had a better sense of when, approximately, some of the most significant experiences had unfolded. Not a perfect understanding (I wouldn't have expected one), but one that I thought was good enough to paint an adequate picture of the ways in which his life had impacted him. I was immensely grateful for what he had done. His autobiographies allowed me to render human that which I had experienced as monstrous. I could now view him with a depth of compassion and understanding that offered me meaningful consolation. I still had formidable damage to contend with in myself and I still found it enormously unpleasant to be around him, but I now also had compassion and depth of insight as a more prominent part of my interface with him and my interface with myself.

The most salient emotion that I experienced when my father died at 94 was relief. I was almost giddy with it. I was no longer required to talk to him, to endure the conspiracy theories and the outrageous bigotries that could punctuate his conversation with me, nor would I any longer be subject to his subversive attempts to undercut and deconstruct me. His funeral assumed a surreal aspect as I was required to hear from various attendees about aggrandized versions of his life he had offered them which they, in turn, thought I would be gratified to be introduced to or to hear confirmed. I had already heard the stories and knew all too well that they were not true (he had worked on the Manhattan Project and would have to shoot me if he told me what he did; he was a member of the first U.S. navy underwater demolition team and had, along with other team members, been responsible for blowing up a battleship at the end of the war in Tokyo Bay). Having always been prone to make up outrageous exploits that attested to his prowess, as he moved further from the centers of power and "greatness" that he had once occupied, he filled in the empty spaces with his wonderful – but apocryphal – self-congratulatory stories. This was particularly true of his recounting of World War II adventures. The summary of his service record in the Navy, which I had seen prior to his burial in the US armed forces cemetery in San Diego, made the limits of his naval service shockingly clear. Under a heading something like "positions occupied" was the entry, "procurement officer," followed, oddly, by a period, as if to place special emphasis on the reality that this was all he did. This odd style of entries in his service record extended itself into the categories of (approximately) "special qualifications and training" and "rewards and citations." Each was demarcated by the word "none" and each "none," as I remember it, possibly imperfectly, had its own period.

With the passage of time, my sadness about the kind of life that he had lived and about the terrible losses that he had endured became more prominent. Would that I, as a child, had been capable of the understanding that I enjoy now I might have been able to offer him more support or, at least, more forbearance rather than the largely secret war that I waged with him. Such insights are, however, not possible for children. I have to accept that his life irretrievably damaged him. He had to endure the pain that it occasioned without any real recourse to set a different direction for himself. What I can do, however, is to try to elucidate his pain and penetrate it as best I can so that I can better grasp my own realities and so that others may better appreciate how narcissism – at least some forms of it – can potentially grow out of the human experience. It is my belief that my father's autobiographies render his narcissism – perhaps I should say salient parts of it – accessible. That is to say, accessible in human terms rather than simply as a manifestation of what we have come to think of as evil. To my mind, it is essential that we make sense of this very fundamental and potentially very disruptive, destructive human condition that has helped set the stage for cataclysmic human suffering in the form of war, economic privation, psychological trauma, and suffocating oppression.

Perhaps one of the first things that one will notice looking at the autobiographies is the reappearance of many of the same stories framed by almost identical words and phrases. Initially striking me as somewhat odd, I quickly remembered that my father had told his stories over and over again, dozens and dozens of times during the course of my acquaintance with him. Stories retold, possibly, in search of resolution or understanding that always eluded him, hence the need to endlessly revisit them. Many of the stories were also trauma stories, capturing pain that seemed to serve a number of functions –

consolidation of entitlement, confirmation of his endemic cynicism, investiture in an embattled solitude that admitted little help from others, and invigoration of vigilance, contempt, and rage. There was also, unmistakably, a deeply plaintive cry for help that he would say never came and that he certainly could not have accepted, had it presented itself. His obsessive oral history giving found the words to express itself and, once found, ossified itself in fixed forms – in the words and phrases that he used over and over again to express himself. A man caught in a maze, increasingly, of his own making, moving down the same blind alleys with the insistence that this time he could find new answers.

Many of his stories were presented as accusations: "Why did this happen to me and not to you? Why were you favored while I lived with such punishing deprivation?" The tone of accusation that attended his storytelling, as I have said, always filled me with dread. Because dread dominated my experience with him in these moments, it was harder for me to appreciate that at these times he became the desperately wounded child he had once been. Not that I was unaware of his suffering or untouched by it – I was – but my fear of him soon displaced any compassion I was capable of feeling. I suppose I dwell on these feelings because I think it is important for the reader to be reminded of the ambience that surrounded his storytelling, both in him and in me. What I see on paper as I read the autobiographies doesn't begin to capture the immensity of injustice and suffering he conveyed as he told his stories.

From the vantage point that I occupy towards the end of my own life, I can now better set the dread I experienced in association with his storytelling aside and hear the anguish that they represent. Endless, tortured appeals for someone to free him from what was undoubtedly a tormented existence.

Before I begin my commentary on his autobiographies, I wish to emphasize that of course I am very mindful that his retellings of his experiences are likely distorted by the vagaries of brain function and memory and by the emotions that help compel and shape memories over time. I don't doubt that in some respects his sense of injustice, for instance, had become increasingly hyperbolized as years passed, lending his stories the sometimes frantically indignant quality that they assumed, but I also have little doubt that the pain he displayed was very real. I could see and feel and taste the damage that he had endured (much of it described in the first seven chapters) through his impact on me. I also recognized in the coherent patterns of suffering my father presented patterns that I was seeing in many of my patients. It further struck me that the dissociation (emotional numbing) his trauma experiences created for him could conceivably mean that in some respects he was not well-equipped to appreciate (to feel) how fully devastating they had been.

What was also apparent in his appraisal of his life was his inability (his reluctance?) to acknowledge the damaging impact he had upon many of the people close to him. My mother and I had certainly cried out in pain and in protest often enough – for me, particularly during my adult years when I was more capable of confronting him – so I knew he had to be cognizant of our respective agonies, but he seemed not to be able to incorporate them into his narrative, as if he had no means to address this part of his experience. He attempted to resolve this omission by casting an idealizing glow over the latter part of his life that was meant to create an impression of resolution and growth the actualities of his life could not support.

With respect to memory, I would note that there are inconsistencies in the autobiographies. Virtually any history I have acquired from my patients is marked by inconsistency. In extended therapy work I have the advantage of investigating incongruities and, if I'm lucky, eventually coming to understand them. It was not possible to do that with my father's stories, though, as previously mentioned, some attempt was made to do so. This surely represents a limitation of the autobiographies. Nevertheless, I'm reasonably content that in spite of occasional contradictions and disrupted chronologies the autobiographies tell a poignant and evocative story about my father's life journey. I am, after all, primarily interested in tracing major themes that seem to inform his movement towards a narcissistic posture. I think that the autobiographies so prominently display these themes and allow them to stand out in such relief that matters of inconsistency or contradiction in the storyline recede in importance. I admit that I am departing, to a degree, from the position that I have always taken in my work – that the devil lies in the details. The reader will have to decide for themselves whether I am justified in doing so.

Finally, before actually delving into the autobiographies, it is important to note that at the time my father gave them he was in his early 80s and was beginning to struggle with the effects of the congestive heart failure that eventually ended his life at 94. When he constructed them, I regarded him as being intact cognitively. He remained quite lucid up to the end of his life, but the oral histories that he has given may not be truly reflective of the intellectual capabilities that typified his functioning at the apex of his career. What they do offer, I think, is an appreciation of what his spoken language was like – not a perfect one, of course, because he was engaged in dictation, but a reasonable facsimile of the kind of language that he used when he spoke to others, as I remember it. Notwithstanding his disclaimers in the autobiographies about a lack of skill with English and grammar, his written business communications struck me as quite articulate: focused, succinct, and effective. In a business context, his vocabulary and his use of language embraced complex constructs and organized them, to my eye, very successfully; in contrast, in a personal context – perhaps as one might expect – quality of language appeared to degrade, subject both to the impact of his narcissism and to the informality that characterizes spoken language.

As he surveyed what he had written in his autobiographies, my father reflected upon what his experience had been like for him:

In looking back over my younger days, I think it's very difficult for me to recall many happy circumstances. My mother and dad did everything in the world they could for me though we just plain lived in poverty, real poverty and I was bound to be envious of what the other kids had and what they were doing and being unable to go along with them, in terms of having various toys and amusements and going places and that sort of thing...

My father's life statements document crushing poverty and hardship. Beginnings possibly as early as seven or eight years old marked by soul-sapping responsibilities that only increased throughout the course of childhood and early adulthood. Wherever this demarcation began, it seems that at the latest by the time he was nine or ten, my father was tasked with supplementing a very meagre family income with inordinate – and he would say (and often did) – backbreaking physical labor that made the difference between whether the family had enough to eat and whether it had enough coal to heat the house in wintertime. As best I can tell, by the time he was ten (and probably well before that time), he was supplementing his mother's desperate efforts to keep the family afloat by holding 4 different jobs that filled his after-school hours and his weekends (operating the washing machine crank in 3 or 4 half-hour sessions each night, stringing up the clothesline and hanging out the washing to dry, beating carpets in the neighborhood, and mowing between 8 and 20 lawns in season). He also seems to have been accountable for shoveling coal into the furnace when it was available and for helping his father plant a family garden that the Overbrook School for the Blind had made available. My father's workload appeared to escalate rather quickly rather than diminishing with each passing year of childhood. While there seem to have been brief periods of respite when the family did a little bit better for itself, almost inevitably, it must have felt, things seemed to get worse again, necessitating more crushing responsibility.

By the time my father was 11 or 12 years old, by his account, there was enough concern about shortage of food in the family that he was sent down to the family farm in Virginia called Nimrod Hall where it was expected that he would be fed better than he could have been in his own home. Once there, however, he found that he was responsible for working for his own keep in the summer months "by milking the cows, bailing the hay, weeding the garden, and such joys as that." While at the farm, he was also tasked with driving 1,800-pound loads of ice down an adjacent mountainside to the family farm, having been taught to drive by one of his uncles at age 10 (this reference and the associated chronology implies that summers at Nimrod Hall may have unfolded a little earlier than he suggested they did at one point in his narrative). The end of grammar school (what sounded to me a reference to grades 1 through 8) and the very beginning of high school saw him continue to fill the hours after school and on weekends with work. He obtained a license at age 14 after lying about his age so that he could qualify himself to drive a grocery truck. Work at the grocery store began as he finished school, evidently at two and extended until six when he took another job working at a local candy store that required his presence until 11pm. Weekend work included work at a garage that was as much as a 10-mile bike ride or caddying 2 full rounds at a local golf course, whenever possible, that involved 10 miles of walking with what would have been a heavy bag for a youngster who had not fully reached physical maturity.

Such work was necessary, my father maintained in his autobiographies, to pay rent, buy food, and look after other necessities of life. Although the autobiographies do not say so explicitly, my own conversations with my father confirmed that after my grandfather left the family to live at Nimrod Hall on a full-time basis when my father was in his freshman year of high school (I assume this is an approximate estimate), my father's earnings also helped fund a series of psychology lectures that my grandfather presented in different cities. One of his autobiographies also made it sound as if he began making contributions to his father to help his father buy a house around the freshman year time mark, but my own sense, again from conversations of my own with my father, suggests to me that my father offered help with a house purchase either much later in high school or at some point in his early 20s. I acknowledge that I may be mistaken and that my father's account in the autobiography may be accurate.

In addition to these burdens, my father also found himself partially supporting the physician, Dr. E. F. Williamson, who was looking after my grandmother's now compromised health, by sharing the meagre supplies of food available to the family. My father implied that it was only as a result of pressure that he placed on Dr. Williamson that the latter eventually relented and began to offer the family limited financial support.

At the end of high school my father faced the financial burden of paying for his own university at the same time that he continued to help support his mother and, to some degree, possibly his father as well. He seems to have done so by maintaining multiple jobs and long hours of work. A summer job at a miniature golf course in what he described as a rough part of town extended from the morning until well past midnight, but it did offer my father opportunity to save a meaningful amount of money as a result of his ability to capitalize upon a betting scheme he organized after hours. In between two summers at the miniature golf course, he commented that "I worked at gas stations, delivery trucks, soda fountains, painter, etc. for the rest of the year...," further augmenting savings in the process. He did pay for his university (it sounded like he attended a pre-med course for one or more years) as well as his first-year medical school and several weeks of his second year before another crisis presented itself in the form of a bank failure in the midst of the Great Depression. This event resulted in loss of all of his savings (approximately $10,000). Though he resolved to walk away from everyone at this time, in actuality his resourcefulness and ingenuity as well as some unexpected luck insured that he had the means to continue to support his mother, which he seems to have done up until the time he was nearly 30. At that point his mother and Dr. Williamson finally married, probably, my father seemed to suggest, as a result of pressure that he placed on the latter.

After walking away and finding himself on his own, my father gave me to understand through personal communication that he continued to support his father and his father's new wife on a limited basis that was sufficient for them to sustain themselves and that eventually culminated in shouldering the costs for nursing home residency for each of them.

During my childhood when my father talked about the extraordinary burdens he felt he had been required to assume from a very early age, his tone reflected a mixture of bitterness, rage, injustice, and at times, childlike despair. Underneath the acrimonious outcries and the accusatory tone he directed towards his listeners, one could hear the helpless, terrified child that he had once been. I should add that I don't think he fully occupied the psychological space of that terrified child; rage and indignation and his sense of injustice easily eclipsed the profound vulnerability and probably equally profound despair that his experiences had undoubtedly instilled in him.

His life seems to have been a terribly precarious affair, lurching from one daily or weekly financial crisis to the next, never offering any real measure of certainty that now everything was going to be okay. His own father's singular devotion to the church meant that family needs could be pushed aside so that my grandfather's income could be redirected to the church building fund. Perhaps not surprisingly, my grandfather's insistence in doing so was cause for bitter arguments with my grandmother that infiltrated my father's home life.

One can imagine a child's growing bewilderment and hurt in such circumstances. Why won't dad help? Why aren't we important to him? Does it not matter that we often don't have enough to eat, that we often can't keep warm, that we don't have enough money for decent clothes (requisite for both dignity and for warmth in the winter in the absence of coal), that we can't afford Christmas, that we rarely have money for pleasure, and that my mother and I have to work so hard? What must my father have felt about himself and how much more precarious must existence have felt in the absence of paternal commitment to the family?

Each time the family seemed to get a leg up, things fell apart again. The promise that a completed new church and a regular pastoral salary seemed to offer evaporated with my grandfather's unexpected blindness. Return of sightedness in one eye offered hope that my grandfather might work again, but his attempts to reengage himself with his ministry as well as efforts to redirect himself as a vacuum cleaner salesman and as a psychological lecturer all miscarried, leaving my grandmother and my father to somehow fend for themselves. Tragically, the best that my grandfather could do was absent himself from the family home and re-situate himself in Virginia so that my grandmother and father didn't have to continue to pay for his food. Shortly after these terrible disappointments, my grandmother's health began to fail as she was subject to increasing bouts of asthma. And in spite of the financial relief that my grandfather's absence offered, foreclosure on the family home approximately a year after the occurrence of blindness was followed in succeeding years by multiple evictions from increasingly meagre dwellings that my grandmother and father had trouble affording. At least one eviction seems to have resulted in a sheriff garnishing both my grandmother's and my father's wages for back rent. One gathered that these evictions were also disruptive to my father's schooling, occasioning attendance at three different high schools and, in at least one instance, a commute to school that was experienced as daunting. For a young man who decided at an early age that he wanted to be a doctor, school disruption must have felt quite threatening, intensifying the sense of instability that attended his life.

In the midst of all of this, the Great Depression presented itself. Evidence of financial disasters were everywhere to be seen, often in the form, in my father's world, of people desperately trying to eke out subsistence by selling apples. The Great Depression, of course, eventually did catch up to my father, occasioning the bank failure that denied him continuation at medical school.

So much of my father's early life seems transactional to me: you're only as good as the work you contribute and, at best, you could only buy yourself and your family another day's food and shelter. There seems to have been little room and little enough resource for parents to invest in him. His and his mother's life were subordinated to his father's dream of church and ministry. My grandfather took him on bike rides, but mostly where he wanted to go, as my own father said, rather than soliciting his son's wishes. The point of the bike rides, it seemed, was more work: the vegetable patch that the family needed for food. The radio that the family treasured was a product of my father's labor and his windfall; his parents decided he should have the money, but for educational purposes. Parents did buy him a train set, but reminded him continuously about its cost. The most unconditional presents he seems to have received were a skateboard his father made for him and an aerial that his father had installed on the roof for the radio (the latter actually served the family rather than my father alone, but one got a sense that the time my grandfather spent with him doing this was meaningful). Otherwise, there seems to have been very little affirmation of either their investment in him or the pleasure he could give just by being him. There appears not to been much solicitation of interest in his tastes or his sensibilities or much real appreciation of his uniqueness.

He was there to serve others. To serve their dreams and their needs. Much the same appears to be true of his many relations on the Virginia farm. He regarded "typical" Wood family men as lazy, unproductive, and often unsuccessful people who, like his father, failed to adequately look after their families, putting their own needs first instead. Tellingly and sadly, my father recalled his grandfather as a guy who spent most of his time relaxing in a rocking chair eating fried chicken who was disinclined to make much conversation with his grandson.

In my clinical experience, families that demonstrate joy in response to the personal gifts (not monetary ones) that a child can bring consolidate attachment and generate meaning. I can see I'm important to you. I can make you laugh or you like the way I think or recognize I'm a good artist or you can see that I'm a kind person or that I love music. My qualities make you happy and when I make you, my parent, happy I feel like I have a place in the world and that I have value. In the absence of this kind of feedback – and these are exchanges, by the way, that more or less unfold on a daily basis – a child feels rootless, functionally unable to make the parent they belong to feel happy or experience joy. Similarly, a parent's investment in a child's interests (What can we do that you would like? How can I help you do the things that are important to you? Or, even better, I know you like X, I've arranged for us or for you to do that) also affirm value. In a context in which there is a substantial absence of such experiences, I think a child must inevitably endure doubt about their importance to others, save for the utility they can offer other parties. Such a connection is certainly not a sustaining one. It also must exacerbate the sense that one's place in the world is very tenuous.

Aspects of the reality my father had to contend with must have made him feel very disposable. Imagine being required, as either a 10-year-old or 13-year-old (depending on which account of my father's one reads) to drive down a roller coaster like mountainside by yourself with breaks smoking and reverse pedals to the floor carrying six 300-pound blocks of ice in the back of a broken-down truck. My father's half comical account in one of his autobiographical statements of doing so belies the immensity of risk he faced. In other conversations about this incident and in the record he provided for the Wood family tree, however, it becomes apparent risk was very acutely felt. His retrospective humor in the autobiography likely not only offered him the opportunity for a colorful story that could augment the larger-than-life persona he was eager to create for himself; it also disguised the terrible reality that his family was all too willing to lose him to the chores they assigned him. He never explicitly talked about such feelings of disposability, but I can imagine they were a very prominent part of his psyche.

I wonder if the reason that my father's memory at seven or eight of a young boy run over by a truck (and killed) was as indelible as it was, remaining with him throughout his lifetime, because it captured his sense that life and survival were tentative and that he was discardable.

His comments about this incident are quite poignant:

> I saw a little boy cross the street and a truck hit him and he fell down in front and the truck ran smack over his stomach and the front wheels and then I saw the back wheels do the same thing and there wasn't any visible

evidence, outside of the fact that I learned later he was, when they finally got the ambulance there and all, that I learned he was dead – it had squashed his insides and broken his back and all kinds of things and it's just something that stuck in my memory all my life and it was a sad thing to watch, but it was another important incident in my growing up days.

I think an eye injury he endured in the schoolyard in primary school must have had a similar impact as well as the death of his dog Nix and his encounter with a bear that scared him half to death while he was collecting blueberries for the family, chasing him all the way down the mountainside. I believe that, in part, this is one of the reasons that he returned to these memories so often throughout his lifetime.

I think it's important at this juncture to continue to reflect upon the parsimonious nature of the transactional world my father lived in. It was parsimonious, as may be apparent now, both materially and spiritually. Subjectively, I can imagine my father only ever felt good enough for used clothes and toys or that he was only ever deserving enough on rare occasions to have money for movies or spending money (a penny) for candy. It would have been easy for him to feel that neither he or his mother were important enough to induce my grandfather to share more of his money with the family or, alternatively, to develop a supplementary income. My father could work his heart out, in other words, for the people around him, but they had very little to give back in the form of either gifts or personal interest. The world wasn't receptive to his needs; on the contrary, as I have said previously, he was there to look after others. He was required to give everything that he earned to his parents or to the summer family at Nimrod in Virginia, but very rarely got to keep much, if anything, for himself.

His world was punishingly withholding. When he did manage to save money as a consequence of heroic effort or attempted an emotional investment, it must have begun to feel inevitable that the world would take what little he had away (see, for instance, his one-week old reconditioned car utterly destroyed by fire, the little dog Nix that he accidentally killed and, most poignantly, plans for medical school disrupted by both depression related bank failure and by his mother's possibly vindictive new partner who denied him a relatively small loan that would have permitted my father to carry on with his intended career). Even practical joking that he engaged in on the farm had its costs (fearsome switching from grandma).

I've included descriptions of some of these losses in his own words in the passages which follow below:

> While living in Kirkland, I found a little, lost dog – a puppy. I asked my dad if we could keep it and he said nix. So, to make a long story short, after many tears and wheedling I kept the dog and named it 'Nix.' Over the next little while I got very attached to this dog and one day swinging

a golf club in the yard he jumped, hit the head of the club and it killed him. I was one sad little kid at the time, boy around 13 years old.[1]

I finally had enough money, about $300 to buy a car. I bought a little red Chevrolet roadster and paid $300 for it. I redid the engine and the brakes and all the things I learned to do with the gas station. After about a week and it was working pretty well, and there was no place to park it at our little apartment (it was a very small apartment) so, I got a deal with a little garage across the street where I worked part time. I was so proud of that car, I can't tell you. I went to bed that night, woke up and saw flames through my window coming out of the garage just down the street. I jumped out of bed and ran down in my pajamas. Those flames were coming from that garage and for sure my little car was burnt to a crisp. The tires were burnt off it, it was melted down. Even the upholstery had been burnt off. Total loss. As luck would have it, no car insurance and the car was totaled. I was pretty sad, was without a car, which was needed to get to one of my jobs. I didn't know what the hell to do, but couldn't do much about it.

I was so damn broken hearted about leaving medical school – I can never describe the feeling in my stomach; no money, had no job and didn't know what the hell to do. I was just about ready to get a job in a boat and go away…

The vindictiveness I think my father experienced with Dr. Williamson seems plausible to me. Reading between the lines in the autobiographies and, as well, having had the benefit of listening to my father tell this story repeatedly, I had the unmistakable sense that he believed Williamson meant to punish him because my father had demanded payment for either food or rent in response to Williamson's persistent use of these resources. I think my father was attempting to impose the same rules on the world, in the form of Williamson, that he felt the world had imposed on him throughout most of his life. In response to this act of assertion, the world (Williamson) fought back, withholding my father's most precious dream (medical school) by refusing him the loan that he needed to continue with school after his bank's failure. I met Williamson at various points during my childhood. He struck me as a fearsome, forbidding man whom I tried to avoid on my visits to my grandmother. As a footnote, when he died my father and I discovered that he was indeed rich. My memory is that he had accumulated well over a million, if not $2 million in US stocks – quite a sum at the time (60+ years ago). Williamson's will seemed to confirm his emotional and material parsimony, a kind of implicitly vindictive meanness of spirit. All of his money was to go to his medical college with the exception of a monthly subsistence allotment for my grandmother. While I did not think my father recognized the parallel, I think he must have experienced it: like my paternal grandfather, Williamson was turning most of his resource back to his profession rather than making enough of it available to offer his wife even a modestly comfortable lifestyle. The terms of Williamson's will clearly placed much of the burden of support for my grandmother on my father. My father readily reached an agreement with the medical college to provide my grandmother with adequate income; the medical college also agreed to pay for my university and to establish a scholarship for either my sister or I or any of our children to go to medical school, if we or they so wished. I'm sure in that moment my father must have felt that he had managed to partially redress a terrible injustice he had suffered, although too belatedly, of course, to give him the career that he had wanted.

The import of the kind of life experience that my father had, I think, was to confirm his aloneness, save for his relationship with his mother. She and he worked side-by-side to ensure that life could go on. What she could not do, however, given her harsh circumstance, was protect him from the inordinate hardships that defined his life as well as hers. My grandfather, in turn, seemed almost entirely unable to afford my father meaningful shelter from the variety of threats that assailed him. Even an injury like bullying incited a response from grandfather that pushed my father back into the world on his own to somehow deal with the two school bullies jeopardizing him. Grandfather threatened such "drastic" punishment that my father became too afraid not to fight back. The message that repeated itself over and over in my father's life, consistent with this experience, was don't depend on others – you're in this more or less by yourself. You have to figure it out. Others are unlikely to help you much.

I think my father remembers his experience with Boy Scouts and with the church basketball team as fondly as he did because in both instances other people made an effort to help him. While he had to buy his scouts uniform himself, the church provided him and the other boys with instruments to play and some lessons. What sounded like a different church community provided its neighborhood children, including my father, a place to play basketball and team uniforms. I suspect that in part my father felt as good as he did about these experiences because he was dressed just like the other boys unlike his daily garb of second-hand clothes his poverty necessitated. I do think he was genuinely, deeply appreciative of the clothes and the toys that the DeLong family gave him, but they came at a cost: charity was diminishing, probably earmarking him as different than many of the children around him.

As an aside, I was struck by some of the comments my father made about his encounters with school bullies. After successfully vanquishing them by fighting back, he considered that maybe he subsequently developed a reputation as being a tough little kid, saying that he didn't really think that he was. Was this the beginning, I wondered, of his reliance on bullying others to secure his own space? I don't feel the evidence in the autobiographies is strong enough to draw that conclusion, but the question nevertheless nagged me, prompting me to mention it here.

Notwithstanding what my father said about Christianity in his auto-biographies, he remained deeply, bitterly opposed to Christianity up to very nearly the end of his life, feeling that it was self-serving and hypocritical. He saw Christianity as the origin of much of his family's suffering. He expressed deep resentment about the extensive Christian devotionals he was expected to participate in, probably seeing them as another obligation that his father imposed on him without having much to give back in return. On a deeper level, one could speculate that he saw Christianity as a ruthless competitor, an enticing and irresistible siren that consumed all of his father's resources, robbing the family of what they needed from him.

My father was exposed to profound and frankly shocking adultification during his childhood and young adult years. This is to say that he was expected to shoulder oppressive adult burdens throughout this period of his life before he had opportunity to form a self or to develop resources appropriate to the responsibilities he was carrying. The lion's share of whatever personal resilience he possessed was directed towards looking after others. One can imagine that he felt extraordinarily depleted and all the more so with each passing year. Little opportunity to be a child. Little chance to explore the world as a child so that he might discover facets of himself that he wanted to develop and express. Little reason to feel safe and protected. And little freedom from the constant fear of survival that dogged his steps throughout these years. A pretend adult in a child's body and a child's half formed psyche desperately trying to be so much more than he was so that he could get by and so that he could ensure his one close companion in this journey, his mother, could continue to stand by his side. He had to find the means to convince himself that he was bigger than he was, stronger than he was, more resourceful than he could be. He consolidated such belief with grandiosity – grandiosity and self-idealization that his mother in all likelihood encouraged. I could hear her hyperbolized and aggrandizing adorations of him during my childhood, over the top devotionals that always made me feel awkward, as if something was terribly skewed in their relationship. I felt a measure of embarrassment around them that I recognized later in my life reflected my sense that their relationship felt too close, too affectionate, almost incestuous. The portrait provided was a confusing one as they seemed to swing back and forth between two frightened children clinging to one another and two battered partners beseeching one another for comfort. Accepting her aggrandizement confirmed their bond, confirmed his worth, and afforded him reassurance that maybe he could be all that she needed him to be. If he could accommodate his aggrandized status, they could and he could assuage his loneliness. If he could accept the position she probably assigned him as surrogate husband, he could feel special, powerful, and attractive. The sexualized undercurrent passing between them would have also helped confirm grandiosity.

Whether the reader can accept some of the Oedipal themes that I have just outlined, it can probably readily be appreciated that aggrandizement and adultification carry within them impossible contradictions. The more the child accepts the adult role, the more precarious the entire venture becomes. The child, after all, is only a child, not the adult he purports to establish in his own and others' eyes. The more he pretends to be what he is not, the more impossible the whole venture must feel. Attempts to reassure the self through adultification only generate more fright and more aloneness. Fright, however, is vulnerability badly tolerated in the rickety structure of adultification. It must somehow be set aside and repressed. Not an undertaking marked by a sense of much surety or certainty. Many children compelled to adultification fail. Significant life disruption often ensues. Aggrandizement and idealization can help hold people together, but, as is obvious, at potentially terrible cost. My father, I believe, was able to maintain his aggrandized stance because he was so talented, so improbably resourceful and creative, and so unexpectedly resilient he could pull it off. One breathtaking high wire act after another after another. Each one affirming his larger-than-life status. And, for better or worse, he had the "benefit" of early physical maturation – which is to say, like me, relatively early on he looked much older than he was for his age. Looking the part, I'm sure, meant getting his driver's license at 14 and meant getting jobs he otherwise might have been disqualified from. It could be said of my father that he grew up too fast and that he never grew up at all.

All of the above is not to suggest that my father was free from suffocating despair. Such despair must have repeatedly punctuated his life as he and the family moved from crisis to crisis. It is perhaps most obviously apparent in the autobiographies in his description of his feelings following abrupt termination of medical school and his reaction to loss of his car. One can also guess that his mother's escalating bouts of asthma must have portended a kind of abandonment foretelling even greater burdens for him to carry, not to mention the potentiality of mother-loss. One would also think that his mother's growing dependence on Williamson might have increasingly occasioned powerful jealousy. The one dear heart he had always held close was being withdrawn from him. In some ways probably a relief, but in others an unbearable absence. Improbably, he seems to have survived innumerable crises like those I've just referenced, but one does not have to extend oneself very far as one reads his autobiographies to appreciate that such reversals were searing experiences for him – ones that he carried with him and struggled with the rest of his life.

Once established in one's adult life, self-aggrandizement associated with adultification requires defense; having been won at such cost, it is not easily yielded. That which threatens the bearer's grandiosity must be opposed with ruthless vigor lest the self is flooded with remnants of crippling panic and helplessness set aside, more (or less) effectively, during childhood years.

My father's relationship with his mother bears further exploration. I think his compulsion to feed her was an attempt to feed himself by participating vicariously in the nurturance and support he continuously offered her. I'm reminded of a poignant incident that I experienced with one of my daughters. During toilet training she contracted diarrhea. Because she could no longer fully control elimination, she became afraid, as best we could tell, that she was losing parts of herself literally down the drain each time diarrhea struck. Tying a little rope to the toilet paper dispenser helped, but she remained obviously quite terrified. She very quickly recognized the association between eating and the urge to go to the bathroom (gastrocolic reflex). In response, she tried to protect herself by refusing to eat anything at all. She was able to maintain this strategy for perhaps a day or a day and half before a curious thing happened: gently at first, but with increasing ferocity, she began to put food into my mouth. By the end of the second day, she was quite desperate to feed me. She was participating vicariously in my satiation. Her insistence was quite striking.

I think my father must have done the same thing with his mother. He couldn't lean on others, but he could feed her and, in the process, also help save her, of course. I think, in part, it became compulsive for him to feed her because no one could feed him very effectively. As an adult, I think he found himself caught between his fear of leaning on other people and his need to offer some form of substance to others as a way of satiating himself. Doing the latter, however, was a very angry undertaking. How do you demonstrate generosity towards others when you're starving yourself? He certainly mana-ged to be a far better provider than his own father by several magnitudes of difference, but his giving was always infected with hostility. As noted earlier in the book, acts of generosity almost always evoked anger. One heard endlessly about how much things cost and about what extraordinary effort my father had made to offer even simple necessities; lavish, exaggerated praise was demanded in response to even small gestures of generosity. One was even coached on what to say back. Being called upon to mimic the exaggerated praise that my father wanted for himself felt awful, like one was being required to dance like a puppet on his strings. Tragically, he repeatedly poi-soned his own well, denying himself the heartfelt appreciation which his reci-pient might have otherwise offered.

There is another theme that I alluded to earlier in the book that I think it makes sense to return to now. My father's history offered me confirmation of the enormity of need that must have piled up inside him as a result of not having others in his life who could adequately attend to his human wants. In my clinical experience, as such needs accumulate and as individuals become increasingly frightened by and mistrustful of others' abilities or intentions to be able to appropriately nurture them, it becomes too dangerous to acknowledge need. Like a child with his or her finger in the dike and a deluge waiting on the other side, such people are frozen in place, afraid that acknowledgement of need would unleash a flood of hunger they have no sense how to manage.

Reference to a brief vignette with a patient may be helpful here. Many, many years ago I was working with a young woman (now deceased) who had faced similar circumstance in her own childhood to my father's, but she had somehow managed to retain more of her humanity than he did. Relatively early on in therapy when I empathized with her suffering, she quickly and forcefully cautioned me to stop, explaining that my empathy was moving her to tears and that once she started to cry, she would not be able to stop. Thereafter we collaborated closely on the way that she responded to any empathy that I offered and, having been appropriately cautioned, I took care in the way that I handled empathy. Throughout a very long course of work together, she made a number of attempts to enter into a constructive dependence with a man, but could never do so. We both came to recognize that the risks associated with letting herself consummate intimacy with a male partner were too great. What she could do, however, was deepen friendships, borrowing some of the tolerance for dependency and intimacy she had acquired in therapy.

Learning to tolerate dependence is a foundational skill that hopefully one acquires in childhood. As an aside, it is one of the critical skills that is often disrupted or denied in a complex Post-Traumatic Stress Disorder context. Children begin by expressing their needs in diffuse, unfocused, and inappropriate ways (tantrums, for instance), gradually progressing, through parental tolerance, guidance, and support, to increasingly more successful and constructive ways of asking for that which they need. It's a long process, consuming a substantial part of parenting effort and virtually all of childhood and adolescence. If parenting has been "good enough," a child will have learned how to navigate their way through their own wants with relative confidence, allowing them to extend and deepen any intimacies which they attempt. Trusting the self to be able to do this is critical to the endeavor. I would argue that my father never reached the point of being able to do so, though he certainly could not have put any of this into words. Insight would have been experienced as a source of jeopardy and a diminishment and, as such, would have been resisted vigorously.

Now I would like to return to the theme of depletion. I think the specter of my grandfather's inability to effectively care for himself or his family and my grandmother's eventual decline into a clingy, dependent relationship with her doctor caretaker must have been quite disconcerting for my father. It meant that people could run out of gas and that when they did so, they substantially became unable to tolerate the responsibilities life required of them for survival. They found themselves at the mercy of whatever dependence they could establish to ensure that they had enough to get by.

It probably would not have been apparent to my father and my grandfather why my grandfather found it so hard to cope with life. In one of his autobiographies my father reported that he and his father had often talked about my grandfather's limitations, finally simply accepting the reality. As I look back, I do wonder what might have happened to my grandfather to set the stage for his relative inability to sustain work. I do have access to some of his diaries and to brief vignettes of his early life he provided for a Wood family tree document. The sense I got was that he experienced his early life as demanding and harsh. I wondered whether being the eldest of 15 children might have placed him in the position of having to assume inordinate responsibilities himself at an early age. Surprisingly, diary entries that characterized his experiences later in life (late 1940s/early 1950s) were possessed of a sense that life was enjoyable and meaningful. His stance appeared to be an optimistic one. I've entertained the idea that during my father's childhood and adolescence, however, he might have been living with poorly understood and unrecognized depression. It did occur to me that his unexpected blindness might possibly have arisen from psychological cause. Having gotten his church substantially off the ground and having acquired a reasonably good-sized congregation, was he intimidated by his success and by the demands that it implied – i.e., having to deal, for instance, with contentious congregants who were split ideologically? Every undertaking thereafter seemed to defeat him, eventually leading to a kind of retreat from life on the family farm. It did sound as if he managed to preach again, earning, as my father said, "a few dollars," but his success was never big enough to allow him independence. He remained essentially reliant on my father for the rest of his life for much of the money he needed to pay for himself and his wife.

My grandmother did evidently demonstrate quite substantial capability to endure and mount persistent, perhaps even heroic effort in the face of poverty, but she, too, was eventually defeated by the depleting effects of her burdens. As I knew her, she was frighteningly clingy and demanding, burying her listener with unending lists of physical complaints and entreaties for support – an open mouth that the unfortunate bystander could never fill.

The twined fates of my two grandparents must have dramatically intensified my father's own fear of dependence. Let go of self-aggrandizement and omnipotence and see what happens to you. Never stop. Always keep moving. Keep the show alive. The choice was binary. You either kept up the frantic pace or you drowned.

Fear of depletion and of the disorganizing, diminishing dependence it could impose remained a core fear of my father's throughout his life. He was utterly contemptuous of anyone who was unable to take care of themselves, engaging in lengthy, bitter soliloquies when he felt he encountered such people. Needy people frightened him. One can recognize, given the context of his early history, that he must have been frightened – deeply frightened – that others could drain him with their needs. Drain him and reduce him to the skeletal reality that eventually defined both parents and that had presumably nearly overtaken him.

The key to feeling safe was to hold others at arm's length, to resist the entitlement and the encroachment that others could realize if they succeeded in inspiring loving feelings in him. Love, for him, had very understandably come to represent threat. If you let people love you and if you let yourself feel love for them in return, they could exploit you and exhaust you with their demands and their needs. Now I understood with greater confidence. That's why "nice" never lasted for long. That's why he had contempt for everyone. Nobody gets in. Nobody matters. His words to Williamson were prophetic: "I don't need you, I don't need anybody...." It had required 40+ years for me to finally make these connections.

Paradoxically, I think my father may have made such extraordinary effort, year upon year, to help save his family because he had been "blessed" with a relatively greater capacity for empathy than the average person. His empathy drew him into caregiving effort again and again. He noticed his father's exhaustion and his disappointment. He desperately wanted to protect his mother. His empathy drew him into very deep waters, creating more jeopardy for him the more he extended himself for the people he cared about. Empathy was not his only motive force (survival and the need to protect the people he relied upon had their say), but I believe it played a significant part in informing his larger-than-life devotion to his parents. Learning to turn empathy off, as he eventually did, helped ensure that others could not encroach with love and associated entitlement. Doing so, like his need to obliterate loving feelings in himself and others, would have been essential for safety. In muting empathy, he could protect himself against obligation he might feel towards others.

Turning back to earlier speculation I offered in this book, I could now confirm for myself that someone who could not allow himself to love or be loved in return so that he could feel safe was instead exposing himself to another kind of starvation. He couldn't give, or give for long, without feeling angry, but if he could not take pleasure in giving or loving, if those acts were too profoundly dangerous for him to undertake, how was he to sustain himself? Connection and generosity are core building blocks of human relationships, rendering our lives meaningful, rewarding, and sustaining. My father had protected himself against the risk of one form of starvation only to impose another. Perpetually alone, perpetually and profoundly – one would say indelibly – mistrustful of virtually everyone around him, voraciously hungry, and willfully blind to the growing ugliness inside, he tried to feed himself with stuff (money, power, status) that had been denied him as a youngster and that had caused such enduring envy. Believing that getting all the things that he missed and believing that standing apart from people behind walls of contempt would protect him, he exposed himself to an even more devastating form of envy, one occasioned by his envy of other people's humanity – that is, their still relatively intact capacity to give and to love. As I have reflected previously, his envy was endemic. It manifested itself in all of his relationships. Looking back, I can remember him offering prerogatives and gifts to me or to my mother he had been denied, only to poison them in very short order with dark resentment. Why was I getting so many of the things he had never been given, secure in a world where food and shelter were certainties? I could see now, from the context of his history, why he so compulsively and sadistically tried to evoke envy in other people. He perceived them to be complete in a way that he was not and satiated in a way that his mistrust would never allow him to be. They had each other; he had no one.

As a manifestation of the starvation occasioned by blunting his capacity to love, one could recognize, again within the context of his history, how terribly acquisitive and rapacious he must have felt. He could never feed himself adequately and feel sated. Always ravenous, compelled, as he was, by his own oral rage, he experienced other people as hungry mouths attempting to encroach on the meagre, subsistence nourishment he relied upon to feed himself. He could never authenticate their voices or make room for their personalities; he needed all the air in the room and, at that, it was never really enough. Authenticating others and respecting their voices created unbearable risk. Newly empowered, they could turn upon him with the same ferocity and hunger that he directed towards them. Projecting his rapacity onto the world around him and substantiating it with his unyielding cynicism made the world a very dangerous place.

The parallels between my internal realities while I was growing up (and for a long time thereafter) and my father's stood out in greater relief and could be seen with greater clarity once an appreciation of his history had been developed. Both of us had faced adultification, he because he had been tasked with carrying his family financially and me because I had been tasked with carrying my family psychologically. Both of us faced formidable threat of depletion and endured starvation, though in different forms. Each of us had been encouraged to develop a sense of grandiosity, me because I acted as my parents' therapist as a child and him because he was asked to believe he could shoulder all the physical burdens assigned him. Each of us accommodated incestuous attachment to our mothers. Each of us struggled with a sense of inner deadness and each of us also contrived our lives rather than living them. Both of us spent much of our lives feeling unsafe and scared and both of us were hypervigilant. And each of us was haunted by the monsters we were afraid we carried within us. His capacity to love was fundamentally compromised; I worried that I would never be able to. So many secrets for each of us to carry, so much to try to hide.

It can be seen now how my father's experience in his formative years set the stage for the narcissism he acquired that dominated the remainder of his life. He couldn't feel love, at least not in a sustained way or to a meaningful degree. It was too jeopardizing. So, too, was empathy. He shut it down in order to afford himself protection against others' need and others' ungovernable hunger. He had powerful reasons to be mistrustful of other people and so he was. Unrelentingly. Unyieldingly. Mistrust bred vigilance and was supported by obdurate cynicism. Always on guard, looking for the worst, to ensure that others could not exploit him. Continuously affirming his strength and his dominance so that he might reassure himself no one else could overpower him or deny him that which his feral instincts told him he needed to survive. Shutting down other voices and other personalities. Making them feel afraid – too afraid to challenge him. Always the only man standing and the last man standing. Tragically, using hostility and contempt to obliterate love, to ensure that others could not touch him, and to affirm his ability to crush others so that he would not have to worry about being crushed or displaced himself. Voraciously, inconsolably, ruthlessly hungry. Trying to address all his pain and all of his gaping hunger by pushing others aside, greedily consuming that which he imagined would fill him, but never could. Always prepared to annihilate the other to fight for the last scrap. Relentlessly pursuing the trappings of wealth his early life denied him in lieu of connection, community, and humanity. Endemic starvation side-by-side endemic, toxic envy. Incapable of looking at himself because of the horrors he was afraid he might encounter. Eschewing insight, as a consequence, and replacing it with action.

Formidable, life-sucking poverty, nearly unceasing exploitation by people that he loved all too ready to sidestep his needs to meet their own, and interminable threat and interminable depletion wrought by his life circumstance all conspired, it would seem, to construct my father's narcissism.

As I write this, my heart breaks yet again.

As a postscript to this chapter, I want to reflect for a moment on my father's feelings towards my grandfather. On the last page of his most extensive autobiography, he made some effort to reassure me and himself that the life story he had provided was in no way meant to reflect criticism of his dad. I don't think his self-appraisal, or at least this aspect of it, is accurate. He often expressed rage tinged with bitterness towards his father in response to the latter's rigid devotion to church at the expense of family. At times he tried to escape such anger, but it always seemed to reassert itself. He did intermittently make efforts to reassure both of us that his father was a close comrade, as he would put it, and that his father had been forgiven for all the shortfalls that he created, but these reassurances usually presented themselves in a context in which my own anger towards him had become more manifest. He was effectively carrying out an invidious comparison – "look at how my father hurt me, notice that I was never angry with him in the way that you just were with me even though I had greater cause."

Unbeknownst to my father, I discovered a number of letters my grandfather had sent him over a period of many months beseeching my father to send on desperately needed support checks. These letters made it clear that my father had not only withheld support, but had refused to respond to my grandfather's entreaties or to communicate with him in any way, despite the latter's obvious desperation. I could certainly understand, once I enjoyed the benefit of my father's autobiographies, why my father might have acted as he did. Tragic for both of them, but understandable.

Notwithstanding the foregoing, I do think my father tried to sidestep anger that he felt towards my grandfather. I think it was genuinely disconcerting for him, but I also believe that it was so intense that at times it could not be denied. Part of managing what must have been rage entailed diverting anger towards Williamson and, however momentarily, idealizing his own father. It was somehow safer to experience Williamson as the devil incarnate then it was to consider the implications of my grandfather's apparent inadequacies.

Upon reviewing my father's autobiographies, my wife observed that my father never seemed to have raised questions about why my grandfather had not taken him and his mother down to Nimrod Hall at the point at which my grandfather had effectively given up on himself. I realize that she was right. My father had seemingly always accepted my grandfather's life transition back to his home of origin with a kind of sad resignation. My father never considered in any conversation I had with him that his parents might have arranged for him to go down to the farm with his dad so that he could enjoy a more stable life. As I thought about the question my wife had raised, I could guess – but certainly didn't know – that my grandmother was probably already involved with her doctor, hoping that he might provide her and her son with a better life. That, tragically, was not to be. My grandmother, instead, seems to have replaced my grandfather's personal limitations and daunting ideological fervor with parsimony and ideological fervor of another kind, occasioned by Williamson's mean-spiritedness (he, of course, has a life story of his own that, if it could be understood, would allow one to better appreciate how he came to be the person that he was). In retrospect, I wondered whether my father's attempted, but usually failed idealizations of his relationship with his father were meant to mitigate the pain that father's abandonment was felt to have caused. In my father's world, people were experienced as looking after themselves first, much as he might have felt his father did when he left and his mother did when she invested herself more deeply in the relationship with Williamson. I do think my father was touched by my grandfather's end-of-life gift to him. I'm referring to a sum of $10,000 my grandfather had saved from the support money my father had sent him over the years. While the gift was not significant monetarily to my father, it did at last confirm that my grandfather understood that he had a debt to pay. He could pay homage to my father by denying himself comfort so that my father could see he was worth making a sacrifice for.

Towards the end of his autobiographies my father reflected upon what it might have been like for him had he accepted another executive position, this time as a president of another large American retail operation. I think I can hear in his tone a sense that such an endeavor, while appealing as a possibility, felt beyond his grasp. He and I often talked about his regret that he had not carried on. He had hoped that a new experience might redress the sharp disappointment he had faced during his final years at Wards. He imagined he might have a successful leadership experience somewhere else that Wards was felt to have denied him. He also very much wanted to redress Wards poor stock performance during his years there by creating a retail success elsewhere that would lead to an immense stock payout. He was frequently preoccupied by the money which stock options as president of Target might have yielded, a position he had bypassed for Wards. From my perspective, it struck me that he remained compelled by the idea that a large payout could make everything else all right inside. The allure of pursuing this kind of victory, however, was offset by what I would guess was an immense sense of exhaustion – a feeling that he could no longer safely expose himself to the rigors of executive combat. Had he been able to do otherwise, I think he would have. Instead, he had to content himself with the reflected glory of his earlier and rather astonishing accomplishments. He could never live comfortably with the personal reduction that his diminished status created, hence his increasingly outrageous attempts to aggrandize the self by attributing improbable, apocryphal achievements to himself.

I don't think my father ever did find the peace that he was looking for, even though his new world of retirement was smaller and less demanding. He continued his wars with everyone around him with much the same intensity, but on a smaller, less epic scale than his executive battles. He never found the replenishment that he was seeking, only more struggle. How could it have been otherwise? Without empathy, human connection, and the ability to feel love (to both give it and receive it), he was fated to endure everlasting starvation in the absence of satiation. Everyone else always looked like they had so much more; his magic trick was to make other people, including himself, feel that he was richer than they were. His narcissistic defenses denied him the very tools necessary for meaningful, fulfilling engagement with others: the ability to sustain warmth, openness, and vulnerability and the capacity to celebrate generosity and generativity.

It is important to underscore, as an aside, that my father's envy of other people's humanity was largely unconsciously held. It was not something he could have articulated or recognized in himself. Had he been able to do so, one can imagine it would have horrified him to have made such an admission. Even though he lacked awareness of the core nature of his envy, I would argue that it still had enormous impact on him, rendering the rest of the world unbearably more vibrant and attractive than the world he occupied, in spite of the virulent cynicism he relied upon to taint others' decency. So many riches so close at hand, but always out of reach.

His resulting sense of personal deficiency was also largely unconscious, I believe, but it nevertheless impelled him to take desperate measures to hide his terrible shortfalls. A powerful motive force behind his endless efforts to draw people's attention away from his core deficits with threats and bullying, with deflections and distractions, and with re-direction towards the shiny objects he paraded in front of them.

In his autobiographies and in his relationship with me, he made transparent attempts to idealize the manifest suffering that continued to express itself during his retirement. The effect was poignant. I wondered how conscious he was of this misrepresentation. Sometimes I think he believed it, but at others it was hard for me to conceive that he was unaware of his immense pain. What was unconscious, I think, was any substantive awareness of both why he lived his life the way that he did and why he felt compelled to hurt the people around him, nor was he fully cognizant of the costs that he was imposing on himself. Accordingly, his last years looked to be as awful as the first part of his life had been: fights for dominance and fights for scraps. Disturbingly, I watched the same Oedipal battles I had endured play themselves out in his new family, as he experienced poisonous outrage whenever my stepmother's attention was turned toward parenting rather than him. So far as I could see, his final years were, in the main, not very happy.

I suppose before I end this chapter, I would like to allude to a part of the autobiographies that keeps nagging at me and seemingly will not let me alone until I mention it. As I reviewed my father's narratives numbers of times, I kept noticing how often he used the word "little" to describe his possessions or aspects of his experience. This word called me back over and over to the injured child I had come to appreciate that my father was. An injured child who never healed himself and who felt left alone to deal with his own pain, without real hope of solace or support. As I become older, that child feels increasingly like the biggest part of who he was.

As beguiling and as coherent as my understanding of my father might appear to be to some readers, I must caution the reader, as I did at the outset of this book, that science is a process of successive approximation. My grasp of my father's experience and of my own can at best represent only a partial appreciation of our personal journeys. As others consider what I have said, ideas may be elaborated, discarded, and amended. Potential causalities that I have identified can, at best, capture only part of the reality I'm attempting to investigate. Within the world of mental health, it is generally accepted that most phenomena are multi-determined. I have only looked at limited forms of environmental trauma that would appear to make a contribution to the development of what I have called malignant narcissism. Genetics, epigenetics, biochemistry and physiology, and complexities of brain function acting in concert with one another and upon one another side-by-side their interaction with "nurture" will eventually allow us (if, indeed, we are ever capable of doing so) to truly grasp what malignant narcissism is. And, finally, to more fully set context, I must take care to add that while malignant narcissism is a compelling construct for me, I am very cognizant that many clinicians would argue that malignant narcissism is either a misleading or an inappropriate descriptor.

Completing this book won't end my investigation of narcissism nor will it offer the full measure of consummation I would like to experience; I will continue to feel restless and dissatisfied with the ideas that I and many others like me have pieced together to penetrate narcissism's veil. I would ask my readers to do the same.

Note

1 In my father's conversations with me, he identified his father as having swung the golf club that killed the dog.

Chapter 10

The Case for Narcissism as Psychopathy

In exploring the theoretical underpinnings that anchor my conception of narcissism, I'd like to set context by talking, in very broad terms, about diagnostic formulations pertinent to narcissism and psychopathy.

Psychopathy, at present, is not a distinct diagnostic entity, at least not in the framework that the *Diagnostic and Statistical Manual of Mental Disorders* – 5 provides (DSM-5). The DSM-5 is the reference work that mental health professionals use to confirm diagnosis. With few exceptions, the DSM-5 sidesteps etiology or causation, focusing instead on clusters of symptoms that are believed to characterize various clinical entities like mood disorders, anxiety disorders, sexual disorders, etc. Many diagnostic categories share marker symptoms, meaning that there is often considerable (and sometimes confusing) overlap between clinical entities. Classification in a young science is challenging. Practitioners and research scientists do the best that they can defining diagnostic categories using very imperfect and very limited knowledge. At times, they are reduced to making decisions about what they think a particular clinical entity is by relying on consensus rather than being able to access definitive scientific data. It is assumed that practitioners will not regard diagnostic categories as hard and fast rules – fixed truths, if one likes – but rather phenomena subject to the shifts and changes (and ongoing discussions) that characterize the evolution of a given science. Many divergent opinions feed the discussion and help refine it. It will be important to keep these caveats in mind as this chapter unfolds. We will not be talking about unyielding realities, but rather fluid truths that we hope to approximate with ever greater success as our efforts play themselves out.

Currently the DSM-5 recognizes a single diagnostic entity, Antisocial Personality Disorder (ASPD), that can be seen to embrace what has been referred to, variously, as psychopathy, sociopathy, and dissocial personality disorder. Noting that Narcissistic Personality Disorder shares much the same symptom cluster that typifies ASPD, the DSM-5 suggests that the two can be distinguished from one another because NPD is not characterized either by the presence or, alternatively, by the prominence of impulsivity, aggression, and deceit.

DOI: 10.4324/9781003246923-10

To remind my reader, as I extend my consideration of psychopathy literature in this chapter, I will be referencing broad trends and themes I have dis-
tilled from my reading of it rather than presenting specific research citations. I
would again reference Christopher Patrick's *Handbook of Psychopathy* as
essential reading for anyone who wishes to explore this subject in greater
depth.

The current and, one should say, very voluminous research on psychopathy proposes multifactorial models consisting of either two or three
factors, each of which represents a cluster of traits (stable, enduring personal dispositions that characterize people over substantial periods of
time). Although component traits are organized differently in the two and
three factor models of psychopathy, they are strikingly similar in both
conceptions.

For simplicity's sake, I will not compare and contrast the two- and three-
factor models of psychopathy. Instead, I will briefly describe the three factor
or triarchic model that Christopher Patrick developed. Providing a description of the triarchic model will, I hope, give the reader a strong sense of
contemporary conceptions of psychopathy. The three factors that Patrick
proposed were called, respectively, boldness, disinhibition, and meanness. As
may be apparent from earlier discussion in this book, boldness refers to a
constellation of traits including venturesomeness, willingness to take risks,
relative imperviousness to fear, the drive to dominate, and confident personal
assertion. As an aggregate, these traits could be subsumed under a heading
like fearless dominance. Disinhibition, in turn, not only encompasses impulsivity and compromised personal controls, but also irresponsibility, poor
decision-making, and deceitfulness. Meanness was construed to reflect markedly diminished capacity for empathy, compulsion to exploit others, an
orientation marked by dislike and distrust of others, and an inclination to
take pleasure in others' pain.

Most authors seem to view psychopathy as expressing itself along a continuum of severity, depending upon the degree to which a given individual
demonstrates traits along the three axes of boldness, disinhibition, and
meanness. Such a conception denies a unitary model of psychopathy – that is,
one in which psychopathy is conceived of as a unitary entity producing a
relatively consistent emergent clinical picture.

Implicit in the triarchic and two-factor models is anticipation that there are
probably subtypes of psychopathy one could expect to encounter depending
upon which factors in the two or three factor model are more evident than
others.

Two major subtypes of psychopathy have received a great deal of attention
in the literature, primary and secondary psychopathy. Formulations of these
two subtypes have varied, but very generally speaking, it is perhaps fair to say
that some research scientists would regard primary psychopathy as real or
actual psychopathy and secondary psychopathy as a mitigated version of the

former that produces a more limited rupture of conscience. Primary psycho-pathy, at times, has been seen as a core deficit shaped by genetics or biology that springs into being fully formed; it has also been viewed as being asso-ciated with, variously, many of the characteristics that typify both boldness and disinhibition as well as, interestingly, a core of narcissism defined by the need to exploit others ruthlessly. Secondary psychopathy, in contrast, often seems to be regarded as a consequence of damaging environmental influence that occasions the development of psychopathic traits. Perhaps because it arose as a result of stress inducing adverse nurture as opposed to a primary deficit in fear arousal mechanisms (boldness), it was seen to be subject to higher levels of mental health compromise, like depression and suicidality.

The discussion of these entities is often confusing, bespeaking people's attempts to come to terms with constructs they increasingly recognize are com-plex and elusive. Some authors appear to conclude that so-called secondary psychopathy could potentially produce the same array of deficits and very much the same clinical picture as primary psychopathy. I think, increasingly, that investigators are moving away from concepts like primary and secondary psy-chopathy, redirecting themselves towards consideration of the varied constella-tions of factors that may manifest themselves in psychopathic disorders.

The foregoing does not begin to do justice to the intricacy and nuance of discussion that has attended these issues. We also seem to recognize now, again speaking in very broad terms, that psychopathy is linked causally to a number of possible etiologies including genetics, brain structure (which can include response to brain injury), and a very long list of life stressors that either singly or in combination with one another unfolding at particularly vulnerable points in the developmental process may help set the stage for psychopathic personality.

Because the focus of this book has been upon the disruptive impact that a toxic nurture experience can potentially have upon a given individual, I will simply name some of these influences. They are thought to include: conviction and incarceration of one or more close family members; depression in a mother; age of a mother; paternal uninvolvement; physical abuse; sexual abuse; lack of parental supervision; harsh punishment; childhood neglect; parental conflict; an absent parent; multiple father figures; family size; low socioeconomic status; poverty; housing; quality of schooling; prevalence of antisocial behavior in one's neighborhood; and parental substance abuse. Genetic factors not directly related to the transmission of psychopathic traits might include low I.Q., difficulties paying attention at school, and low school attainment. Please keep in mind that I have provided only a partial list and that confidence in each of these factors or in specific combination with one another does vary, but the overall picture that emerges clearly underscores the importance that our experience plays in shaping who we become. Some evi-dence seems to suggest that a salutary early environment (family, school, community) may dilute the impact of presumably genetically acquired psychopathic traits.

There is not full agreement about the importance of all of the environmental factors I have just listed. Some of the research that surrounds particular factors is contradictory. Some of it is beset by problems because it has been difficult for research scientists to carry out prospective studies (some few exist) as opposed to retrospective studies. A prospective study begins with people that it observes longitudinally, allowing researchers to directly evaluate causative factors unfolding in real time as opposed to looking back (a retrospective study) as one tries to reconstruct, through subject report, what conditions might have been like when trauma was imposed. Research has also been beset by use of multiple instruments defining psychopathic traits, by varying definitions of experiences like abuse, by the difficulty of obtaining clinically diagnosed psychopaths as opposed to high scorers on instruments meant to measure psychopathy, by conflating psychopathy with other criterion measures like incarceration and ASPD, and by the problem of "cart horse" (which came first, bad parenting or psychopathic personality traits that disrupted parenting?). Again, this is only a partial list of research challenges and limitations.

My argument with ASPD as set out in DSM-5 is its failure to embrace the complexity that psychopathy represents as so wonderfully attested to by the impressively extensive research literature that surrounds the subject of psychopathy. I think the weight of the research makes sense. I believe psychopathy is multidimensional, comprising a variety of subtypes of which narcissism is one. So far as I can see, Narcissistic Personality Disorder (NPD) would meet the criteria established for psychopathy in the relevant research literature as specified by both the triarchic and the two-factor models. Moreover, on a purely prima facie basis, it is hard for me to imagine that someone can be possessed of salient NPD symptomatology (as defined by the DSM-5), including, as a partial list, grandiosity, self-aggrandizement, a sense of entitlement, interpersonal exploitativeness, lack of empathy, endemic envy, and arrogance without also being likely to be duplicitous, aggressive, and impulsive. My clinical experience working with limited numbers of NPD confirms my prima facie impression. The DSM, of course, argues the contrary.

If one is to consider that narcissism is a subtype of psychopathy, I would think it would also be true, given that psychopathy appears to be inherently multidimensional, that narcissistic personality could be expected to express itself differently, depending upon which of its core traits stands out in greatest relief. Indeed, it is widely recognized that some narcissistic personalities are able to navigate their way through the world with startling success in spite of their deficits while others are either ineffectual and obviously troubled (subject to a variety of other mental health disorders) or have had the means to cause widespread human suffering. In fact, the DSM does implicitly recognize that one NPD may not be like another. In allowing clinicians a range of symptomatology to choose from (not all NPD symptoms have to be present in order

for the diagnosis to be made), the DSM is recognizing that symptom configuration may be different in different narcissistic personalities. By implication,
if there are different configurations of narcissistic personality disorder, the
pathways or etiologies that produce each may be different in some important
ways than it is for the others.

For me, this discussion is important because it highlights an important
limitation of diagnosis. Diagnosis, at best, is a label that can only capture very
approximate appreciation of a given individual. It may serve a variety of
important needs (categorization, risk appraisal, formulation of prognosis,
treatment planning), but it can never capture the intricacy of a given individual, nor, as a collection of symptoms, can it capture the complex interplay of
forces that lead to the problems that the individual is experiencing. As one of
my colleagues pointed out, it is at this juncture that the distinction between
diagnosis and formulation becomes important. In contrast to diagnosis, formulation attempts to look deeply – or at least more deeply – into an individual's unique circumstances in an attempt to develop an appreciation of just
how that person got to be the person that they are. Doing this places one in a
far better position to start to examine causative factors. It means, inevitably,
constructing a lengthy narrative that, hopefully, judiciously weighs various
hypotheses and informed guesses that one makes about the patterns and the
causalities that begin to declare themselves. It is, at one and the same time,
both more speculative and more precise than identification of a diagnostic
label. It offers one the possibility of spelling out the dynamic interplay of
causalities that produce different kinds of human problems.

Trait-based research attempts to do this by measuring stable dispositional
characteristics across large numbers of people. Its findings are enormously
helpful. I've relied heavily on trait data in this discussion and in earlier parts
of my book. The trait approach currently lacks the means, however, as trait-
based researchers point out themselves, to articulate the mechanisms or
dynamics that underlie some of the broad causative agents it has identified,
like parental neglect, parental separation, physical and sexual abuse, etc.
Intensive observation of individuals, couples, and families in psychotherapy
allows one an intimate view of dynamics close at hand, but doing so means
that one is working with very small numbers of people and that the data one
produces are less amenable to quantitative study more readily accessible to
trait research. For a clinician attempting to understand the complexity of
forces, including psychological ones, that inform and direct someone's life, it
is words, rather than numbers, that become essential. Formulations are words.

My bias as a psychoanalytically oriented psychologist is to believe that an
appreciation of the dynamic interplay of psychological forces is critical to an
understanding of diagnosis. It is, in other words, the mechanisms or dynamics
that drive various human realities which I find most helpful and most informative when I think about diagnosis. Some of the dynamics that I observe
seem to apply across the human condition and some of them, or groups of

them, appear to be distinctive, identifying features of particular clinical problems. Diagnosis based upon etiology and dynamics would, to my mind, be
ideal. The intense idiographic study of each individual's uniquely configured
personality organization, mental functioning, and subjective experience that
the *Psychodynamic Diagnostic Manual* (PDM–2) (2017) affords certainly
helps us achieve the kind of in-depth formulation of dynamics I find so useful.
It significantly extends the nomothetic formulations that the DSM–5 offers us
and, as such, can be used in conjunction with the DSM or on its own, particularly when treatment planning and countertransferential issues represent
prominent concerns, as they do in psychodynamic work.

The best that we can do is try and describe some of the interactive forces
we encounter in the people we work with as adequately we can, biding our
time and re-exploring our ideas endlessly until we begin to have the measure
of confirmation we need to have confidence in them. Articulating patterns of
interaction between psychological forces is just the beginning, as I noted at
the outset of this book. We have to integrate that understanding with an
appreciation of brain function and structure, genetics and epigenetics, and
biology in order for diagnosis to be fully meaningful. At that point it is not
inconceivable to me that we will be confronted with multiplicities of patterns/
dynamics that lead to the same behavioral outcomes and personality structures. And with that knowledge we may discover that diagnosis via etiology is
less desirable than one might imagine it would be. What, then, is the diagnosis? It is our best appreciation, however imperfect, of the form that a given
disorder takes (its expression) and/or the unique pathways that give birth to
it. It is a relatively fluid construct, subject, as it is, to frequent reappraisals
that produce ever more helpful models of human psychology.

What I have tried to do in the preceding chapters of the book is provide a
lengthy formulation that attempts to capture both my own and my father's
salient dynamic patterns. This effort is inevitably flawed. My father's view of
his life experience was, to a significant degree, a retrospective one, though I
did have the opportunity to view him contemporaneously. My view of myself
could also be characterized as retrospective in some important regards.
Though I was part of my experience as it unfolded, in order to recapture it I
had to rely on both memory and psychological reconstruction to be able to
describe it. I relied on these reconstructions as well as my ongoing experience
with myself to extrapolate patterns. While I was seemingly able to provide a
very intimate and focused portrait of my experience and my father's, I am
very much aware that I was only describing two people. In some respects, it
must be true that my experience and his are unique, setting us apart from
other people in ways that I cannot anticipate and from that group of people
that I have identified as having Narcissistic Personality Disorder. The confluence of forces that define each of us are so extraordinarily imposing I
cannot hope to begin to capture their specificity. I must content myself with
moving from the few particularities of our lives I was able to appreciate

towards formulations of patterns and generalities that I think could characterize important parts of the dynamics that typify one form of NPD. That is what I have attempted to do in Chapters 3 through 8.

I am acutely aware that in offering up these patterns and generalizations I am providing the reader with a description of only two of the many pathways that may lead to narcissism. I am referring to the pathway that my father took and the pathway that I nearly took myself.

In the remaining chapters of this book, I hope to restate some of my ideas in a modestly more formal way that further clarifies and extends the understanding of narcissism I have provided.

References

American Psychiatric Association: *Diagnostic and statistical manual of mental disorders* (5th edition). Arlington, VA: American Psychiatric Association, 2013.

Lingiardi, V. and McWilliams, N. (Eds.) (2017). *Psychodynamic Diagnostic Manual*, (2nd edition). New York, N.Y.: Guilford Press.

Patrick, C. J. (Ed.) (2018). *Handbook of psychopathy* (2nd edition). New York, N.Y.: Guilford Press.

Chapter 11

Formulation of Narcissism

My father's autobiographies conferred a wonderful advantage in my patient work. They allowed me the means to build a theoretical model of narcissism that I could test against the realities that narcissistic patients presented me in a treatment context. I found myself engaging with three different groups of narcissistic patients: people whom I never met, but could deduce might be narcissistic given a patient's ongoing description of them in the context of a treatment effort; narcissistic relatives or partners of patients I had a chance to observe directly whose contact with me was, typically, relatively brief (five to six sessions); and people I worked with over a prolonged period of time (nine months or more) who appeared to be compatible with my concept of malignant narcissism. The first two groups provided me with the opportunity to observe, either directly or indirectly, prominent characteristics or patterns of narcissistic behavior alongside its impact on the people in the narcissist's life. There were a relatively great number of putative Narcissistic Personality Disorders (NPDs) in each of these two groups. The latter or third group – pathologically narcissistic patients who sought out extended treatment for themselves – only consisted of six individuals. For the most part, malignantly narcissistic individuals rarely submit to self-exploration, as I commented earlier in the book. It was this last small group of people who afforded me opportunity to compare some of the salient dynamics of my father's history with those of other people I considered to be possessed of malignant narcissism. In such a fashion I could tentatively attribute more or less confidence to some of the patterns of causality I thought I had identified. My comparisons of their histories with my father's were limited by the small number of "subjects" I had to work with, but enriched by the lengthy, in-depth work I was able to do with such individuals.

All of the malignant narcissists that I undertook long-term work with were male. While I met numbers of women who were relations of patients who struck me as narcissistic, I did not have the benefit of having obtained full, detailed histories from them. As a result, the models of malignant narcissistic etiology that I am about to articulate reflect my appreciation of male realities. While I have some sense that at least some of the dynamics and causalities I

DOI: 10.4324/9781003246923-11

identified in men who were malignantly narcissistic could be extended to female narcissism, I have little data and consequently little justification in asserting that this would be so. Because my appreciation of female malignant narcissism is so tenuous, it must remain for other writers who have accrued experience with a female narcissistic population to attempt to describe it.

I should also emphasize that I worked with many people whose backgrounds appeared to be as egregious as my father's who did not adopt a narcissistic life stance. Understanding this group's resistance to narcissistic adjustment represents an important focus of study, but not one that falls within the purview of this book.

I want the reader to be skeptical about the patterns of causality and of narcissistic life adjustment that I have described in previous text and that I am about to reformulate now. I would ask the reader, in other words, to think critically about what I have had to say and to consider alternative hypotheses possessed of greater explanatory value. For my own part, each time I worked briefly with relations of patients who impressed me as narcissistic or heard about people in patients' lives who sounded as if they were struggling with narcissism, I worried about the all too powerful inclination that I think we all possess to see examples of a precious insight where it may not exist. My hunger to find examples of malignant narcissism, in other words, could readily lead to errors in clinical judgement.

I will also caution the reader that while the language that I use sometimes will sound authoritative and declarative, its self-confidence in no way is meant to assert a claim to "truth," but, rather, enables me to outline my ideas with greater clarity and efficiency. To express hesitation about everything that I say would mire text in tiresome, tedious equivocation. Simply put, the assumption should be made that I consider everything I say to be hypothetical and speculative.

Finally, a reminder to readers that I will not talk about patient histories in any depth nor in a way that might expose patient identity. Instead, I will focus on broad generalities that seem to typify histories and life adjustments.

In all of the people that I worked with closely, one powerful dynamic seemed to stand out in great relief: relentless, ruthless early exploitation and adultification of a target individual by parental figures. As was the case with my father, parents were experienced as making unceasing, punishing demands that their needs or their agendas be attended to while providing little sustenance for their child and little recognition of the child's own needs. The level of expectation and commitment that parents imposed upon their children gave little quarter, allowing a child no room to be a child or become the child that they might have been. All was duty. All was work. All was obligation. Listening to these histories was hard. Children dedicated and re-dedicated themselves to their parents' purpose without receiving much reward, save for either indirect or lavishly indulgent confirmation that their soul-destroying effort made them special. Either directly or indirectly (but more typically the former), aggrandizement and grandiosity were the close companions of exhaustion.

As a result of such an experience, love comes to connote toxicity, signifying obligation, exploitation, and terrifying levels of psychic depletion that increasingly confirm love as a dangerous and jeopardizing experience for the self. Others' demands create a measure of psychic and, in my father's case, physical starvation that is felt to threaten annihilation, if not of the person, then of the spirit. Such starvation occurs in a context in which the parental other is felt to be relatively indifferent or at least insensitive to the child's literal struggle for survival. In two of the cases that I saw, parental neglect appeared to be infiltrated with thinly disguised murderous undercurrents. In order to survive the profound threat and deprivation that it faces, the developing self feels increasingly compelled to defend itself against its impulse to love others and to engage in acts of generosity and empathy. Circumstances that might evoke love come to be imbued with risk and lethality for the self.

As exploitation continues, extending itself throughout childhood and even young adulthood, deep and intractable cynicism about the possibility of generosity and meaningful, sustaining caring from others entrenches itself. It is, increasingly, supported by vigilance meant to ensure that the self never lets down its guard, that it never lets others gain traction through love, and that invocation of mistrust is immediate, pervasive, and unyielding. The self has to ensure that it cannot be touched by human hand or heart. The self that emerges is formidably alone and formidably self-interested, determined never again to expose itself to the exploitation and depredation of others.

The emergent self is also profoundly mistrustful of dependence on others, having rarely experienced dependence as a constructive and fulfilling enterprise. The inaccessibility of inter-dependence ensures that solitude becomes more formidable. The terrified, lonely child seizes upon the self-aggrandizement and grandiosity assigned it, clinging to it as a bulwark against all the unrequited need piling up inside that the child has had little opportunity to gratify. Aggrandizement also seems to offer protection against the suffocating helplessness that the child's devastating circumstances have created. "If I can pretend that I'm bigger, that I am more than the defenseless child that I am, if I can believe in my aggrandizement, I can feel safer." Aggrandizement and grandiosity further offer promise that the child can somehow satisfy its needy parent, consolidating connection and belonging and, perhaps, ensuring parental survival. Most importantly – and perhaps more poignantly – the aggrandized self is relied upon to protect the child from too close an acquaintance with the damaged, neglected, inadequate self that exists underneath his surface – the frightened child who is beset by unbearable vulnerabilities.

Parenthetically, I should mention that prominent incestuous/oedipal themes only presented themselves in one patient I worked with. Such themes stood out with relief, of course, in my father's relationship with his mother and my relationship with mine. My sense is that strong oedipal undercurrents or frankly incestuous ones probably eroticize attribution of self-aggrandizement, rendering it well-nigh irresistible, particularly in an individual who may feel desperate for nurturance in whatever form it might present itself.

The "mature" aggrandized self that eventually emerges after childhood is intolerant of vulnerability, intolerant of dependence, and intolerant of others' wants. It replaces the vulnerability that love and human communion entail with predation. It repeatedly confirms its authority to take from others and to dominate them in an effort to create safety for itself in a world that it has experienced as malignant and invasive. Domination and predation become compulsive and defining, both because the self would reflexively find it unbearable to re-experience the agony of childhood and, not insignificantly, because the self is beset by intolerable, insatiable hunger. Defense against love, generosity, empathy, and interdependence denies that which is essential for people to feed themselves: human connection. In the absence of that, the self becomes hungrier, more voracious, more toxic, extending its rapacity. Turning away from that which would be truly sustaining, the self instead focuses upon that which gives the appearance of richness – trappings of power, status, money, possessions, and acquisition of fame and attention. In my father's case, one can imagine how beseechingly desirable these commodities must have seemed, given their absence while he was growing up.

Contempt is the cornerstone defense. It is really pervasive and relentless. The mistake is often made that the narcissist dislikes particular groups of people; sustained acquaintance with a narcissist, however, reveals dislike for everybody, a truly misanthropic stance. Contempt is the wall that keeps the narcissist in and others out, ensuring tortured, aggrieved solitude and the deconstruction of loving, generous impulses both in self and in others. Inevitably, the great charisma of which some narcissistic people are capable is corrupted by contempt. Nice doesn't last for very long.

In the process of pursuing that which can never satiate, the narcissist becomes even less human. His rage, his vigilance, and his rapacity become his defining preoccupations. His inner landscape becomes blighted by the violations he must direct towards others in order to feed himself and in order to ensure that a predatory world cannot overpower him. There is little relief from the cynicism, mistrust, and cruelty that informs his inner world. Rage and cynicism are necessary. They justify his exploitation of others and support a forbidding sense of entitlement. After all, others are just as self-interested as he is, aren't they? He tells himself incessantly that everybody's looking for an angle, that he has the right to get to them before they can get to him. His hostility and depreciation ensure that others will react in kind, further confirming his cynicism.

This process is referred to as projective identification. I feel "X," now I accuse you of feeling X, and then I provoke you to act out that which I project onto you, offering me confirmation that my appraisal of your original intentions was accurate. In even simpler terms, it's kind of like telling somebody you're mad at that they're mad at you, then preemptively kicking them in the shins, after which you get to experience a sense of satisfaction that your assessment of them was fitting when they attack you back. This defense may imply that you're either so convinced or so frightened that you're about to be attacked you feel compelled to act first. It is a particularly toxic and disturbing process to endure if you're the target. Someone else has effectively injected you with their toxic emotions and gotten you to feel and act as if they were your own. Projective identification is widely recognized as one of the core defenses narcissistic personalities rely on. It acts in concert with splitting, another cornerstone defense in narcissism. Rather than seeing the self or others around one as complex human beings defined by myriads of nuanced and often competing intentions and feelings, the narcissist divides the world of self and the world of people into simplistic categories of right and wrong, good and bad. Doing so (splitting) makes it easier to expel or to disconfirm parts of the self that he doesn't like, projecting them onto the people around him, whom he experiences as utterly irredeemable. It also creates opportunity to bask in the reflected glory of those people he venerates, enhancing, in the process, his own grotesque idealization of himself.

In this fashion, people are experienced in either idealized or denigrated terms. The resulting lop-sided portrait either vastly overestimates people's value or impugns them with reprehensible motives. It is important to emphasize that these attributions are not stable, but shifting and seemingly capricious, as can be seen by the manner in which my father responded to the people in his world. In my experience, splitting and projective identification never fully protect the narcissist from an awareness of their own destructive urges; protection is only partial and may vacillate from one moment to the next. It can be seen through some of the examples I gave earlier in the book that my father was at times acutely aware of his own ugliness, often using it to justify his exploitation of others ("See, they're just as bad as I am, if not worse, just as I knew"). Tragically, idealization also never manages to consolidate stability in the narcissist's relationships, nor does it provide the means to incorporate enduring representations of good relationships that the narcissist could rely on to enrich his inner life. The narcissist's relationship with himself and with those around him is constantly buffeted by the shifting perceptions that characterize a life dominated by projective identification and splitting. In part, the offset is that the malignant narcissist ensures for himself no one can ever get close to him and make the kinds of demands of him bonds of fealty growing out of a longer-term relationship could impose. By employing splitting and projective identification, he also benefits by generating an atmosphere of fear and uncertainty he can harness to meet his needs. Like any of the defenses that we employ, the solutions that these defenses offer the malignant narcissist are imperfect compromises, imposing both significant costs and desirable advantages.

Bereft of loving impulse, which he would find too dangerous to experience, his private self becomes a wasteland, populated by grotesque feelings and impulses that further contribute to a sense of inner deadness. There is little that feels alive and attractive. Engagement and aliveness are simulated through acts of cruelty and risk taking that confirm power and that enable him to feel something. In defense against the ugliness accruing inside, he imbues the aggrandized self with desirable attributions, characterizing its rapacity as competence and as strength. In this way he tries to conceal his terrible secret – his inability to love and give – turning tragic weakness into an admirable asset.

The narcissist is quite literally terrified of any confrontation with his damaged humanity. His blindness to his terrible deficits is informed by his need to protect the self from the repellent internal realities that define him. Such blindness is obdurate, inflexible, and intransigent. Its unyielding nature means that he could not admit to himself, much less tell others, that he is terrified of looking deeply into himself; nonetheless, much of his energy is directed towards avoidance of any meaningful exploration of his interior. Accordingly, extraordinary effort is made to construct an exterior or a "surface" that the narcissist wishes to call attention to: one meant to inspire envy, invoke status, convey indomitability, and compel fear. The aggrandized self previously referred to is a central part of such a surface. These surface facets of self are, ironically, the compensatory or aggrandized self that has earned the narcissist the reputation for staring adoringly at his own image.

Remaining on the surface creates great costs for the narcissist. The relative deadness that characterizes the narcissistic interior, save for defining emotions like rage, envy, and acquisitiveness, denies the narcissist access to many of the internal promptings that potentially enrich the self. Spontaneity, playfulness, tolerance for surprise, openness to vulnerability, capacity for self-depreciating humor – virtually any act that enhances one's own and others' humanity – largely elude the narcissistic personality. Instead, such "human" markers have to be contrived. As a result, personality has to be orchestrated, conducted, curated, and manipulated in order for the narcissist to simulate humanity in the world of people. For some narcissistic personalities, particularly those capable of great charisma, fabrication of humanity can unfold with such an ease and plausibility that a casual observer feels like they are interacting with an authentic other who is as caught up in the rhythms and music of the relationship as the observer is themselves. The simulation, in other words, may feel quite real. In the main, though there are certainly moments of real connection, it is not. What feels authentic or substantial or meaningful strikes one, on careful reflection, as empty, vacuous, and insubstantial. Such inter-action is defined by surfaces and appearances rather than by genuine emotional and intellectual engagement – at best, a transfixing embellishment that glitters and bewitches but, confusingly, fails to satisfy or fulfil. While other diagnostic realities in the psychoanalytic world (e.g., hysteria and "as if" personality), may, respectively, either incessantly seek others' attention (hysteria) or contrive their presentation so that, chameleon like, they might blend into their environment (as if personality), neither is dominated by the rage, envy, and cruelty that is characteristic of narcissism.

Hiding his damaged humanity becomes an unconscious burden the narcissist must carry with him into all of his human interactions. If he can dazzle, distract, deflect, and threaten, he can turn others away or, even better, seduce them into believing that his is a rare and enticing world that they must want to be a part of. Encounters with decency are disconcerting. That which is decent must be deconstructed and debased or turned away from.

Protection of the aggrandized self is essential. The narcissist assumes the posture of a fragile tyrant, unable to tolerate any assault on the aggrandized self, frantically parrying perceived or real sleights out of all proportion to their objective value. Doing so is critical to survival. Without the aggrandized self, the narcissist feels exposed to others' predation. And without the aggrandized self, the narcissist faces re- exposure to the devastating helplessness his childhood occasioned. Others' attacks have to be met with counterattack. Each and every time. But the whole enterprise increasingly assumes an improbable cast: incessant domination and hostility breed resistance and pushback. To be safe, the narcissist has to win every time. Incessant winning demands ever more single-minded ruthlessness that, while effective in the moment, generates more injury in those people who occupy space with the narcissist, occasioning future risk that the narcissist inevitably has to contend with. Narcissistic predation, hostility, and need for dominance very effectively protect the narcissist from experiencing loving impulses or from being genuinely loved himself, but they set the stage for endless warfare.

Destined to wander in the wilderness of a disturbingly desolate personal landscape and an interpersonal one pervaded by acrimony, accrual of injury to others, and frantic attempts to prop up the aggrandized self, the narcissist endures extraordinary pain that only accumulates with the passage of a lifetime, incrementally consolidating a sense of badness and injuriousness that becomes increasingly hard to disguise. In an attempt to defend the self from the catastrophic actualities that define it, the narcissist's deep revulsion for the self is projected onto the surrounding world. In consequence, the projected world that the narcissist occupies assumes the same frightening aspect as the inner one the narcissist is attempting to evade and conceal. Danger and threat compound one another; cynicism finds evermore justification for itself.

I would have to say that many of the narcissistic patients that I have worked with, whether my acquaintance with them unfolded in long-term work or through relatively brief contact, confirmed how awful they felt about themselves, much like my father did. The confession was usually very briefly stated (though not always), but was always poignantly given. One was impressed by these people's genuine, but very disturbing appreciation of what they had become. Just as quickly as this door opened, it was usually closed, presumably because keeping it open felt far too jeopardizing. A brief moment of humanity and vulnerability rarely ever revisited. Two of my narcissistic patients, however, could bear the sight of what they saw inside and could talk openly about the agony their confrontation with self caused them. They were plainly horrified by the damage they had sustained to their humanity, re-confirming and expanding my understanding of what my other narcissistic patients were feeling. One of them was obviously clinically depressed and the other appeared not to be (I should clarify that he fell in the short-term treatment group, meaning that I may not have had adequate opportunity to assess depression).

The patient experiencing depression also proved himself to be able to tolerate another facet of his personal experience, one that core narcissistic defenses seem contrived to protect the narcissistic personality from enduring. Rather than relentlessly attacking others in an attempt to consolidate dominance, he could recognize and talk about reiteration of childhood pain and helplessness that surfaced in his adult interchanges. When grandiosity and need for control were challenged, he could acknowledge the helplessness and panic such challenge might elicit and, more strikingly, could tell one that what he was experiencing as an adult reflected facets of unbearable childhood pain. He could afford to set aside his aggrandizement and grandiosity, in other words, and feel the early agony that drove him to act as he did. Not surprisingly, he made more headway in treatment than his compatriots.

A critical part of what I see narcissistic personalities attempting to protect themselves against is what I refer to as regression to an earlier ego state. Regressing to an earlier ego state is something that we all endure as a commonplace part of our everyday lives. Contemporary events elicit re-invocation of deeper early pain that has the capacity to flood us, however momentarily, not only with early feelings, but an early state of being. We feel ourselves to be the helpless or terrified or relatively resourceless child that we once were who, depending upon what our early experience was like, may feel overwhelmed with shame, guilt, utter despair, uncontrollable rage, etc. An encounter with regression to an earlier ego state is both powerful and disconcerting, robbing one, however transiently, of adult competencies and dignity. I remember seeing an old Saturday Night Live episode in which the adult "kids" go home for Thanksgiving at their parents' home. Finding themselves situated in the basement because there is no room at the big table upstairs, they begin to squabble and fight with one another in the way that they once did when they were children. I think we've all been there. For some of my patients, however, re-invocation of early pain can be quite catastrophic, producing, as extreme examples, intense depressive feelings, relationship disruption, violence, and suicidal behavior. Frequently, people have no sense of why they have reacted in the way that they do. Helping them establish links between devastating early pain and contemporary experience can make a difference. People no longer feel as unsafe with the abrupt, shearing emotional distress that regression to an earlier ego state can occasion. They can also see and feel that they are no longer the children that they once were, limited by nascent resources.

In working with this phenomenon, part of the difficulty that one faces is dealing with defenses that curtail regression experiences before they can assert themselves. People develop the means to curtail or short-circuit very aversive regression states before they can consummate themselves. This is what the narcissist does by adopting a dominant, rapacious stance: hopelessness, desolation, and depletion are replaced with the sense of substance that confirmation of power provides. The narcissist never has to go back to the defenseless, humiliating childhood space. As can be seen from the description of narcissistic dynamics, extraordinary efforts are made to ensure that never happens.

Inner deadness I have referenced gives rise to poisonous envy, which infects and directs much of the narcissist's experience and behavior. Though unfolding on a largely unconscious basis, the narcissist is aware that others are much richer than he is. Envy is offset by attempts to inspire envy in others, by continued affirmations of power and expansiveness, and by compulsion to diminish and debase those around him. Desperate to acquire more supplies to fill the terrible, raging empty space inside, envy only intensifies the desire to exploit and to demean. It directs the self to consume everything outside itself, greedily demanding that its voice must dominate, that it must occupy center stage, that accolades are its prerogatives and not others, that its assertions are infallible, etc.

The narcissist's pervasive envy and unquenchable appetites help drive the imperative to dominate space, compelling the narcissist to assert expertise that is either insubstantial or nonexistent. Qualifications that legitimize another voice offend; they represent potential encroachment upon proprietary supplies the narcissist deems rightfully his. Resulting assertions of competence can assume outlandish proportions. The narcissist all too readily becomes an instant expert in fields that he knows little about. Extravagant claims are supported with stridency; objections, however reasonably founded, incite indignation, elaborate rationalization that may strike one as preposterous, and a sharp sense of injury in the narcissistic personality. Appropriate backtracking, acknowledgement of mistakes, and especially apology, are all impossible. Because they authenticate others' voices and are felt to bespeak personal weakness, they are anathema. Apology is unendurable, experienced as exposing the damaged self and compromising the compensatory aggrandized self. Collaboration also essentially remains out of reach inasmuch as it necessitates confirmation of the other, invites the other to create and use a voice, grants space for the other to occupy, and enables the other's personal growth. Instead, relationships are zero-sum games in which one party's win is inevitably the other party's loss; the narcissist can only conceive of acting in his own interest and does not see that generating opportunity for the other also enriches him.

Envy extends to the very selfhood of others. The other cannot be allowed to exist as a separate self; rather it must be subsumed as an extension of the narcissist. The other is asked to feel and think and judge as the narcissist does rather than responding to their own inner promptings. In such a context the narcissist can reassure themselves that the other no longer represents a substantial threat to the insatiable supplies that they need or to their own paradoxically fragile aggrandized self. Others are meant to experience dominance, power, envy, and threat in the narcissist's presence; any intimation of personal weakness on the narcissist's part is felt to be abhorrent and jeopardizing to him.

In the psychological context of narcissism, the self must protect itself from empathic experience. Empathy threatens to expose the self to bonds of attachment, to obligation to look after the other's well-being, and to breach of a tenacious focus on self-interest. For the narcissist, empathy implies exposure to vulnerability and to an exploitation of the self that was an unbearable and pervasive aspect of early experience. Empathy is generally tolerated only briefly and fleetingly before the psyche displaces it with cynicism and contempt. Deep, sustained empathy is rare, though the narcissist may simulate empathy in a transactional context to realize gains.

Horrified by empathy, by intense, rich interdependency, and by the generosity of spirit that supports and extends loving feelings over meaningful periods of time, the narcissist soon finds himself adrift in a love relationship, disinterested and repelled by the intimacy so necessary to extend and deepen it. In all likelihood, the narcissist has probably chosen someone as a partner who is as transactional as he is. The transactional "bargain" that the narcissist enters into with his transactional partner only confirms the narcissist's deeply cynical view of others as essentially calculating and exploitative. After all, the narcissist can tell himself, my partner's manipulation and self-interest confirm for me, day-to-day, what I have always known about people.

Choosing a partner kinder or warmer than the narcissist is may be appealing, however, because doing so offers the prospect that the other may help the narcissist heal himself. Relationships based on the promise of transcendence, though, are often marked by particularly intense, chaotic, and acrimonious exchanges that pervade and essentially define them. The other's humanity threatens to expose the narcissist's own lack of humanity and must certainly exacerbate the narcissist's formidable underlying envy. The other's relative richness of spirit torments the narcissistic personality, soon evoking storms of debasement and disconfirmation intended to obliterate grace and decency that the other possesses. In such a fashion, the narcissist destroys his own best hope of re-invoking his capacity to love.

Restless and bored in a transactional love relationship or tormented and aggrieved by a partner's relative richness of spirit, the narcissist soon resorts to multiple infidelities that suit his taste for risk-taking, indulgence of power, and objectification, moving from one essentially meaningless adventure to another in an attempt to simulate life. Braggadocio, hyperbolized accounts of sexual exploits, and attempts to incite envy associated with extended conquests are all meant to distract and deflect both others and the self from an awareness of the empty, barren nature of such exchanges. Celebrate with me, the narcissist seems to say, and we can both bask in my shared glory. The invitation to do so, however, often seems clumsy, marked by exaggerated self-indulgence and self-congratulation. The aftertaste such an invitation creates may be offset by the possibility that one can be admitted, at least momentarily, to the narcissist's special world, one that promises to imbue the individual with the embellishments of the narcissist's aggrandized self.

What is interesting is that the narcissist's appeals to the other to celebrate reflected glory is often undertaken seemingly without any real awareness of the caricature that the narcissist renders of himself. The appeal appears to be indiscriminate, exposing the narcissist, in the process, to expressions of disapproval or even revulsion in his audience that, in turn, elicits narcissistic counterattack.

Endemic lying both arises from and confirms the grandiosity and omnipotence that are central to narcissistic character organization. The narcissist operates in a world in which his is the only tangible, meaningful presence. There can only be room for his voice and for his perception. Reality is not objectifiable and verifiable; it is, instead, an extension of his needs, whims, and feeling states, confirming what he thinks or wishes simply is. The other does not matter. Others are experienced – if they are to be acknowledged at all – as an extension of the aggrandized self, instruments or "things" to be used and manipulated to achieve narcissistic ends.

Lying serves a particularly critical function. It allows the narcissist to test and retest his relationships, confirming loyalty as his acolytes parrot the latest version of truth he has chosen to sell. Because he is eternally wary and mistrustful, obeisance and loyalty have to be probed over and over. Demonstrations of fealty are never enough. Those who would partner themselves with him must show themselves, literally day by day, in an unselfconscious and enthusiastic fashion, as being willing to replicate the shifting and conflicting versions of reality he concocts. In this way the narcissist can reassure himself that he is in command of his world and of the personalities that populate it.

Perpetual testing extends itself in other ways. Should a subordinate too passionately and too articulately capture the narcissist's own voice, sharp retaliation ensues. The other can find themselves facing contradiction and diminishment for their too successful appropriation of a core narcissistic prerogative: you must always ensure that my presence and the recognition that I enjoy are more prominent than yours. Confusingly, the target can find themselves punished for adhering too closely and too effectively to the narcissist's perspective. Even more bewilderingly, they must somehow gracefully accommodate their diminishment and, possibly, a contradictory version of reality the narcissist imposes upon them ("he's got it wrong – that isn't my position," etc.). Failure to drink this particularly bitter version of Kool-Aid and display unfaltering accommodation generates concerns about loyalty for the narcissist and may begin to spell the beginning of the end of the relationship, which can unfold with alarming abruptness. In this way, the narcissist can ensure that no relationship remains too important to him and that no individual achieves too much purchase in his life.

The narcissist also expects the other to be willing to sacrifice themselves to ensure his survival. This is a presumptive and almost casual expectation that plays itself out with great frequency seemingly in the absence of an obvious business or political crisis that might demand subordinates take a hit for the leader. For the narcissist, in spite of his grandiosity, survival is an ever-present threat occasioned, in no small part, by the unending transgressions which define his behavior. He must know that others will allow themselves to be debased and wounded so that he can carry on in spite of the jeopardy his grandiosity can create for him. For the narcissist, the other is only possessed of value inasmuch as they can demonstrate utility. Someone who places greater value on their own survival insults the narcissist. A subordinate who fails to make the required sacrifice can expect to be characterized as back-stabbing, as perfidious, or as treasonous. The subordinate who chooses to take a hit gracefully and without objection possibly reassures themselves that their act of falling on their sword will earn them eventual rescue through the agency of the narcissist's unconstrained power. As a consequence of close "collaboration" with the narcissist, they may have come to feel that his omnipotence is defining for them, too, imbuing them with the means to respond to others' incursions with indifference or contempt.

Testing and versions of lying also play themselves out in other ways. Subordinates can be repeatedly asked to cross distasteful moral lines. Their willingness to do so confirms loyalty, of course; it also insidiously and incrementally tethers those complicit in immoral acts ever more closely to the narcissist, reassuring the narcissist that individuals who have done so can only turn against him at great cost to themselves. Having compromised themselves in an increasingly inexorable stepwise fashion, their corruption comes to all too closely resemble his. They find themselves fated to cling to his ship. To do otherwise would be to drown. In such a manner, the narcissist expands the moral compromise of those who would be part of the influence and power he wields. It also seems likely that a significant proportion of the people who would choose to work closely with him have engaged in substantive moral transgression of their own, perhaps as a habitual part of their being. By incorporating such individuals into his fold, the narcissist has the reassurance that he is working with others who can follow him wheresoever he chooses to go.

Disagreement with a narcissist's untenable interpretations of reality produces outrage. It threatens grandiosity and threatens belief that only the narcissistic self has the right to occupy space in the world which surrounds it. If the challenges which the surrounding world mounts are meaningful, sustained, and effective, narcissistic response comes to be characterized by outbursts of rage, by genuine bewilderment (as if it is hard for the narcissist to imagine that others are possessed of substance), and, ultimately, by a deep sense of injury that impresses an observer as childlike indignation. All three of these states of being can alternate rapidly with one another. The narcissist variously presents himself as both bully and victim. His presentation is devoid of empathy and insight. It is, simultaneously, often mawkish or even clownish, exaggerated in a way and to a degree that lends the entire response an absurd, arbitrary quality. It is also characterized by ongoing distortions of reality and impelled by the narcissist's needs to re-establish entitlement, to disarm the other, and to portray the self as having endured egregious injury. For those who have not been enveloped by and identified with the narcissist's rapacity and grievance, such behavior feels almost farcical, a surreal drama possessed of only the thinnest justification for itself. Missing entirely is any sensitivity to the injury that continued bullying, misappropriation of reality, and depreciation have had on the narcissist's neighbors. An outside observer not embroiled in identification with a narcissist is likely to experience deep indignation that an individual who persistently and blindly batters others demands that extraordinary sensitivity be accorded to his own feelings. For those people who have accommodated themselves to the narcissist's worldview, finding common cause with the narcissist's deep sense of injury, there is corresponding offence and outrage, mirroring the narcissist's sense that he has been unjustly attacked.

Vacillation between outbursts of rage, petulance, and disbelief that others can push back creates a cacophony of emotions and postures that often feels overwhelming and bruising, a discordant, fractured symphony assaulting all an adversary's senses. Bewilderment, shock and awe, and a sense of absurdity and unreality are its byproducts.

Upon close acquaintance with a narcissistic personality, one realizes that the alienated, wounded child is never far away. That child is very much compelled by its preoccupation with its own egregious sense of loss and injustice for which it can receive no meaningful consolation from the surrounding world. One realizes that this injury is experienced as essentially irreparable, refractory to any effort that others might make to ameliorate suffering. Amelioration and healing could grow out of meaningful connection with others, but the narcissist's profound mistrust, their conviction that love is a toxic, dangerous emotion, their fear of being obligated by others' giving, and their sense that attachment renders them vulnerable to others' rapacity together deny them the possibility of addressing their own agony. With the passage of time, and in the company of the hyperbolized, often maudlin reiteration of personal pain a narcissistic personality can endlessly restate, the narcissist's genuinely soul-destroying early pain comes to elicit impatience, intolerance, and incredulity, especially in the absence of any appreciation of the hurt the narcissist regularly causes others. As previously noted, the other eventually comes to experience a mixture of outrage and disdain co-mingling with a disturbing but often poorly articulated appreciation of the narcissist's fragility.

The guise of wounded child that the narcissist presents is, at one and the same time, both authentic, reflecting very formidable, punishing internal realities, and a contrived posture intended to serve a protective function. In the case of the former, certainly the rage, indignation, and sense of injustice that one encounters when the damaged child is introduced are all very real, but rather than being reflective of early desolation and helplessness, they are extensions of narcissistic rapacity and entitlement. The narcissist is deeply incensed that others have opposed him, but he is not in those moments re-experiencing what I have earlier referred to as regression to an earlier ego state – an experience in which he is truly flooded and overwhelmed by early pain. Instead, what one is seeing are the defenses the narcissist employs to protect himself against the regression experience: faux vulnerability, outrage, and entitlement. Evocation of the wounded child is meant to disconcert others and create advantage for the narcissist. Ironically, were he able to truly re-experience his early pain, rather than disguising it with effrontery, he might genuinely appeal to the others' humanity, an act of real power and authority that the narcissist would experience as repulsive weakness.

Expecting unfaltering loyalty from the other and a willingness on the part of the other to allow themselves, without evidence of hesitation, to let the narcissist fill them and define them, the narcissist offers little reciprocity. Any attempt to use one's voice or to act on personal need, particularly if those needs are declaratively expressed or thwart the ends the narcissist means to pursue, is very likely to produce immediate censure and counterattack. In response to his own retaliatory rage, the narcissist may expel the other from his life, treating them as utterly disposable. Such an act further confirms for the narcissist that no one in his world is possessed of enduring importance, that no attachment can compel him. He has affirmed for himself again that he remains untouchable, standing outside any hold that bonds of relatedness might create for the other. The narcissist may claim friendship, but such friendship is not bound by the usual terms that typify sustained attachment between people: patience, compassion, awareness of the other's reality, willingness to amend the self to help the other, and readiness to make appropriate sacrifice to ensure the other's well-being. On the contrary, calling the other "friend" is meant to serve transactional needs or, more insidiously, to generate an illusion of humanity that seemingly affirms participation in the human community not possible for the narcissist. Put differently, friendship is not intrinsically rewarding, generating deep emotional satisfaction and meaning that grows out of two personalities who can open themselves to one another. It is, rather, an empty vessel filled with narcissistic interest.

Bullying is a core part of narcissistic presentation, as is by now manifestly apparent. It also affirms dominance and entitlement to exploit. It naturally extends itself from the narcissist's cornerstone defense, contempt. And it is readily supported by the rage and envy that drives the narcissist's rapacity. Objectification of the other and significantly diminished ability to tolerate empathy render endemic bullying an inevitability. Most of the narcissist's interactions with others appear to be predicated upon bullying. Respect, inasmuch as it exists, derives from the other's ability to meet narcissistic needs; in the absence of such utility, respect proves to be very transitory, re-emerging or dispersing itself quickly as utility is perceived to vacillate.

Ubiquitous bullying is intended to confirm a sense of limitless power. The world can then be experienced as a place the narcissist can exploit without meaningful constraint. The narcissist is merciless in assault and unselfcon-scious in his efforts to break the other. Punches are rarely pulled.

Vindictiveness grows out of the narcissist's sense that literally every affront to domination, however petty, must be addressed. In order for him to feel safe, the narcissist must be able to demonstrate to himself as well as to others in his world that any individual who has stood in the way of narcissistic prerogative, even on a petty level, must eventually face punishment and must eventually be neutered. Vindictiveness is also relentless, is ruthlessly pursued, and can be remarkably heavy-handed, arising from what otherwise would be judged to be a small slight or injury. Subjectively, of course, such vindictiveness reflects the narcissist's sense that any confrontation, however small, challenges the absolute dominion they require in order to protect the aggrandized self.

Shaming bears a special mention as part of the narcissist's efforts to bully. Shaming, more than other forms of retaliation, serves to still the other's voice, compelling the other to hide the now depreciated self from public view. The "shamed" self is meant to be too horrified by the ugly attributions imposed upon it by its attacker to risk further public exposure. Shaming, too, is unyielding and merciless. It means to obliterate and wreck.

Sadism is both a facet of bullying and an end in itself that renders the wounding and humiliation of others intrinsically satisfying. It confirms for the narcissist, variously, that his depredations are irresistible, that others' loyalty remains uncontested, that his own strength is inviolate, and that, once again, he is an aggressor, not a victim. It also eventually serves the narcissist's needs to poison all his relationships. More profoundly, however, it helps support a sense of aliveness that the narcissist's ravaged internal landscape and con-trived humanity denies him. Unable to feel fully alive, the narcissist takes pleasure in his power to hurt other people and deconstruct them. Being able to destroy or wound that which he can't have himself is exhilarating. Like bullying, sadism is an endemic part of narcissistic experience.

Tragically, to be narcissistic is to be at war. Life is combat. Everyone is potentially an adversary. Alliances are transitory. To be continuously at war and to be fundamentally alone, as the narcissist must essentially be, imposes a state of perpetual arousal. The self supports vigilance by constantly reminding itself that the world is a malignant, exploitative, self-interested place, a pro-jected world dominated by the narcissist's greed and rapacity; the consequent high levels of arousal that permeate narcissistic existence ensure rage is always close to the surface, available to redirect itself towards the acts of hostility and contempt that serve core protective functions. Much like the famous Marvel comic book character, the narcissist is "angry all the time." Projecting his or her own malevolence onto the surrounding world helps confirm the malevolence the narcissist imagines that others would all too willingly direct towards him, save for the hair trigger show of force that his vigilance supports. In a context of florid fear and threat, conspiracy theories find fertile ground; mistrust and fear proliferate. The stage is set for objectification, diminishment of the other's humanity, and denial of empathy, all of which enable entitlement and remorseless obliteration of one's opponent.

Constantly and habitually accusing others of transgressions you've just inflicted on them is extraordinarily provocative. While this strategy may effectively disconcert and flummox one's intended adversary, momentarily robbing him or her of voice, it inevitably instigates a counter-response marked by outrage and a profound sense of indignation. In his quest to deconstruct and disqualify the other by attributing his own dark motivations to them, the narcissist may win a local battle, but he broadens and intensifies others' desire to harm him. Their increasingly transparent antipathy towards him, which in many ways he has manufactured, provides justification to perpetuate and expand the warfare that, paradoxically, he requires in order to feel safe.

War requires preparedness to act in an unrestrained fashion. Hesitation, ambiguity, and concern for the harm which the other endures all constrain action. Action mitigates subjective vulnerability. It also potentially confers significant advantage against an opponent hampered by decency. Overwhelming force can be brought to bear against an opponent whose deliberations about morality and ethics compromise their own readiness to respond. Willingness to engage the other with "shock and awe" tactics precipitously compromises the other's ability to think effectively, flooding them with disruptive affect, including intense fear, much like a dunning phone call. For an individual, like a narcissist, who is on a continuous war footing, the capacity to engage in precipitous action is an imperative that is very difficult to resist and very difficult to mitigate. Precipitous action taking, furthermore, is often impelled by deep conviction, readily supported, as it is, by profound rage that is always close to the surface and by the grandiosity and omnipotence which represent core defining features of narcissism.

The imperative to act without hesitation produces a chaotic, unpredictable, impulse ridden style informed by preoccupation with loyalty, rapacity, and dominance. The predominance of impulse over thought would appear to negate the importance of contrivance in the narcissist's life, but it doesn't; the two coexist simultaneously. The reckless, erratic course which narcissistic thought and action-taking follows further contributes to the sense of threat those around the narcissist experience. The narcissist would have it no other way. His unpredictability protects his prerogatives of voice, of decision-making, and of action.

War readiness and preparedness to act, however, either deny or degrade the narcissist's own cognitive assets. Psychological literature tells us that fear dramatically distorts cognition and perception. Thought form perpetually dominated by fear and threat preoccupies itself with that which is perceived to threaten. Watch the tiger. Don't look anywhere else. Keep your eyes on it. Ability to scan one's environment and see the forest, not just the scary phantom approaching you, is forfeit. Perception and scope of attention becomes narrowed and sharply, rigidly focused. In a similar way, intellect is also compromised. Freewheeling exploration of possibilities becomes very difficult indeed when one is afraid and vigilant much of the time. There is only room for simplicity of thought. Making room for appreciation of complex realities instinctively feels jeopardizing. Solutions must be simple and declarative. Annihilate the other or run away. Consideration of nuance becomes intolerable; so, too, does cognitive flexibility and creativity. Thought compelled by fear and perpetual combat readiness is defined by the need to simplify choices. Decisions become binary. Language faces degradation, too, co-opted by primitive thought forms that demand facile identification of friend or foe. Choice is often informed by concrete markers like race, group membership, political alliance, or, perhaps more typically, by stereotypes that align themselves with bigotry and objectification of the other. The language of fear and combat is brutal, guttural, abusive, and abbreviated. Sentences are short and are often spoken at volume. Their power is visceral rather than intellectual. Forethought, planning, and restraint are readily sacrificed to the demands of an eternal present compelled by the urgency of perpetual crisis. Future, too, is largely abandoned; what matters is the clear and present danger the now constitutes.

An internal environment pervaded by anxiety (anxiety is another word for fear), rage, and vigilance eventually neuters other emotional responses in the narcissist. The self retracts. The world around it may feel surreal and oddly unfamiliar; the world inside becomes increasingly diminished, evermore defined by numbness and disengagement. Capacity for emotional richness and for variegated emotional response married to complex, imaginative thought constructions recedes. The self feels unreal and detached, both from the people around it and from itself. Increasingly, it comes to rely on fear, rage, and self-aggrandizement – the very sources of its pain – to simulate aliveness and connection. Capacity for emotional restraint is compromised; primal emotions like fear and rage dominate intellect, further impelling action and an impulse ridden, chaotic decision-making style.

The foregoing description of narcissistic perception, thought form, and emotional dysregulation is not to suggest that narcissistic intellect and capacity for impulse control is continuously compromised, but rather that, given the inherent liabilities that the narcissist carries within himself, it can all too easily be derailed by the narcissist's other pressing preoccupations. My father was certainly capable of disciplined, sustained work effort; the innovations he generated in a retail context were applauded for their sophistication. This "intelligence," however, was guided by a cunning mind on the lookout for advantages to exploit – a beneficial perspective to be able to adopt in a retail marketplace. As I saw on numbers of occasions when I observed him in his work environment and in the family, it was readily subject to degradation by the cacophony of emotions, profound mistrust, and endemic fear that characterized him.

I have noted that self-aggrandizement and grandiosity support a habit of attributing ability, skill, and potentiality to the self that it does not possess. The almost casual ascription of power and competence to the self that far eludes its grasp means that a narcissistic individual can all too easily overlook his own limitations, claiming potencies that would strike an observer as delusional. Accustomed to believing that he's the most creative guy in the room and the only guy, in the end, equipped to solve problems, it becomes all too easy to unselfconsciously proffer solutions that would strike others as outlandish, conspiratorial, or crazy. Failure on the part of others to accept these "gifts" produces outrage, hurt, and a measure of perplexity, further contributing to the sense one is dealing with a delusional individual who believes everything he has said. Instead, what one is encountering are the facile assumptions that extend themselves from his grandiosity. The phrase "magical thinking" probably better approximates what is unfolding: my thoughts are special and precious, like me, so they must be possessed of greater utility and value than the intellectual endeavor of other people. The magical piece is his assumption that because he feels special his thoughts must be, too, and therefore do not require careful validation. His self-aggrandizement requires constant confirmation and constant expansion; in my father's case, it was the one companion that always stood by his side and kept him safe in the face of life's terrible depredations, even though it imposed terrible costs.

Combat language tends to elicit degradation of thought in the other as well as in the self. In order to protect personal boundaries and integrity of self or, more basically, in order to protect the self from the potentiality of physical harm, the other must use similar thought forms to mobilize their own energy, to incite preparedness for action, and to mount a credible and very visceral threat display to offset their attacker. Attempts to be thoughtful, to employ reason, and to problem solve collaboratively very quickly often fail, creating painful and potentially disastrous exposure to devastating violation. Once a target fully appreciates the nature of the threat being posed and marshals the means to mount an effective counterattack, almost invariably they find themselves compelled to use the same tools that their attacker employs. Emotional restraint deteriorates and so, too, does quality of thought. All is action, fear, and survival. And if a target is sufficiently self-possessed to be able to hang onto their humanity in the face of abusive behavior, the likelihood of doing so decreases with the passage of time.

Dissociation, or emotional numbing, and acquired insensitivity to that which would have previously horrified, acts incrementally, but probably rapidly, to render retention of humanity that much more improbable in those targeted by the narcissist's assaults. Dissociation enables one to better tolerate abuse, chaos, and threat, but it denies one access to compelling emotional responses that would otherwise inform a more humane decision-making process. Terror is diminished, but so, too, is emotional intelligence. Dissociation becomes a habit of being in a threat infested world, having its way years, decades, or even a life-time after the introduction of trauma. It blinds the sufferer to their own pain and the pain that they may inadvertently cause others, preparing the way for bru-tishness to perpetuate itself. As the narcissist traumatizes and desensitizes those around him, escalating dissociation and desensitization increasingly erode humane sensibility.

All of the above is not to suggest that retention of humanity is utterly impossible when we find ourselves in literal verbal or physical combat, but rather that it becomes increasingly implausible. Warfare, whether social, political, or actual, degrades our humanity. Occasionally leaders have under-stood the importance of protecting humanity in the way that they respond to brutality, as witnessed in the extraordinarily brave efforts of civil rights lea-ders in the 60s and Gandhi's determination to sidestep violence during the Indian independence movement. More often than not, however, degraded thought, compulsion to act, and readiness to engage in brutishness has expanded itself, infecting most parties in a conflict, if not wholly, then at least to a disturbingly significant degree.

Propensity to rely on simple, binary thought structures in concert with compulsion to retaliate against real or imagined enemies frequently produces a frenetic, impulse ridden, chaotic cognitive style punctuated by affective storms in the narcissist that compromises collaborative enterprises. Whatever potential for collaborative effort might exist when a narcissist is functioning at his or her best soon collapses once significant threat manifests itself, the caveat being that subjectively significant levels of threat are virtually endemic. In an atmosphere of threat, ideas are not judged by their own merit, but rather by the degree of loyalty they embody. Quality of thought is a second-ary consideration. Attunement with narcissistic affect and perspectives is pri-mary, defining a speaker as adversary or ally. From the viewpoint of an outside observer, narcissistic intellect often appears to be irrational or arbi-trary, but, in fact, it is nearly always governed by its preoccupation with loy-alty and by alignment with perceived self-interest. Intellectual endeavors pervert and degrade themselves to meet these ends.

Others possessed of articulate, thoughtful voices are experienced as deeply offensive and are venomously pursued as mortal enemies. Being intellectual is vilified. Science, as a potential competing voice, is discredited. Questions are not to be asked in any meaningful or persistent way, nor are others' thoughts to divert from the narcissist's acts of will. Intellectualism is viewed as dan-gerous and as both weak and "unclean," at odds with the subversion of self, which the narcissist demands. Adherents are given to understand that accep-tance of narcissistic rapacity not only enhances the group's greatness and strength, but that failure to do so jeopardizes the group. Outliers, including intellectuals, are ruthlessly deconstructed and – where sufficient power has been consolidated – annihilated. The threat of social or virtual physical excoriation renders disagreement a very jeopardizing undertaking, to say the least. Dissent can lead to punitive marginalization or to death.

When narcissistic intellectual assets are directed towards acquisitive ends (wealth, power, status), they may be harnessed effectively to generate new ideas or new technical forms that significantly advance the narcissist's interests and, almost serendipitously, may advance society's interest as well. Just as probably, however, narcissistic creativity may impose terrible social costs because narcissistic intellect is not informed by concerns about social justice or others' well-being; on the contrary, it maintains a terrible and deliberate indifference to any consideration compelled by humanity or the constraints of decency. Awareness of decency and humanity can be entertained only fleetingly or sporadically, but certainly not as an enduring and foundational part of an enterprise that the narcissist embarks upon. Intelligence that is not directed, shaped, and, importantly, mitigated by compassion and empathy seems particularly likely to produce destructive progeny.

Intelligence constrained by narcissism renders the narcissist not only blind to but repelled by others' ability to initiate and innovate. Considerable intellectual and emotional resources have to be devoted towards negation of the other. In the process, richness that the other possesses that might otherwise be harnessed to enhance narcissistic creativity is either diminished or obliterated, denying a narcissistic personality the opportunity to enhance and expand their own ideas through the contributions that others can make to them. Contributions from others are only acceptable inasmuch as they can be rebranded or reformulated as extensions of the narcissist's creativity (e.g., stolen) or, alternatively, if they can be squeezed and exploited out of others who participate in a world over which the narcissist can exercise punishing control. In such a world, punishing narcissistic authority might stimulate innovation and productivity in the interim, but it must inevitably have the effect of eventually diminishing any creative or intellectual product the other is able to construct, wearing down and eroding the selfhood of the other until output becomes increasingly sterile. When a countervailing voice intercedes to mitigate narcissistic constraint, human ingenuity seems to be able to restore itself surprisingly quickly. Some historians would argue that Hitler's willingness to empower Albert Speer during the last years of the war to grant German industrial leadership greater latitude in finding their own innovative ways to increase production helped account for the dramatic increase in Germany's industrial output during that timeframe.

The narcissist's reliance on contempt as a core defense also compromises judgement; risk-taking accordingly becomes more extravagant, informed by arrogance and by reliance on danger to simulate engagement. Successes inflame aggrandizement. The self becomes untouchable, directing scathing disdain towards others who stand in its way. With the inevitable escalation of risk-taking that ensues, inevitable failures accrue. When they begin to jeopardize the aggrandized self, cracks in narcissistic adjustment develop; renewed triumph confirms and exacerbates grandiosity while persisting failures associate themselves with invocation of the narcissist's damaged child persona, escalating outbursts of rage, hysterical derision of enemies, and increasingly compromised judgement. As the narcissist faces mounting questions about the competence of the grandiose self, his ability to sustain absolute dominion over the people in his world feels increasingly precarious, instigating reinvigorated efforts to dominate and invade. As this destructive cycle extends itself, so, too, do acts of oppression and brutality that fall within the narcissist's grasp.

In the context of the cognitive and affective limitations that have just been described, narcissistic intellect can be seen to be extraordinarily dangerous in an individual occupying a position of significant leadership, particularly of a national entity, not only because they can be expected to visit acts of rapacity and aggression upon a neighbor or upon internal enemies, but also because a cognitive style uninformed by wisdom is likely to fracture human and non-human environments with little regard for consequence. Without empathy, compassion, generosity, generativity, and a moral sense informed by respect for others, how could any of us harness intelligence, however formidable it might be, without causing great harm, particularly if we occupy a position of imposing authority?

Now imagine that such an intelligence is informed by a personality characterized by rapacity, need to dominate, prevarication, grandiosity, ruthless self-interest, cruelty, and the capacity to devastate a perceived enemy without hesitation – all unfolding in a psyche that lacks meaningful awareness of why it acts as it does. No substantive internal checks and balances and little responsiveness to the limits others may attempt to impose. Perhaps a formula for success in a tribal society and a tribal world, where strong homogeneities define culture and perception of truth and where interests of state and leader merge so that one is indistinguishable from the other, permitting the state to act with ruthless alacrity and aggression to further its interests in expansion and conquest. Indeed, one could argue, as I have earlier in this book, that in a tribal world narcissistic leadership ensures that the most dominant forms of technology and governmental organization prevail over weaker neighbors, thereby advancing and protecting a given civilization's interests.

But what of the world that we actually live in – one defined by complex, global interdependencies and by technological, economic, social, and health care concerns that have potential planetwide impact? In the newly emerging modern world, the complexity of the issues that we face, I would suggest, can no longer be addressed by the territorial imperatives of tribalism; they require collaboration, mutuality of respect, the ability to look beyond our own personal and national horizons to understand one another's position, an enhanced measure of compassion for all humankind, and a willingness, increasingly, to rationalize resources so that they can better serve the entire human family. In fits and starts we appear to be moving in these directions, but the journey is understandably a very frightening one as we call upon one another to leave behind some of the core strategies (like tribalism) that have reassured us the world could be apprehended in familiar, comforting terms and that have allowed us to feel we could successfully protect those we love and the culture we have relied upon to define us. Old truths that we considered absolute and that beguiled us with their simplicity are being replaced with new, more intricate, and certainly more bewildering realities we are being asked contend with. Some of us can embrace this journey, finding it exciting and full of promise, in spite of its attendant ambiguities. Some of us respond with deep alarm and panic, afraid that without the clarity that the old forms provided us, we will never survive.

Of course, the transition I am referencing is an immensely difficult one that is having a tremendously divisive impact in many if not most parts of the world. Consider that many nations and many peoples are still engaged in various forms of tribal combat with one another. Consider also that a significant proportion of world leadership is defined by fascism or by exploitative oligarchies. Forces like poverty, disease, and war have produced mass migrations of people – "others" – that various host cultures are being called upon to accommodate in numbers (but probably not proportions) that sound untenable. With diverse groups of migrants come diverse cultural practices. How, so many of us wonder, can we still retain our identities in the face of so much change? Will these newcomers push us aside, change our institutions, adulterate our religions, transform our values, take our jobs, overload our welfare systems, and generate economic and political instability? How could there not be fear, particularly amongst those people who already feel marginalized in their home culture?

Surely, many people think, some of our worst fears must be justified (and some of them undoubtedly are). But who can tell them? Who can they believe? A leader who provides simple, declarative answers infused with unbreachable confidence? Or a leader who acknowledges complexity and nuance, promising to work flexibly and thoughtfully in response to a shifting, ambiguous landscape? If you're really afraid, which style of leadership would you prefer? If the leader who proffers simple answers also promises salvation, directing contempt at competing voices who may bring less conviction and certitude to the challenges that are to be faced, doesn't he become irresistible to some of the people who are really scared? Fear dictates choice rather than discernment and judgement. In response, political competitors may become equally emphatic, or nearly so, offering assurances of leadership and outcomes impossible for anyone to realistically promise. In such a context, there is a risk that everybody's voice can become more strident and possessed of greater ideological fervor. Trust in government and leadership, as a result, diminishes. How, people wonder, can any of you do all that you say you will? Look at your track records. None of you contenders can really make this work, so who can I count on?

The answer, for many people, is, I'll go with the leader who speaks to my alienation. He's the one I can trust, especially when I'm really afraid. In such a fashion, narcissistic leadership all too readily and all too easily insinuates itself into our lives. The alienation and mistrust of the governed finds common cause in the narcissist's own acute sense of alienation and injustice, not realizing that what appears to be an empathic exchange is ultimately only defined by narcissistic self-interest.

The reality, I would maintain, is that we don't have good answers yet for many of the formidably complex human challenges we've been trying to address. We simply don't. It's going to take us time. Probably a lot of it. Maybe time, with respect to challenges like climate change, that we no longer have. Can we get there, however, by pretending that we know a great deal more than we do? Or do we best get there by acknowledging through civil, thoughtful discourse that we are going to make mistakes, that none of us has all of the answers, that – in essence – we're living in an immensely complicated world that's profoundly difficult to make sense of? If we expect a leader to provide us with all of the answers that we need or want, we're going to be in trouble. In the process, we're going to allow ourselves to be misled or, worse, badly led. I would say we must beware of the messianic voice. And, most especially, guard ourselves against our hunger for it. Knowledge seems to accumulate from many voices and many perspectives, building itself incrementally as it is tested and retested against our grasp of reality. Nobody does this all by themselves. Climate change is a nice example. Hard work, verified and checked over and over again, by countless researchers. That's knowledge.

I want to caution the reader that all of the people that I worked with closely whom I deemed to be narcissistic were very successful in their professions. In this sense, they could be superficially described as high-functioning narcissistic personalities. I emphatically do not wish to suggest that narcissism and success are somehow intertwined with one another. Many of the qualities that typify narcissism could be expected to ensure a disrupted, unsuccessful professional life in individuals not blessed with the resilience, the personal resourcefulness, and the intelligence that led to the professional triumphs I saw in my long-term patients and in my father.

Chapter 12

Legacies of Narcissism – Impact on the Psyche

In this chapter I hope to outline ways in which narcissism appears to perpetuate itself, both in its own form and in forms that can be seen to typify other variants of psychopathy. I will draw heavily, but not exclusively, upon my own experience growing up with a narcissistic father, outlining the pathway I found myself drawn into that I was afraid might have eventuated in my becoming psychopathic. As an aside, I should say that I was always aware that the face my psychopathy wore would be different than my father's. In addition to my own personal experience, I will also be referencing broad, but consistent patterns of compromise that I felt I was able to identify in patients who had been subjected to a narcissistic surround during their growing up years. I believe it would be fair to say that I have modestly extensive experience working with such people.

I understand that some of the material I am about to present may be hard to read – a litany of damage and suffering that the narcissist visits on the people close to him. I ask the reader to bear with me. In considering how narcissism and psychopathy may replicate themselves in a personal and a family context, I will be articulating dynamics that I believe play themselves out in much larger entities, like nations, that accommodate narcissistic leadership. The next chapter, Chapter 13, will devote itself to the relationship between narcissistic leaders and the states that they govern.

So that the reader might more closely appreciate the disruptive impact of the forces I am about to describe, I will begin the chapter by talking about that which I think benefits us in our early experience, contributing to our prospects of being able to fully consummate ourselves as human beings. I will expand some of the constructs that I described earlier in the book, extending them in a fashion that I hope will render our current discussion more meaningful.

I very much recognize that people manage to grow and to transcend themselves in spite of the adversities that they face, sometimes exceeding, by a wide margin, the potentialities they might have been expected to realize otherwise. I do not wish to imply that having less than an ideal childhood utterly and terminally disadvantages people. I very much subscribe to the

DOI: 10.4324/9781003246923-12

notion that adversity and mistakes on the part of both parent and child are necessary for us to learn and to expand ourselves. I also believe that if parenting manages to be good enough, generally meeting children's core needs in a more or less consistent fashion, most children will have the opportunity to enhance themselves, save for children who may carry specific vulnerabilities into the parent–child relationship. The good enough formulation leaves room for growth through adversity as well as for individual differences that render parenting in one parent–child dyad successful and in another compromising.

Attachment plays a foundational role in the formation of identity. Healthy attachment offers confirmation that the self is valuable and is possessed of poignancy – the developing self can feel, on a visceral level, that it has the capacity to generate joy, celebration, and meaning in the lives of those people with whom it establishes intimate relationships. The other confirms – through their own unmistakable responses to the gifts that the self offers – that the self matters and is a source of richness to the people most important to it. In this way, others mirror what the developing self learns to deeply appreciate about itself. These elements form the touchstones of emergent identity: such beginnings empower the self to take risks in the world and to expand the self through new forms of thinking, emoting, communicating, and behaving that allow the self to discover altered forms of being that enhance identity. Creativity and risk-taking, so necessary to such an endeavor, are possible because the self feels relatively safe in a world that has affirmed its basic value. Mirroring positive attributes, of course, need not unfold with flawless consistency; it is enough that one's emotional ambience is in the main caring and affirming, reassuring the self mistakes are possible and that recovery from them is manageable without creating catastrophic outcomes. The ability to tolerate risks helps beget identity. As risk-taking generates rewards for the self, greater risks can be taken and pursued with more tenacity. In this fashion, a sense of resilience begins to accrue that imbues identity and the self with an awareness of its own resourcefulness.

Healthy attachment (what is alternatively referred to as secure attachment) exists in an environment in which the other is reasonably closely attuned to an intimate's internal realities. The other demonstrates the capacity to more or less accurately read an intimate's feelings and need states, confirming that the other can be counted upon to provide protection when it is required in a fashion that relatively closely conforms to the unique characteristics of the person they're attempting to look after. The more accurately uniqueness is appreciated, the safer the self feels and the more likely it is to risk experimentation. Awareness of uniqueness also conveys a willingness to tolerate the self's hunger to expand and differentiate itself. Demonstrating respect for uniqueness helps create an increasingly rich internal environment evermore capable of generating resources like imagination, creativity, intuition, eccentricity, and courage. In this environment there is room for the self to feel safe enough to challenge its protectors and mentors, testing values, perceptions, and ideas it recognizes may antagonize the other. Doing so means the self must balance its needs for succorance and approval against its desire for expansion and growth. Inevitable riffs that arise between the parties may challenge the self to define new ways to think, feel, and communicate that alleviate conflict so that an important relationship can continue to be supported. In circumstances where differences feel too imposing to accommodate, the self that has been supported by healthy attachment can more readily affirm perceptions and values that constitute its identity through spirited, respectful debate or by seeking out other intimates or mentors who offer better opportunities for personal enhancement. Investing in a new attachment that better serves the self may not mean leaving an old attachment behind; on the contrary, old attachments may remain immensely important to the self and may continue to contribute to its growth and differentiation in spite of differences.

Making its immense contribution to internal richness and to formation of a well-articulated, variegated sense of identity, healthy attachment helps insulate the self against otherwise unbearable, disorganizing pain which permeates ruptured relationships occasioned by death or by conflict. The self is far better able to tolerate loss and separation, buoyed by an implicit understanding it likely possesses the means to survive and to begin life anew. This is not to say that separation does not cause profound pain, but rather that such pain is not imbued with a sense that the self is too depleted and too impoverished to be able to survive without the other. Because of its richness, the self is afforded choice that a more damaged or more incomplete self feels incapable of making or only makes in the presence of suffocating terror.

Consider, now, the nature of attachment that unfolds in a relationship with the narcissistic other. Uniqueness is shuttered. The self is called upon to orchestrate itself, simulating a presence it vainly attempts to contrive to appease the other whose moods and perspectives seem to fluctuate arbitrarily. And the self is given to understand it must negate itself and render itself invisible so it can be receptive to the narcissistic voice, which expects to still the voices of those around it. Internal richness is forfeit; so, too, are opportunities to expand the self and enhance identity. Safety and resilience are, in the main, compromised; instead, the self is largely defined by its desperate and often covert attempts to survive its own desolation. The self is denied value and is denied the opportunity to feel and give love, which the narcissist would find unbearable. Instead, as the self is subjected to repeated assaults and acts of cruelty, its capacity to experience a broad range of emotions becomes blunted; in their place, shame, vindictive rage, and envy flourish. Shame arises from a sense that the self is defenseless and ineffectual, unable to protect itself in the face of incessant violation. It asserts itself because the self feels unworthy of the other's love (your failure to love me confirms my defectiveness). And it is experienced because the self increasingly recognizes that it is skeletal and emaciated. The self's inadequacies and distortions feel agonizingly transparent; transparency further exacerbates the exquisitely painful levels of vulnerability the self must live with. Perpetual, unrelenting vigilance ensues. In spite of its best efforts to hide vulnerability, its struggle is all too readily apparent to the surrounding world, marking it for predation (bullying).

With the passage of time and the accumulation of disturbing, monstrous, vindictive feelings, shame becomes particularly acute and particularly private. No one must see the horrific realities inside. An individual so affected looks greedily at those around him or her who seem to be more complete or more gracious. Depth of attachment becomes ever more untenable; dissociation, contrivance, and an indelible sense of one's own unattractiveness render the possibility of ever becoming an accepted or even esteemed member of the human community seem increasingly remote. Depression flourishes, imposing its own attendant consequences that further subvert personal value, that exacerbate depletion and emaciation, and that erode whatever shards of hope remain that one can construct a life of one's own. Thinking about suicide offers avenues of escape in an otherwise impossibly bleak landscape; so, also, does avoidant behavior (including addictions) that is relied upon to provide momentary relief from unbearable suffering, but which only intensifies personal inadequacy arising from compromised productivity. And, finally, set upon by a surrounding world and an internal one that both assume an increasingly malignant aspect, the self endlessly tries to prepare itself for expected new incursions through perpetual rehearsals of responses to worst-case scenarios that, tragically, it is rarely able to consummate. This form of anxiety disorder – what is now conceptually being referred to as complex Post-Traumatic Stress Disorder (PTSD) – becomes an early friend and oft times life-long companion for those who endure narcissistic invasion in their childhoods.

In the face of all of its burdens, the self becomes preoccupied with annihilation – both literal and psychological.

I have watched the pattern of dynamics described in the preceding paragraphs that typified my adjustment to a narcissistic surround unfold countless times, in its various forms, in great numbers of patients that I have worked with who had suffered exposure to a narcissistic parent or parent surrogate. For some patients, it unfolded with a terrible inevitability, producing devastated, chaotic lives marked by addictions, by daunting levels of psychological pain (including depression and complex PTSD), and by the inability to reliably sustain independence and fulfil the potentialities that the self-possessed. Some few people were able to transcend the damage that they had endured to a very meaningful degree, establishing successful lives they found fulfilling, but even they would say that they were still haunted by many of their early ghosts in ways that they understood they would probably never escape. The great majority of people that I worked with managed to forge compromises with their suffering, moving ahead in some areas of their lives, but having to accept painful limitations that continued to constrain and hurt them in numbers of significant ways.

Starvation and depletion proved themselves to be the legacy of growing up in a narcissistic surround. Many patients experienced themselves as skeletal and emaciated; others would say that they had felt unattractive and unlovable much of their lives, extending the blight and starvation that characterized their childhoods up through their adult years. Struggle for voice was a defining part of their reality. One subgroup of patients appeared to have concluded that they were too stupid or too uninformed or too insubstantial for anyone around them to be interested in what they had to say. They experienced themselves as indelibly defective. Those that were acutely aware of how hard and how dangerous it had been to use their voice could also tell me that any assertion of personhood – even in limited ways – met with fierce, if not brutal, resistance. This group of people were more likely to be able to recognize that it was the narcissistic parent who was damaged rather than feeling that their inherent flaws accounted for their parent's discordant, rejecting response to them. Both groups, however, would say that the narcissistic voice got inside, robbing them, in spite of any resistance they might mount, of their sense of worth. Both groups struggled to regain it with varying degrees of success. Recognizing that the narcissistic parent had problems rather than utterly disqualifying the self-made recovery of self-esteem somewhat easier, but only somewhat. One can guess that those individuals who disqualified the self did so as an unconscious means of appeasing the narcissistic other, trying, in the process, to protect what few shards of selfhood remained to them.

Whether a given patient blamed themselves or their parent for their parent's behavior, everyone came to feel that the world was a malignant and unwelcoming place. They learned that it was dangerous to be a person. They expected to be attacked and diminished. Many of them were all too acutely aware that they mistrusted others and many of them felt that others had the power to utterly devastate them with a disapproving or, worse, cruel voice. Some could acknowledge that they feared their own annihilation; others acted as if they did, retreating from the rest of the world in an effort to make themselves feel safer. In the longer run, retreat never worked. It always exacerbated anxiety and depression. Without recourse to human warmth and support, people were left to their own thoughts, which increasingly assaulted them with reminders of their fears, their deficiency, and their hopelessness.

The cruelty of the narcissistic other that infused and defined these patients' worlds eventually seemed to get inside everybody, poisoning their interiors, filling them with vengeful, sadistic fantasies. Many patients backed away from what they saw in themselves with horror, quite terrified to talk to anybody about what was happening inside them. Some few had managed to entirely turn away from these parts of themselves, possibly by employing a psychological defense called repression (as previously referenced, the ability to wall off unpleasant memories and feeling states from consciousness). While one could infer, given all the cruelty they had been subjected to, that emergent sadistic feelings and fantasies must have represented an important part of their experience with themselves, they had been able to disguise and hide these pieces of themselves from their own and others' view. It was only with great care and after considerable trust had been established in the psychotherapy process that one attempted to explore such issues with them, ever mindful that they might need to shut down exploration of this facet of themselves. Considering that they carried darkness inside them that mirrored the ugliness they saw in their assailant was, understandably, a very threatening idea for people to entertain. Making these connections or at least understanding their plausibility helped people better appreciate why they felt so unsafe in the world, if only because they could feel somewhat safer with their own impulses. For some, less energy had to be devoted towards walling off parts of the self; as a consequence, they could afford to be less judgmental and brittle with the people in their environment because they were more accepting of themselves. For others, the walls could never come down.

Some of my patients who had grown up in a narcissistic surround were able to tell me that they felt like monsters – or, at least, potential monsters – waiting for the right triggers and the right circumstances to set off what they feared was inevitable. They were all too aware that people who reminded them, whether obliquely or directly, of the narcissistic personality who had assaulted them in their early lives might set them off, unleashing murderous retaliation. They lived in fear that the surrounding world would attempt to re-violate them and they were equally afraid that if they fought back, they would become the monster inside they had always tried so hard to hold back. They also imagined that the counter response of an enraged world would expose them to more brutality, further compromising the humanity they had assiduously tried to safeguard. Fear of the monster inside – a reposit of all the darkness of their childhoods – dogged most of this group of patients, sometimes throughout their lives. Their fear of their own monstrosity and of compromised humanity made them feel unsafe when they attempted to sustain intimacy with the people that they loved.

Absorbing narcissistic assault and predation seemed to mean, for a substantial portion of the people that I saw, that the world inside eventually replicated the searing, lacerating contempt-filled narcissistic voice they had lived with. Fantasies about success or actual successes produced devastating counterattacks inside. Attempts to use one's voice or to render oneself more visible in the human community elicited a similar internal response. It felt dangerous to be seen and to be heard. Simple and inconsequential acts of assertion, or even the thought of them, could produce tortured rumination. Human interaction became, for many of these people, unbearably threatening, but isolation meant having to contend with murder squad in one's head stuff. It was very, very hard for people to find peace and safety. Vigilance was nearly an omnipresent part of their lives, sometimes fading into the background, but all too readily and easily evoked.

Fear of abandonment assumed immense proportions for many of these patients. Some imagined that their neediness would drive their partners or their family away. Others worried that the rage they were struggling to contain would eventually burst free of its bonds and terminally wreck relationships – and at times it did elude people's self-control, re-inflaming their fears of inflicting devastating harm on people they loved. Other patients anticipated that intimates would eventually understand either how valueless they were or how damaged they were, fatally compromising their important relationships. Or people simply didn't feel safe enough in relationships, yearning for intimacy but too scared of predation or of the immensity of their own need to tolerate it.

In the context of so much fear of intimacy, many of my patients presented a history of destructive relationship choices. The list of possible destructive partner choice was long and varied. Partners who were narcissistic themselves who "partnered" a patient's efforts to diminish themselves. Partners whose own towering neediness promised protection against abandonment, but whose reciprocal fears of intimacy eventually sabotaged a relationship. Partners who could share addictions. Partners who became attractive because their psychological problems seemed bigger than my patient's, offering reassurance that my patient wouldn't be turned away because his/her own problems seemed so imposing ("if you're too healthy, you'll abandon someone as damaged as me"). Partners who were too remote and too inaccessible to offer hope that one's own frightening, mountainous needs could be met, protecting patients, in the process, from the disorganizing impact that a caring or empathic response might have produced ("if I let you touch me, move me with your love, you'll see how terribly needy I am and flee"). The foregoing, of course, represents only a partial accounting of damaging relationship choices people could make.

Interdependency was inherently frightening for my patients. Besides the threat of negotiating identity, many of them had not had the opportunity to engage in a constructive dependence (some few had a parent who was able to oppose the narcissistic other in a way that at least afforded a patient some measure of protection and inoculation). Dependencies did not feel like safe places for them. Setting aside all of the deficiency and sometimes ugliness that they saw in themselves, how could they count on others not to exploit them if they rendered themselves vulnerable? And how could they trust themselves to express their needs in an appropriate way without compromising dignity and attractiveness? To my surprise, however, many of these people readily managed to establish very constructive and productive dependencies in therapy. I was often taken aback by the relative ease with which this happened. Subsequently, these patients were able to take intimacy risks in relationships outside therapy.

Depending upon the receptivity of the people that they chose, risk either paid off or was, for some individuals, catastrophically damaging. Their fragility and pain limited their resilience. As a therapist, I was cognizant that the risk-taking process was, to a degree, ungovernable. I couldn't always protect people effectively and I couldn't always anticipate whether they were exposing themselves to a good choice or a damaging one. So many unpredictable and unanticipated variables could intervene in a given instance. Forewarning patients and attempting to insulate them, ahead of time, against unexpected and unfavorable consequences was sometimes not enough to ensure that they would not be badly hurt or, if they had been hurt, that they would find the courage to take risks again.

Almost all of my patients struggled with depression that was either a constant companion or an intermittent one. It disrupted their lives in myriad ways. It, too, was immensely frightening, as depression is. Within a psychoanalytic framework, depression was both anaclitic (reflecting a response to relational concerns and losses) and introjective (bespeaking preoccupation with achievement standards and expectations). Suicidal ideation was a frequent companion of such depression. In some of my patients it was obsessive, frighteningly seductive, and disturbingly intense when it was present. It often created multiple crises in psychotherapy. Very generally speaking, as people came to feel more comfortable with the dependence that psychotherapy offered, only gradually did suicidal ideation seem to lose its potency.

Finally, many of my patients also demonstrated PTSD marked by irresistible, interminable preparation and rehearsal for catastrophic possibilities. The PTSD process presented itself unbidden in people's daily lives, was extremely hard to short-circuit or mitigate once it had onset, and was a source of agony. It could also contribute to suicidal risk and to susceptibility to addiction. The myriad forms of pain that this group of patients lived with rendered susceptibility to addiction quite high. Addictions offered momentary reprieve in the face of ongoing suffering patients became quite desperate to escape. It probably also served the function of helping them sabotage success and undercut their lives, accommodating an internalized narcissistic dictate to diminish the self.

PTSD reflected people's sense that they were not safe in the world. Endemic bullying and disconfirmation that the narcissistic other had directed towards them subverted their sense that they could protect themselves in the face of expected onslaughts from a predatory and malignant surround. Many of them struggled lifelong with assertion. I have seen, in my clinical experience, that early, sustained bullying sometimes has an enduring impact on people that never fully relents.

I found that the level of "pushback" that my patients were able to direct towards a narcissistic parent could tell me a great deal about people's prospects for a successful future life adjustment.

One distinctive group of patients that I described earlier in this chapter focused on trying to hide the ravaged parts of self left to them, making themselves small enough to be sufficiently unobtrusive so that they might escape further narcissistic attack. Recourse to this strategy might mean that one remained trapped in a small space throughout much of one's life, too afraid to engage in acts of self-assertion required to affirm and enlarge identity. For others, resistance took the form of explicit acts of defiance and opposition that brought them into open combat with their narcissistic adversary. People who chose this strategy – or rather, were capable of it – were conceivably in a better position to protect the self, but they were, simultaneously, almost inevitably exposing themselves (singling themselves out?) to more intense and probably more frequent combat. For some of this group of people, soliciting combat was, in part, an often unconscious attempt to draw fire away from other people in the family that they loved whom they perceived to be more fragile. If they could somehow tolerate the escalating assaults their pushback produced, they could reassure themselves that the self was capable of surviving. The liability that this particular strategy carried with it seemed to be directly related to the ferocity of a patient's defiance. The more patients depended upon counter-aggression to protect themselves – the harder they fought, the less restraint they used to modulate their aggression – the more likely they seemed to be to call on brutish forms of aggression to make themselves feel safe in the intimacies they attempted in adulthood. In the face of real or perceived threat, they reflexively adopted an "eviscerate your opponent before they could hurt you" approach which, of course, mimicked the way they had protected themselves against the narcissistic parent. They also seemed to have great difficulty modulating their emotions, responding to and acting on what they felt rather than being able to think about it. These people often found themselves in stormy adult relationships marked by lots of out-of-control conflict they were at a loss to know how to prevent. While their behavior might deeply trouble them, occasioning suffocating remorse as they confronted the injury they had caused in people they loved, they were loath to give up the one defense that had safeguarded them earlier in their life. They seemed to prove less amenable to psychotherapy and less likely to seek out treatment than people who had not adopted an extreme aggression strategy.

There did appear to be an optimal level of aggression to use to fend off the narcissistic other. Not so little that one was constrained to occupy a tiny space that left the self little room to grow and not so expansive that it had to be supported by ungoverned aggression. The "just right" range of aggression seemed to allow people their best chance to preserve enough of the self so that future intimacy and future growth were possible. These were the people who seemed to do best with themselves in the long run. The capacity to fight back at just right levels was probably mediated by a number of factors including, perhaps, the presence of a supportive or protective parent, access to a mentoring relationship in the family or the community, a rich native endowment of social and intellectual potentialities, avenues of escape from the narcissistic other, etc.

It is striking to me, as I have reflected previously, that the narcissist replicates many of the conditions that define his own inner life – starvation; enduring, suffocating hunger; envy of all that others appear to have that the self is missing; fear of dependence; contrivance; a taste for cruelty; a blighted, rage-filled interior; a profound sense of inner badness; a sense that both one's inner and external worlds are infiltrated by threat and malevolence; and high levels of vigilance.

There do appear to be important manifest differences between narcissistic personalities and people who mount resistance, in one form or another, to narcissistic incursion. Unlike a narcissistic personality, shame is a prominent experience. So, too, is fear of abandonment, depression, subjectively high levels of self-hatred, inertia, and ruminative equivocation. And, unlike the narcissist, rather than feeling the need to occupy center stage continuously, there is a strong drive to disappear and erase oneself that includes a need to back away from successes and disconfirm them. Sense of inner badness and of one's own unattractiveness is exquisitely apparent whereas in the narcissist it is hidden. The self is also experienced as helpless and powerless as opposed to being infected with grandiosity and indomitability. Healthy entitlement is damaged and certainly not inflated in the way that it is in a narcissistic personality.

All of these differences help set a different course for some of the people targeted by narcissism than the course which the narcissist follows himself. It is a course, as I have said, that is fraught with terrible risks. Some people either don't survive or barely survive. Many have to contend with lifelong sequelae. And some few transcend their pain to a significant, but always very imperfect, degree.

One of the potential outcomes of living in a narcissistic surround that I want to consider now is the pathway that I saw myself moving down in what felt like an almost inexorable fashion. Being called upon to accommodate my father's shifting interpretations of reality, facing the necessity of disguising my own counter responses to narcissistic violation, and being able, more or less consistently, to respond to a threatening environment in a chameleon-like way contributed to a self that was ravaged by pretense, by a habit of pervasive dissociation and numbness, and by profound, underlying rage incited by the devastation that pervaded and defined my sense of self. Chronic exposure to abuse and bullying evoked murderous retaliatory fantasies and acts of cruelty I directed towards easy targets, helpless animals. The momentary aliveness that my cruelty generated in me provided some relief from the numbing effect of dissociation, giving me the opportunity to at least feel something. Apart from transient relief, however, my engagement with cruelty horrified me. Why was I unable to feel untouched by the suffering I was witnessing? Could I not feel anything beyond the boundaries of my own pain? Was I too dead inside to be able to engage with life except through sadism?

I had another fear. I felt so devoid of self I could feel the urge to try to copy someone else, to replicate their personality as closely and as completely as I could so that not only could I look like a real person, but I might actually feel like one as well, offsetting, in the process, the skeletal self I had to live with. It's challenging to capture this subjective state in a way that adequately describes it. I can recall being afraid that my emptiness would prove to be so unbearable I would be compelled to give up what few shards of identity I possessed, replacing them with the newer, bigger, more sustaining identity that somebody else offered me. At the same time, the idea that somebody else could possess me and define me terrified me. There was so little of me, after all, maybe I would disappear altogether if I made too much room for somebody else.

I learned to rely on my ability to simulate socially appropriate responses to hide my secrets, but my underlying transformation increasingly horrified me. Could I become – in a different fashion than my father had – someone largely devoid of humanity whose ravaged insides would lead me to hurt people in the way that I had animals? In the midst of the intense darkness that had enveloped me it seemed plausible to me that that's where I was heading. Numbness and cruelty were such big parts of me I could not imagine that I would ever be capable of experiencing loving or communal feelings. It was dauntingly scary. I suppose the fact that I was scared by what was happening to me offered some testament that I could be somebody else, but, honestly, as I look back, I'm not sure my observing self could have saved me.

In actuality, it did not take much (or perhaps it was a lot) to make a difference: the (to me) improbable mentorships of a few coaches and teachers who demonstrated obvious affection for me. Had I been possessed of a less attractive personality to them or had I not been in as supportive a school environment, I think I might well have found myself trapped in a psychopathic existence. My psychopathy would indeed have looked different than my father's narcissism, a parade of obvious weaknesses and vulnerabilities contrasting his contrivance of strength. Psychopathy literature makes reference to so-called secondary psychopathy, which is thought, by some authors, to be reflective of people with a psychopathic core who are obviously tormented by their existence rather than appearing to be impervious to various manifest forms of mental illness, like depression. That, I think, is who I very nearly became. With just a little of the right help at the right time from my teachers and coaches, however, the stage was set for me to find a way out of my black space. The journey was interminable, requiring a lifetime of effort and help. At many points along the way I found myself utterly bereft of hope. How could I ever find someone to love me? Or support myself, never mind a family? Where was the energy and discipline I would need to sustain a career? What could I possibly have to give to friends that they could value? Every time I saw someone begging on the street, I palpably cringed. I saw my own future.

I want to mention another pathway that I think people might follow in response to threat a narcissistic other creates for them. I have not directly observed people who have moved down this pathway as part of my clinical work. I only have the examples that my father's subordinates provided of what might possibly unfold in a narcissistic family context. Could children, I wondered, living in such a frightening and stressful environment try to protect themselves by identifying with the narcissist's perspectives and values, mimicking the aggrieved, entitled, bullying postures so pronounced in the narcissistic other? I have often read about the kiss ass up, kick ass down mentality attributed to Nazi hierarchical structures. Could children do the same thing? Could they walk the walk that the narcissist required of them, later playing the part of the narcissist themselves with someone more vulnerable than they were? "I'll give you the obeisance and the pliability that you want from me, but when I'm dealing with someone I perceive to be weaker than me, I get to be the bully, just as you have been with me." A child, I would imagine, might make such a choice almost intuitively, instinctively. Once they had done so, identity would begin to consolidate around the posture of alternating obeisance and bullying that they had adopted for themselves. The whole process would probably unfold largely outside the child's conscious awareness.

I think this process would be facilitated if the child came to understand that the narcissistic other was prepared to reward them for adopting a narcissistic stance. Identification would not just represent an escape, then, from narcissistic invasion and diminishment, but rather a potentially effective way to win praise and respect from the depreciatory other as well as a means of consolidating one's own version of grandiosity. For a self that would otherwise feel beset by emaciation, starvation, and incompletion, the inducement the narcissistic other offers to identify with them might well feel irresistible. Taking in the narcissistic other and refashioning oneself in their image, however, might depend upon whether one is possessed of constitutional givens and proclivities of personality that would render such a transformation both bearable and actionable. What may well have saved me from being ensnared by such a process was my mother's obvious distaste for my father; had she not resisted him, I wonder whether I would have been able to protect myself from a devastating identification with him.

For me, the fulcrum in this process is not threat of humiliation if the child resists identification, but rather the spiritual withering and identity dissolution that appears to be an inevitable consequence of narcissistic predation. Partnering in a relationship with the narcissist, whether as a spouse, child, or colleague, progressively exposes one to erosion of identity. This erosion of self, particularly in family members close to the narcissist, does represent a kind of soul murder that produces agonies of suffering and often results, as it did with my mother and with me, in a fragmented self that denies one a sense of personal cohesion. People who face profound struggle with these issues can sometimes be described as Borderline Personality Disorders (BPD). The portrait I provided of my mother in Chapter 3 offers one an in-depth look at the ways in which BPD tragically manifests itself.

But what of adults? While I understand that fear could impel adults to make a choice like this for themselves, I would think that they would have to sacrifice self-awareness in order to facilitate movement towards the new self their fear propelled them to acquire. How could you make such a shift, in other words, if you were aware of what was happening to you, unless, of course, you deliberately contrived your new face to make you more acceptable to the threatening party? If deliberate contrivance was not informing your behavior, how could you embrace such a shift if you allowed yourself to be at all thoughtful about what was happening to you? Wouldn't the cost feel too high? You would somehow have to shut down your capacity for critical thought, allowing yourself to swallow holus-bolus that which the other party required of you. In return, you would get to experience relief from fear and you would also get to feel strong and perhaps indomitable when opportunities for you to aggress against others presented themselves. Fear shutting down selfhood and our ability to think for ourselves. A powerful testament to the extraordinary effect fear potentially has on the human psyche. Such ideas took me back, again, to a reconsideration of the events of 1933 Germany which Eric Larson so powerfully documented in his book, *Garden of Beasts*.

It is important to remind the reader again at this junction that other clinicians/researchers have identified additional pathways that might potentially lead to psychopathy. Genetics would appear to play some role. Multiple environmental factors beyond those that were part of my own and my father's histories have also been seen to make a contribution. People who might potentially be described as psychopathic also appear to be possessed of specific patterns of brain function observable through specialized imaging techniques. With respect to the latter, what I think we don't know at this point is whether the psychopathic brain could learn to acquire some of the responsivity that is characteristic of "healthier" brain function. Intriguingly, one clinician investigating imaging characteristics of functioning psychopathic brains discovered that his own brain imagery was compatible with that of psychopaths. In the context of this discussion, one wonders whether patterns of brain function typifying psychopathy must always express themselves as a manifest psychopathic personality. If not, what factors might mediate the difference between underlying functional brain realities and clinical presentation? We just don't know yet – or, at least, we don't yet have the compelling answers we want.

Chapter 13

Legacies of Narcissism – Malignant Narcissistic Leadership and the State as a Narcissistic Entity

We have seen that a narcissistic presence in the family produces terrible disruptions of selfhood, some or many of which may reverberate throughout a person's life. Depression and anxiety are its common offspring. People don't feel safe. The ability to trust is ruptured. Both the world around them and inside them assumes a malignant aspect. Capacity for intimacy is damaged or forfeited. The acts of cruelty that invade them and the profound dissociation that they rely upon to protect themselves compromises empathy and facilitates brutality. The self is starved and ill formed, primed to take in identities others might attempt to impose on them. For some, the stage is set for predilection to psychopathy and narcissism.

I would ask the reader now to project the effects of the narcissist on a family onto the state he governs.

Because the narcissist is himself at war, as he dominates his culture, he places it on a war footing. Everyone is potentially suspect and anyone can become a potential target. Threat is an omnipresent, crushing reality. Like him, members of his culture learn to become hypervigilant, on guard against predation and violation. War requires enemies. The narcissist provides them. Enemies are identified within the host culture and outside it – in either case, unfortunates who are seen to disrupt or stand in the way of the narcissist's entitlements. The "moral" imperative of the narcissist is acquisition of resources of all kinds, save for decency and love. Just as is true of the narcissist in his personal life, pursuit of desired supplies that an enemy within the state or a designated enemy outside possesses can unfold with terrible ruthlessness. The narcissist is driven by his own subjective starvation. With suppression of freedom, selfhood, and personal initiative, those he would govern endure erosion of spirit as well. His imperative to engage in predation becomes theirs. Their reactive, but poorly understood, starvation helps drive them.

The narcissistic leader promises compensation for the spiritual emaciation he has helped create. The governed are invited to bask in narcissistic self-aggrandizement, attributing to themselves aspects of "potency" and "strength" that the master purports to possess. They, too, can share in his spoils, enjoying the fruits of predation that he sanctions. If only they would surrender themselves to him, allowing him to

DOI: 10.4324/9781003246923-13

define them, he would enhance them. They can become bigger and more powerful than they have ever felt themselves to be.

In circumstances in which national identities may already have been compromised by a sense of acute and unbearable vulnerabilities, by humiliation, and by unmanageable subjective levels of fear generated by previous privations and suffering, the narcissistic promise is a seductive one. Conditions of economic contraction, defeat, war, political chaos, and widespread disease all help set the stage for receptivity to narcissistic leadership. If a real crisis doesn't exist, the narcissist may invent one, or may exaggerate an existing one, emphasizing their unique capacity to save those being threatened. Visionary leadership is his prerogative. Only he can solve the problems confronting his people.

His seeming capacity to appreciate others' circumstances is illusory. He always serves his own ends.

The bargain that the governed enters into with him requires utter subordination of the self to his wishes. People that the narcissist leads are impelled to surrender old and possibly more humane versions of the self for the new self the narcissist offers them, one seemingly more powerful and certainly more entitled than the old self. This new self must be aligned with the narcissist's rapacity. Absolute loyalty and subjugation of the self is required. Because the new self accommodates escalating erosion of humanity, its bearer must endure increasing starvation and withering of spirit. Hate and fear begin to replace both love and sustaining communion with others.

Projection of the aggrandized self, or part of it, onto an entire country is a complicated and inherently unstable undertaking for the narcissistic leader, characterized, as it must be, by efforts to diminish followers so that they represent extensions of narcissistic will at the same time that he attempts to empower them – the latter being an implicitly threatening endeavor for the narcissist. After all, much of the narcissist's energy focuses itself upon preventing growth and expansion in adjacent personalities.

Having imbued his followers with his greatness, he must now ensure that they never exceed him, that their voices never assume more authority than his. Only he can be the potentate, but he must somehow feed the aggrandizement he has encouraged in them without antagonizing them when he subjects them to diminishment. He relies on fear to accomplish this end. Fear is the deliberate by-product of the chaotic, arbitrary, shifting moods he adopts, his shearing positional changes, and the bullying and the cruelty he so frequently enacts. Making people afraid serves him well. Anyone, even those close to him, can become an enemy, as those around him must be acutely aware.

The narcissistic leader is himself afraid all the time, though he would rarely acknowledge it as fear. In an attempt to confirm domination which, unconsciously at least, must always feel in jeopardy, the narcissist must continually test others. They must show themselves willing to accept his version of the truth, even though it may change from moment to moment. They must also show themselves ready to make unconscionable sacrifice should he require that of them. They must endure his contempt, his ethical lapses, and his breaches of loyalty, which he requires in order to ensure that no one can realize enduring purchase in his life. Satisfactory testing produces momentary reassurance, but exacerbates longer-term fears. At some point, as the narcissist at least subliminally appreciates, drinking from the poisoned chalice must eventually produce resistance among those he commands to do so.

Having assigned himself visionary powers and having perpetually reconfirmed his expansive abilities, he must somehow keep afloat an outsized version of himself (much like my father and I had to do as adultified children) that can never admit to fallibility or error. This, too, is an impossible proposition and an inherently unstable one. Errors of judgement must be projected onto subordinates. Cracks in the aggrandized self that failures occasion are very badly tolerated, producing hysterical outbursts of rage fueled by a measure of panic the narcissistic leader can never acknowledge.

All of these sources of instability continually feed a narcissistic leader's sense that his war footing must be maintained. No one can be trusted for long. Cynicism reinvigorates itself. Vigilance never relaxes. The self is always prepared for combat.

The war footing that the narcissistic leader maintains – supported by pervasive rage, unyielding mistrust, and destructive, out-of-control appetites – requires perpetual combat. So long as the narcissistic leader can fight, he can create a measure of safety for himself, reassuring himself through combat that he is the biggest, baddest cat on the playground. Others must be subjugated before they can hurt him. The rage and pain he so effectively mobilizes in his followers needs targets. So long as he can draw his people together with the endless combat he requires for himself, he can turn their attention away from the depredations he visits on them. He can keep the show going a little while longer. In part – but only in part – his grandiosity protects him against the sense of instability that the whole endeavor possesses.

The effect that narcissism appears to have on individuals growing up in a narcissistic family offers a glimpse of what can happen on a larger, or national scale, in the context of narcissistic leadership. Narcissistic leadership creates imposing threat that members of a given culture must find a way to accommodate themselves to. The ambience of fear and uncertainty that the narcissistic leader creates pervades people's lives. The more power the narcissist has, the more crushing and the more invasive fear becomes. Threat generates dissociation and overall blunting of emotion. It creates erosion of humane sensibility, of capacity for empathy, and of capacity for thoughtful discourse that appreciates nuance and complexity. It demands an action-oriented, friend or foe orientation in which delineation of bad guys becomes a primary concern. Because thought is framed in simpleminded dictums, objectification and dehumanization of the other is facilitated. It becomes easier to experience revulsion for an adversary because we don't see them as fully human, but rather as cardboard cut outs worthy of the aggression and debasement we direct towards them.

In such an environment the narcissist possesses frightening opportunities to exploit his rapacity and his taste for cruelty. He finds ready and willing allies. People enduring endemically high and unsupportable levels of fear become desperate for safety. For many of them, safety will reside in the tyrannies that the narcissistic leader allows them to exercise. This is what I referred to in the previous chapter as a "kiss ass up, kick ass down" mentality. The chance to bully someone else even as you yourself have been bullied helps many people feel stronger, better protected. Such bullying can be carefully orchestrated by the state and can be expected to unfold more or less within prescribed limits. In effect, a kind of institutionalized bullying. It may be embedded in a Byzantine, deeply competitive, bureaucratic fabric that pits various bureaucratic arms of the government against one another, as seemed to be characteristic of Germany in World War II. Bullying and threat serve the narcissistic state well, generating a cadre of angry, frightened people who have learned to mitigate their own fear by beating up their neighbors. A cadre of angry, frightened people whose own habits of predation can be all too readily harnessed by the narcissistic leadership. People who become inured, through a habit of predation, to the harm that they routinely cause others and to the harm that they routinely endure themselves.

Perhaps counterintuitively, investment of power in an autocratic leader and the kiss ass up, kick ass down bureaucratic fiefdoms autocracy births, each headed by their own potentate, exacerbates inefficiencies, obstructing attempts to rationalize resources rather than facilitating them. Too much energy is consumed by fear and by fractious rivalries that, while serving the narcissistic leader's needs to wrongfoot those he governs, badly compromises productivity. Democracy, with its relatively greater reliance on collaboration, proves to be more successful.

Outright persecution of internal enemies sanctioned by a narcissistic state also ratchets up fear that everybody in the state, whether they have been targeted or not, must live with. The more vicious the persecution of a given group, the greater the fear that everyone endures. In a setting of such suffocating fear, people can feel relief – perhaps a mixture of exhilaration, pleasure in others' suffering, and a sense of power – that they themselves are immune to the devastation that the other must bear. Schadenfreude becomes a widespread, culturally sanctioned experience. Underlying "relief," however, there is unspoken dread that one's immunity is not indelible. A dread that one can become a hated outsider. Moral frameworks that the state provides justifying targeted persecutions help support people's sense that they, themselves, will not be touched by the state's wandering hatreds. In a state where fear fills so much of the space in people's lives, the moral justifications the state provides for its actions reflect the quality of thinking that fear imposes: simplistic, ugly generalizations possessed of visceral appeal that offer only the thinnest veneer of a rationale for prejudicial rage. What is important is identification of enemies through language dominated by contempt. Being able to incite prejudice through the use of such language allows the state to quickly shift rage and fear in its populace towards the new targets it finds desirable. People's identification with the aggrandizement of the narcissistic leader helps them to continue to feel out of reach of the prejudices and manufactured bigotries swirling around them.

Acts of cruelty can unfold with numbing regularity. The unthinkable soon becomes commonplace. There is so much assault on people's sensibility and humanity that it becomes impossible to respond to all of it, much less process it. The more persecutorial the narcissistic state acts, the more frightened everyone becomes. Fear begets rage, which is easier to experience than helplessness and vulnerability. The pool of people whose fear and rage the state can marry to its own intentions grows. It befits a narcissistic leader's preference that these are people, increasingly, whose humanity has been diminished. They can be more readily paired with the narcissist's ruthless intentions.

Survival in a fear drenched environment becomes everybody's primary concern. To separate oneself from the narcissistic leader's voice is to identify oneself as "other" or enemy. As state and leader become ever more powerful, acts of resistance become ever more dangerous and ever more improbable. People's fear transforms itself into bullying directed at state sanctioned targets. The state institutionalizes its prejudices and provides rationalizations for them. Acts of bigotry eventually become second nature for a dissociated, frightened populace. The acculturation of objectification and depreciation of others makes it ever easier to swallow justifications for rapacity that state and culture continue to elaborate. So justified, entitlements extend themselves, becoming culture wide "givens" or "truths" that are experienced as self-evident. Lies about others insinuate themselves into consciousness, unfolding reflexively and casually. Prejudice and brutality barely disconcert, becoming commonplace acts that express themselves in everyday life quite unselfconsciously. People who act thusly would be shocked and offended if an outsider questioned their decency; they would point to the respect and everyday acts of kindness they direct towards their own kind or members of their own tribe, decrying those they exploited or persecuted as unworthy of humane consideration. In such a fashion, decency and brutality come to coexist comfortably with one another. Dissociation and compromised empathy render this marriage possible. And in such a context, various inhumane practices, like slavery, can become institutionalized and flourish. Even as a cultural milieu becomes less oppressive, bigotries continue to express themselves. Those who oppress would find it far too hard and far too jeopardizing to acknowledge the cruelties they enact. Looking at the collective damaged "self" they embody would feel too dangerous and potentially too compromising to endure. Only with the passage of time marked by painful and fractious self reflection could such a society effectively transform itself, moving towards a gentler and more caring version of its former self.

People who support the narcissistic leader, representing the apparatus of state, also suffer diminishment of humanity as they are called upon incessantly to betray themselves, to betray their colleagues, and to betray the truth. The lapses required of them violate their integrity, which, increasingly, is forsaken. That which they might previously have found intolerable and objectionable becomes acceptable as they, too, become inured to the ugliness that surrounds them and fills them. Whatever moral authority or individuality they might once have possessed becomes suborned to leadership.

The narcissistic leader finds resources in unlikely places in the populace he governs. People who share his bigotries and prejudices are drawn forward. They are granted stature and offered political opportunity that allows them to enact policies consonant with their own natures, but at odds with respect for diversity. In a tribal environment, "same" connotes friend and safety; "other" represents enemy and unwelcome adversary. These new leaders further fracture society, inciting old and new hatreds that serve up an ongoing supply of targets that the narcissistic state requires for itself.

The narcissistic leader also finds himself comfortable with people who have compromised themselves for personal gain, whether it takes the form of status, money, power, or thirst for notoriety. Such people can be trusted because they have shown themselves willing to sell themselves for the price that they want. Their presence in the apparatus of state ensures that there will be fewer voices to oppose the narcissistic voice. Their presence also compounds the brutalities that the state enacts and the erosion of sensitivity that unfolds.

Under narcissistic leadership, everybody endures at least some erosion of their humanity. If the narcissistic leader extends his rapacity and embroils the state in a live fire war, damage to humanity is corrosive and extensive, not only for the inhabitants of the state but for those that they batter and destroy with their armies. War shatters attachments, creating losses and wounds, both physical and psychological, that may not heal themselves for generations. It requires that one shut down one's sensitivity to suffering. In a narcissistic context, effective soldiering requires abandonment of conscience. The extraordinary breadth and scope of suffering that war occasions diminishes people's ability to recognize their own pain or the pain in others. Stoicism becomes a prized and necessary commodity.

Thus, the state and its people join with the narcissistic leader, increasingly assuming the attributes of psychopathy. Not everyone in the state, of course; some few individuals show themselves capable of surmounting fear and engaging in acts of resistance. Sometimes resistance flourishes and a narcissistic leader is deposed, though not always to better effect. Compromised authoritarian leadership seems to result in an extended period of chaos and violence before a more respecting form of government can be established.

Narcissistic leadership may unfortunately follow itself with another authoritarian presence. Contemporary human affairs continue to struggle with these
themes, though, thankfully, not on the scale that we once did. This is a
struggle that has played itself out throughout recorded history.

I believe that what people do in warfare remains with them, whether
unbidden or not, haunting their conscience. If war was undertaken largely as
an act of exploitation at the behest of a rapacious other, how does one
reconcile the injury that one has caused in war with one's membership in the
human community? What of the acts of deliberate cruelty that war and a
terror filled existence instigate? How does one explain that to oneself? If war
has been lost, the tribal narcissistic society must retreat into itself, shuttering
itself away from others' view lest the indiscretions of a bad war become too
transparent and too personal. Tribalism therefore extends itself, perpetuating
an "us and them" state of being that is all too easily exploited by another
narcissistic leader. Dissociation, erosion of humane sensibilities, and devastating postwar privations all make their own contributions to this tragic
vulnerability.

The film, "*Labyrinth of Lies,*" provides a thoughtful and disturbing look at
postwar adjustment, in this case, German home front realities following
World War II. Participants in the war struggle with their place in society after
the war is over. For many, what they did in the war becomes unspeakable.
They retreat into silos – small societies, like the remnants of a particular
combat organization – where discourse of some kind is possible. The outside
world, including the larger world of Germany, is shut out. As the title implies,
Germany devolves into fragments, each with its own closely guarded indiscretions – a broken mosaic of dissonant tribal interests that coalesce around
secrecy.

Accommodating ourselves to the breadth and the diversity of experience
that the human condition imposes on us is a challenging, if not terrifying
endeavor. We come into this world and this life understanding very little
about it, save for the genetic proclivities we possess that equip us to make
some sense out of what is happening to us. In the main, we need other people
to show us how to interpret that which takes place inside us and around us.
That which unfolds in our private worlds can all too readily assume a frightening aspect because it is seemingly so ungovernable, so illogical, so reckless,
and so amoral. How do we accept the many faces that present themselves to
us internally, some of which inspire creativity and offer intrinsic satisfaction
and some of which strike us as horrifying, repugnant, and dangerous? Our
parental guides need to help us make our way. If they are themselves repelled
by parts of their inner world, then we, too, are likely to feel the same way.
Those strictures and taboos that they rely upon to wall off parts of self they
find unacceptable we import into our own psyches, probably all too easily,
employing the same tools to keep ourselves safe that they did. I would think
that discomfort with our insides has dogged humanity from its inception. In

our primitive tribal iterations, frightening images and impulses that arose internally were experienced as out-of-control and threatening to us; we mitigated the terror they caused us by projecting them onto the world around us, treating them as gods, and appeasing them by offering them fealty, worship, or supplicant fear. Institutions of worship and governance legitimized rules for us to follow so that we could manage that which frightened us most – our inner life. And we needed the means to manage our insides. Without the constraints we created, our efforts to incrementally civilize ourselves would have failed.

It is only by degree that we have come, gradually, to acquire a measure of comfort and equanimity when we attempt to explore what we live with inside ourselves. It has taken much of our human history to reach a point at which we seek out treatment so that we might know ourselves better. Knowledge of all kinds, including religious "truth" and self-knowledge, was largely a prerogative of an authoritarian other. Someone else told us what to think and feel and when to think and feel it. Art, science, literature, and commerce offered the individual increasing opportunity to make their own decisions about the conduct of their lives and the kind of relationship they would establish with their own psyches. People enjoyed greater freedom to construct their own moralities and to decide for themselves what was acceptable and what was not about their inner lives. This evolution has been stormy and challenging. It seems likely that individual freedom will continue to expand and express itself, but it is hard to imagine that we will ever free ourselves from reliance on authority and the structures that it imposes. We inherently want and need oversight to feel safe with ourselves and to be safe with other people.

Though we may think of ourselves as mostly intrepid explorers of our psyches, many of us continue to find a trip through our own interiors to be a very aversive and dangerous endeavor; even the most experienced of us will acknowledge they still find aspects of this journey pretty daunting. Many of us require oppressive strictures enforced by an overriding, implacable authority to feel safe with big parts of ourselves that would otherwise seem frighteningly out-of-control. For many people, stability and safety can best be realized through authoritarian/fascistic hierarchies that appropriate morality and its compatriots, fear and punishment. Such people want to be provided with a clear and inviolate sense of what we can and cannot do. Unyielding consequences and authority define those boundaries. A strong state and a strong leader tell us who we are, who we ought to be, and under what circumstances we are to be the things we are told to be. It can be comforting for us to know that someone else will tell us when it is moral to unleash our most unacceptable impulses and when it is not, relieving us of a burden many of us would rather avoid. Authoritarian and fascistic structures continue to seduce and beguile us, then, offering to absolve us of carrying responsibility for our own actions. We don't have to worry about our inner lives anymore – at least not to the degree that we might otherwise have to in the absence of a punishing surround. Leader and state take care of it for us.

Authoritarian structures also solve another important problem. No longer is the individual confronted with difficult existential questions about how to create personal meaning; the state tells one what is important and even what function one is to serve. If a citizen colors between the prescribed lines and does a good job of it, rewards are to be had as is a strong sense of place in a cohesive community. We are given purpose and belonging rather than having to construct them for ourselves. Thus armed – part of something much bigger and more powerful than ourselves – we can even defer dread about our own mortality.

Authoritarian and fascistic structures will continue to draw many of us to these forms of government and leadership. The costs that they can be seen to impose in an increasingly complex, interrelated global village are formidable. My sense is that autocratic forms of leadership will continue to seduce us, creating sometimes unbearable tension between those of us who wish to expand their prerogatives of freedom and those of us who wish to constrain them. In delineating the liabilities that narcissistic leadership carries within itself, it is my hope that we can develop more thoughtful and more extensive conversations that better inform us about the choices we make and why we make them. We have allowed ourselves to be persuaded by malignant narcissism throughout our history; now we must find the means, at last, to step away from it and direct ourselves.

American Army psychologist Capt. G. M. Gilbert, tasked with observing defendants at the Nuremberg trials at the end of World War II, developed a simple, but compelling, appreciation of what he thought evil was:

> I was searching for the nature of evil and I now think I have come close to defining it. A lack of empathy. It's the one characteristic that connects all the defendants, a genuine incapacity to feel with their fellow men. Evil, I think, is the absence of empathy.

Totalitarian states compromise empathy with terrifying efficiency in a fashion that is consistent with the interests of both state and leader. I have also suggested, however, that the ability to compromise empathy exists within all of us, independent of totalitarian influence. We turn empathy off to protect the self or, I would maintain, to protect the tribe. We do so with a frightening and casual automaticity. The easy facility with which we can turn off empathy appears to be built into most or all of us. In many respects, negating empathy has been an adaptive quality for us in the past, allowing ascendant forms of civilization to triumph over neighbors and expand themselves, thus furthering the broader interests of civilization itself. On a personal level, we can all too readily harm others with either full or partial ignorance of what we have done; when we act as part of a larger aggregate, neutralized empathy can enable acts of extraordinary cruelty as part of either predation or defence against others' predation (or both). In a group context, we can violate others with extreme prejudice at the same time that we demonstrate kindness and empathic attunement with the people we care about. The transposition of these realities captures, for me, an unintended implication of Hannah Arendt's phrase "banality of evil": our capacity to accommodate both brutality and decency in ourselves more or less simultaneously. The discourse between these two contradictory parts of ourselves, however, sooner or later proves to be a fractious one. We pay personal and social costs for the harm we do others.

Given our propensity to turn away empathic feeling, even outside the damaging impact that totalitarian leadership has on our humanity, we must be ever mindful, as a species, of our need to support, enhance, and protect empathic response in ourselves. Empathy rehearsal that the arts compel in us – theatre, dance, music, literature, visual arts – is more than pleasure: it is necessary for our continued survival.

The arts serve another crucial function: they help us accommodate ourselves to the breadth and diversity of our inner life, including our many dark corners. Much as "Alice in Wonderland" and "the Wizard of Oz" provided me with a kind of road map to unconscious experience, reassuring me that I could survive my own nightmares, the arts enable us to explore, in a relatively safe way, facets of our experience that might otherwise be too frightening for us to look at. In so doing they extend our appreciation and our acceptance of human realities, reassuring us we can not only endure what we might discover inside ourselves, but become, as a result of our arts' journeys, kinder, more curious, more fanciful and imaginative, more flexible in our thinking, more creative and innovative, and more humane. Cultures that support rich diversity of arts expression potentially help us expand ourselves, encouraging us to take risks with ourselves so that we might evolve and become better, more thoughtful versions of who we are.

The evolution of self and of culture that unfolds, however, is not without jeopardy, as I have said; not everyone moves ahead at the same pace and in the same way and not all change is beneficial. Cultures need time to digest new forms. And new ideas don't always work well. Here, too, the arts help us. Vigorous reconsideration and re-exploration of emergent frameworks through the arts can be – and invariably is – undertaken. In a very imperfect and often uneven fashion what unfolds is an even more accurate appraisal of both our humanity and our possibilities. Gradually – incrementally – we start to move away from the rigid defensive postures we have felt compelled to protect at all costs – often through injurious acts towards ourselves and others – that have so typified our history.

Would that this evolutionary process were easier. With the passage of time, we do seem to be making more headway with ourselves, but my fear is that time is a commodity that may soon fail us. Such a large part of humanity continues to yearn for some of the "safety" that oppression and autocratic forms seem to promise.

In addition to protecting the arts, there are other measures we must take on our journey to move towards and enhance that which is best in ourselves.

My father's life story offers a passionate argument against the potentially devastating effects inequality and poverty have on an emerging personality. The resulting distortions in development lay the groundwork not only for personal suffering, but for devastating injury for other people whom such an individual touches with their pain. Remember now that the personality that emerges from such suffering may be particularly well-suited to exploit opportunities for leadership of large communities of people. The damage that can be wrought can multiply itself to an incalculable degree. Over 60 million people are thought to have died in World War II. This astonishing number, as intimidating and imponderable as it is, is eclipsed by the numbers of people enduring starvation, crippling wounds, displacement, shattered attachments, and psychological injuries. It is for this reason that I think it is important to append the word "malignant" to "narcissism" in the descriptive phrase malignant narcissism, which forms part of the title of this book.

The word malignant is not meant to reference a judgement about the personality organization I and others have described, nor does it excuse us from responding to such people with compassion and understanding, as hard as that may be. It is, instead, intended to remind us of the extraordinary calamities such personalities can visit on humankind. As a descriptor, then, malignant calls our attention to a distortion of the human character that is extremely dangerous when allowed to govern communities and nations. Malignant prompts us to be ever mindful of the risks we face when we permit ourselves to be led by malignant narcissists. Vigilance and an awareness of the destructive potentiality malignant narcissistic leadership embodies helps us better protect ourselves against future, and probably unimaginable, catastrophes. In this way, we are better equipped to avoid devastation and pain that might impose itself in the presence of persisting blindness. Malignant, then, also applies to the horrifying consequences ignorance creates for us and, as such, implicates everyone; malignancy, after all, is a quality that all of us possess and that all of us must recognize and understand if we are to be safe with one another. Not an easy thing to do. I have to acknowledge that I might have become my father. And the collective "we" need to acknowledge we can be badly led, seduced into expressing the most blighted corners of our souls.

Ian Hughes poignantly reminds us that we need to erect enduring, resilient structures around us to ensure that we don't get lost in our own darkness. In his powerful and important book, Dangerous Minds, he identifies democracy as the governmental form we probably conceived to help us contain our worst impulses, including our willingness to be directed by tyrants. Like all else about the best parts of the human character, democracy requires attentiveness, commitment, and a full and accurate appraisal of its importance if it is to survive, never mind flourish. We dare not let ourselves believe that, once it assumes the appearance of being well established, its self-protective functions will never fail us. We have only to consider the experience of the past four years in the United States under the Trump administration to remind us how vulnerable democratic institutions can be, even in a relatively "old" democracy. Democracy, as Hughes points out, has only recently proliferated as a popular governing form; throughout most of human history it has been eclipsed by the autocracies and tyrannies that have defined the human experience and that, even now, continue to struggle for ascendancy. We don't readily or easily leave the destructive parts of ourselves behind.

There is another terribly important function that democracy serves that I think is implicit in Hughes' work: democracy emphasizes the importance for each of us of assuming responsibility for what we think, what we feel, and how we parse morality. It implicitly requires us to stand apart from our conventions to construct a point of view reflective of our individuality. It calls upon us, in other words, to become responsible for our own value systems. It tells us that if we disagree with government, we not only have the right, but the responsibility to say so. The imperative for individual members of a democratic society to express themselves thusly, however, has been a very uneven and often deeply flawed undertaking. We are still torn between the desire to encourage people to think for themselves versus our need for members of a given society, including democratic ones, to act in concert with one another and confirm perspectives that serve society's stated ends. These are, admittedly, often very hard choices to make.

Complicating the picture is what I see as a profoundly powerful human yearning for affiliation and belonging that induces us to surrender ourselves to context driven values, conventions, and "wisdom." In effect, we give ourselves permission not to think and feel so that we can confirm our place in the group that establishes context for us. This is an extraordinarily powerful human phenomenon, so far as I can see. It may also be reflective of our desire to be led, often badly, by "strong" personalities who are willing to tell us how to see ourselves and how to define our place in the world.

Receptivity to leadership and to conformity has in some respects worked quite well for us, but it often means that we sidestep the discomfort of separating ourselves from the group, wrestling with our prerogatives, and formulating a position that may identify us as outliers. Very, very hard to do, even when the group we are part of encourages us to take such chances. The desire to be led and the desire to belong helped me better understand why subjects behaved as they did in the famous Milgram (1963) and Haney et al. (1973) studies and why people could accommodate the destructive value systems of the Third Reich (as I have said earlier in this book, intolerable levels of threat and terror also made their contributions to German conformity). Disturbingly high percentages of Milgram's subjects were willing to shock another person at dangerous levels each time they failed a learning trial simply because they were told by an authoritative other to do so, unaware that the shocks were not real; subjects assigned the role of prison guards in the Zimbardo experiment, in turn, showed themselves all too willing to accommodate themselves to a punitive guard mentality which they directed towards subjects who had arbitrarily been assigned the role of prisoners. A sort of context overwhelms conscience kind of scenario. Both of these studies have been subject to extensive criticism, but each has nonetheless produced almost indelible concern about our malleability.

Arendt (1963) has warned about people who avoid thinking and feeling for themselves and who surrender their personhood to a larger totality; Dabrowski et al. (1973) has suggested that education which promotes conventionality interferes with our capacity to be discerning; Fromm (1941) drew our attention to our need to escape freedom of choice. It does seem that the burden of assuming responsibility for ourselves as individuals is often intolerable. I believe that we have to be taught to do so, taught to be able to take the kinds of chances that using one's own voice requires. The caveat – and it's an enormous one – is that the less we understand about ourselves, about our own pain, and about the shared human condition, the more unlikely we'll be to make choices that truly reflect our individuality and our capacity for decency. Which brings us back to the arts, to respect for democratic values, and to cultivation of individuality, most especially in the way that we educate our young. Without such assets to draw upon, it will be all too easy for many of us to become defined by context, whether such context represents a small group or micro-cultural experience or a larger macro one. The world is, in fact, cut up into myriad pieces, each characterized by its own attendant perceptions and appraised realities. Somehow we need to render these differences subjectively smaller than they feel so that our commonalities loom larger. We have to come to believe that we are all part of the same human family. Nationalism, elitism, exceptionality, and prejudice will only continue to divide us and alienate us from one another, offering the most destructive parts of ourselves more prerogatives to express themselves.

As I am putting these ideas into written form, I find myself wondering – can we really do it? Can we pull off this piece of magic, effecting a paradigm shift that moves us away from the fractured mosaic of self-interested silos currently defining much of our world? If our response to the ongoing Covid-19 pandemic serves as a metric of our capacity to shift our focus towards the well-being of all humanity, we can see that our vaccination efforts have often been compelled by the advantages that wealth and scientific privilege have offered the world's most resource-rich nations, many of whom appear to have elevated the importance of their own political concerns and a "me first" stance. Of course, there has also been generosity, but it has been very uneven, very piecemeal, and not reflective of a coordinated, overall global response that makes a rational, compassionate effort to address worldwide health compromise. We may be able to make our patchwork quilt solutions work this time, but what of the next? Of the waves of immigrants, the massive economic and social disruptions, and the upsurgence in populism that we will soon face as the effects of climate change accelerate?

References

Arendt, H. (1963). *Eichmann in Jerusalem: A report on the banality of evil.* New York, N.Y.: Penguin.

Dabrowski, K., Kawczak, A., & Sochanska, J. (1973). *The dynamics of concepts.* London, U.K.: Gryf Publications.

Fromm, E. (1941). *Escape from freedom.* New York, N.Y.: Farrar & Rinehart.

Haney, C., Banks, C., & Zimbardo, P. (1973). A study of prisoners and guards. *Naval Research Reviews*: 26.

Milgram, S. (1963). Behavioral study of obedience. *Journal of Abnormal and Social Psychology*, 67, 371–378.

Chapter 14

Reflections

In describing my father's personal struggles with himself, I have suggested that his challenges can be best understood as a unitary personality organization (malignant narcissism) rather than an intersection of various personality disorders (Kernberg, Kohut, Hughes, Malkin, Gartner, Stone) or as an expression of an altogether different unitary conception of personality (see Tansey, Dodes, Friedman). Of course, parsimony is beguiling. As I have noted elsewhere, it is, however, important to acknowledge again that my appraisal of my father's personality and of the personalities that I worked with that I designated as malignant narcissists may only capture a limited set of realities that attend this most dangerous variant of the human character. We can only expect real clarity to emerge after many clinicians have added their voices and tested their ideas alongside mine. What then emerges may be substantially different than the portrait I have painted.

As I have also pointed out elsewhere in this book, diagnosis is a very challenging concept. The DSM–5 currently conceives of diagnosis as clusters of symptoms, behaviors, and traits that are felt to manifest themselves in the framework of a particular diagnostic category. The resulting patchwork quilt of diagnostic "realities" we have conceived, many of which include overlapping clusters of markers or symptoms, is hard to grasp except as distinct categories, especially in the absence of psychodynamics and etiologies that might allow us to better interrelate the "siloed" diagnoses we work with day by day. If we include as part of the diagnostic process delineation of specific psychodynamics and/or etiologies associated with a diagnostic entity – an approach that I prefer – the complaint can be made, with some justification, that making a diagnosis is less "objective" than our current consensus driven system. But I would maintain that unless we include psychodynamics and etiology as part of our appreciation of diagnosis, we sacrifice richness and depth of understanding in preference for avoiding a bit of mess. Even more importantly, we deny ourselves opportunities to capitalize upon the imprecision and messiness that a focus on psychodynamics and etiology occasions, which, while creating ambiguity for us in the short run, begins to open doors for us in the longer run we must not turn away from. This is the kind of

DOI: 10.4324/9781003246923-14

messiness, in other words, that is heuristic and is therefore essential to scientific endeavor. As I noted earlier in this book, use of a diagnostic tool like the PDM-2 helps us more fully capture the complexities and important realities that attends each individual's unique life experience, further extending diagnostic appreciation that the DSM offers.

As I have indicated earlier, I don't find investigation of critical phases of development (narcissistic, oral receptive, oral aggressive, anal sadistic, phallic, genital) to be nearly as helpful in understanding personality distortions and challenges as I do elucidation of overall patterns of being, thinking, feeling, acting, and experiencing that present themselves in our relationship with ourselves and that are embedded in our relationship with others. In my book, I have attempted to articulate some of those patterns and the ways in which they are informed by defenses we rely on to protect the self. In this respect, my position is more similar to Shaw's than to Kernberg's.

In endorsing a relational perspective, I am very much aware that my father's autobiographies do not permit one a glimpse of what my father's pre-oedipal life experience might have been like. Accordingly, I don't have the means – other than engaging in extraordinary supposition – of weighing the kind of contribution early trauma of the sort that Kohut, Kernberg, and others envisioned unfolding at critical phases of development might have made to my father's inflexible investment in grandiosity. I would say the autobiographies do attest, however, very compellingly to relational patterns of trauma that iterated themselves seemingly endlessly throughout my father's later growing up and young adult years.

Like Fromm, I believe that we are possessed of a variety of innate drives we feel compelled to try and consummate rather than believing that we begin with two core drives (libidinal and aggressive drives) that eventually differentiate themselves into a multiplicity of felt intentionalities. Among the core drives that I see expressing themselves in people are the desire to love and to be loved; the drive to be autonomous; the drive to be competent; a proclivity to be empathic and consolidate our relationships with others through empathic attunement; a need for belonging and affiliation; and an abiding hunger for meaning. I would also say that there are powerful drives for symbiosis and for aggression, both of which may express themselves in myriad forms. In my clinical experience, frustration of any of these drives can produce what we call pathology, but I would also say that disruption of our need to both express and receive love makes a disproportionate contribution to human suffering. In this respect, again, my views are closer to Shaw's and, in this case, Hughes and Kohut's, than to Kernberg's.

I do find that there are numbers of points of agreement between Kernberg's formulation of malignant narcissism and my own. I very much agree with him that grandiosity in a malignant narcissistic personality protects such a personality from identity fragmentation. I think the underlying, but probably poorly articulated threat of such dissolution probably compels the malignant narcissist to cling evermore desperately to personal aggrandizement, though he would be horrified to confront such a reality in himself and/or to make such an admission. For my father, grandiosity appeared to be the means he relied upon to survive in a world and in relationships where he was required to carry everyone else's burdens on his shoulders. It insulated him against the helplessness and terror that must have pervaded his early life. Through its agency, he could assure himself, however improbably, that he could gratify the mountainous oral rage his background had incited. It also reassured him that in spite of his repeated violation of others, his grandiosity and self-aggrandizement would see him through. So, like Kernberg, Mika, and Kohut – in contrast to Shaw who emphasized the traumatizing narcissist's unconscious fear of shame or Fromm, who identified the malignant narcissist's vulnerability to underlying depression – I see the malignant narcissist as being inherently and probably unconsciously frightened that his whole being faces unbearable jeopardy should he fail to protect his outrageous, larger than life self-attributions. On the other side of such a failure is personal disintegration.

I also see strong similarities between borderline personality organization and malignant narcissism, as Kernberg does. Both personalities employ many of the same defenses (splitting, projection, projective identification, idealization/denigration), both are impelled by oral rage, and both are preoccupied with concerns about abandonment, though this concern manifests itself in very different forms. For people grappling with Borderline Personality Disorder (BPD), abandonment is an ever present and all too painful focus, one that shapes much of their behavior and experience. The malignant narcissist, in turn, has seemingly neutered vulnerability to abandonment by refusing to engage in loving exchange, but is nevertheless endlessly beset with obsession about loyalty, which is tested compulsively and interminably, never yielding him a secure position. He lives his life on this knife's edge, always looking for the next betrayal, ready to react to it with ruthlessness. His world must feel like a very precarious place indeed as he lurches from one failed relationship to another, much like the experience people with BPD endure. Both of these personality organizations are also profoundly engaged in their attempts to maintain cohesion. In BPD, however, identity diffusion and fragmentation are painfully apparent and painfully persistent facets of their reality, while in malignant narcissism, personality structure appears to be strongly cohesive, but cohesion is established at the price of great rigidity and inflexibility. The entire structure strikes one as frighteningly brittle, but I have seen that malignant narcissistic personality organization can endure far longer and demonstrate far more resilience than one imagines it would, even though it appears to carry the seeds of its own destruction. Stalin and Mao are two probable examples.

One readily sees that the malignant narcissist probably carries far fewer positive representations of self and of relationships than a person struggling with a borderline state, although the person presenting a borderline state has great difficulty establishing stability for any of the rewarding images he or she can introject. Notwithstanding such painful limitations, it appears to me that people struggling with borderline states have a greater capacity, however fleetingly and in spite of their obvious torment, to express their humanity and to engage in acts of love and caring than the malignant narcissist does. And, finally, both "disorders" are marked by a chaotic, impulse ridden presentation that seemingly lurches from one personal disaster to another; difficulties with self-regulation in both of these entities contributes to a stormy, sometimes volatile and often unpleasant therapeutic relationship. In my clinical experience, people living with BPD would appear to have a far better prognosis than people with malignant narcissism. I agree with Kernberg that malignant narcissism is "almost" untreatable and I agree with Kohut and Shaw that malignant narcissists (or traumatizing narcissists, a term that the latter prefers) are very unlikely to present themselves for treatment.

I am appreciative that Shaw has identified the destruction of one's subjectivity as perhaps the most devastating wound one human being can inflict on another. Importantly, these dramatic wounds may not arise from dramatic and highly visible forms of abuse, but rather from relatively subtle insults (from the perspective of the outside observer) that belie the extent of damage being sustained. When we look for etiology that may set the stage for intergenerational transmission of narcissism, we must be aware that the source of injury may not be readily graspable, instead being embedded in a matrix of destructive interactions that progressively compromise selfhood, but do not do so in an obvious or declarative way. As I have said, I see disruptions of subjectivity as empathic failures that visit themselves repeatedly during the course of an entire developmental process as opposed to empathic failures that occur at very early, vulnerable points in the affected person's childhood (Kohut). I think it has probably been our inclination to look for hyperbolized examples of brutality in the childhoods of tyrants, but that may not be where we find our most important explanations.

While I have argued that malignant narcissism is a subclass of psychopathy, I am less certain where it might fall along a spectrum of psychopathic disorders or even if various forms of psychopathy ought to be characterized as falling along a spectrum (I don't think they do). Though it is certainly true, like many clinicians, that I have had the opportunity to work with psychopaths (almost exclusively in an assessment format), I don't feel my grasp of the dynamics that might characterize psychopathy is as solid as my putative grasp of the dynamics of malignant narcissism. Is it most appropriate to define psychopathy by criminality, injuriousness to others, and profoundly impaired (or utterly compromised) capacity for empathy or should we, instead, think about severity in terms of a given psychopathic personality's propensity to inflict devastation on a great number of people, like a nation? I'm not even sure how I want to frame this question. The distinctions that I'm attempting to address in rudimentary form will begin to emerge with greater clarity once we know more.

Kernberg (1984) proposes that we consider the malignant narcissist as being possessed, albeit in a very limited way, of greater capacity for relatedness than the psychopath, whom he regards as utterly unable to establish a constructive attachment. My formulation of malignant narcissism suggests to me that the malignant narcissist rarely "sees" the other, save as a tool to be used to gratify exploitation. As I reflect on my experience with my father, I can't find convincing, substantial evidence of meaningful attachment. What I think I see instead is his investment in the idealized parts of himself that he projected onto me rather than substantial recognition and, crucially, appreciation of my individuality. I wonder if I'm being too harsh. I kept looking for points of genuine connection, but they remained elusively, tantalizingly just out of reach. Maybe my rapt attention to his storytelling approximated experiences of connection for me, but I was well aware that I was participating in his world rather than him attempting to reach into mine. Storytelling was infiltrated by a kind of empathy on his part, however, which I would define as his ability to read the pleasure that his stories created and as a capacity to take pleasure in what he was doing for both of us. I can see that among the malignant narcissistic patients with whom I worked there were also points of genuine connection; the longer I worked with them and, importantly, the more successful my work was, the more the real relationship between the two of us advanced itself – but, in fairness, with one exception, I have to admit that actualization of a real relationship was always extremely limited. I haven't been afforded the opportunity to undertake long-term work with people who could otherwise be defined as psychopathic, thus I am not in the position to say whether a relationship with them would have also afforded moments of authenticity and shared humanity. Traditional formulations, of course, maintain that the classically psychopathic personality is entirely bereft of empathy, save for an ability to read what people want and then contrive a seductive presentation that serves the psychopath's unique ends.

Shaw's framing of the differences between psychopathy and malignant narcissism is also worthy of further comment. He saw the malignant narcissist as harming others through a delusional conviction of righteousness while the psychopath was felt to demonstrate thoroughly deliberate efforts to harm. Unlike Shaw, I do see the malignant narcissist as predominantly engaging in deliberately harmful acts. These behaviors serve the function of generating a sense of aliveness, of confirming ascendancy and therefore safety, and of reminding people to be afraid of him. Shaw's wonderful phrase, "delusional conviction of righteousness," does, however, describe significant aspects of malignant narcissistic dynamics.

I'd like now to draw attention again to Shaw's, Kohut's, and Kernberg's delineation of the psychodynamics potentially contributing to development of malignant narcissism. As the reader has probably already noticed, their formulations of etiology closely approximates some of the major dynamic forces that pervaded my father's early life experience. Shaw's suggestion that cumulative relational trauma visited upon the child throughout the child's developmental years is a foundational part of malignant narcissism can be seen to be consistent with my father's growing-up experience, but shaming did not appear to play the central role in my father's emerging narcissism that Shaw's formulation anticipated that it would (it certainly made a contribution, however). Shaw's comments, on the other hand, that the parents of a child who becomes a traumatizing narcissist either implicitly or explicitly require the child to recognize the exclusive validity of parental needs and wishes is very much consonant with the trauma that my father endured. It is also consistent with the emphasis I placed upon early adultification as a contributor to malignant narcissistic character formation. So, too, was his suggestion that such a child develops inflexible, manic defenses as a way of protecting themselves from susceptibility to dependence. His view that a child likely to become a traumatizing narcissist would probably be raised by traumatizing narcissists was not fully supported by my father's history (depending upon how one might characterize my grandfather).

Kernberg's belief that chronically cold parental figures possessed of intense covert aggression often typified the history of a malignant narcissistic individual appears to be somewhat at odds with my father's experience, though it could be said that his mother's preoccupation with survival and her anger towards her husband might have rendered her functionally insensitive to her son's emotional and material needs while his father's ideological fervor and his preoccupation with consummating it might have been reflective of a profoundly narcissistic orientation (bringing us back to Shaw).

Kernberg's and Kohut's suggestion that children who become malignant narcissists often demonstrate unusual characteristics or gifts earmarking them as particularly attractive or talented does seem to be very much reflective of my father's realities as was Kernberg's sense that a mother's exploitation of such qualities invited such a child to feel special, culminating in the child's inclination to pursue compensatory admiration and greatness. One might add that such a dynamic helped the child consolidate identity around an idealized, grandiose self, which I think was Kernberg's intention. The only caveat, for me, in this aspect of Kernberg's formulation was his expectation that mother was probably narcissistic herself. I'm not sure that such a characterization accurately described my grandmother in her younger years, but she certainly evolved into a terribly self-centered, needy, angry person whose own oral rage never enjoyed satiation in her later years.

As I reflected earlier in the book, Kohut's concept of "self" was absolutely critical in helping me conceptualize the devastation my father experienced and that he visited on the people around him. Paired with Kohut's emphasis on empathy, the construct of self allowed me to visualize malignant narcissism as a nearly unceasing series of empathic failures that left my father essentially alone in the world of his childhood, bereft, as Kohut might say, of caring parental presence – a kind of dreadful, extended abandonment denying my father essential psychic sustenance necessary for him to evolve into a loving being.

As I'm writing this last chapter, I also find myself returning to a theme that I highlighted earlier in the book – my father's experience, which paralleled my experience with him, that he was, quite literally, disposable. I wonder if that translated itself into a sense that he was living in a malignant world he could only protect himself from by investing in his own grandiosity. I saw him replaying this theme with me as he episodically acted out lethal intentionalities towards me I think he unconsciously felt he had endured himself.

As I explored malignant narcissism and attempted to make sense out of it over the course of decades, I think the most helpful insight that I enjoyed – the one that was most effective in unlocking the puzzle – was my appreciation that malignant narcissism, at least for my father and for some of my patients, is meant to serve as a defense against love. Almost equally important was my growing awareness that malignant narcissism appears to represent a re-enactment not only of early trauma, but of trauma dynamic that I see as having entrenched itself early on in the lives of these people, compelling them to forever remain vigilant in a world that they can never feel safe in.

Importantly, as I have noted previously, both perspectives permitted me to experience compassion for individuals who must live with this condition. Experiencing informed compassion was a kind of magic, enabling me to distance myself from some of the black forces that have piled up inside over the years. Depth of understanding, the detachment it engendered, and the compassion it enabled allowed me to diminish the imposing and menacing proportions of the monster inside to a frightened, damaged being riven with terrible suffering that my father actually was. This is a process very much akin to the pathway to mitigation of one's own suffering Daniel Shaw (2014) movingly describes in *Traumatic Narcissism* in his chapter entitled "But what do I do?" In Kernberg's terms, I have replaced a "bad object" with a representation of someone else's nearly unbearable suffering.

When I was invited to think about images for the cover of this book that might best reflect its content and its message, I stumbled upon a piece of what I believe to be tattoo art: a portrait of a skull, head inclined forward, defined by swirling smoke that renders the skull almost indiscernible. What could be seen relatively more clearly was a black rose at the top of the skull which it seemed to want to call the viewer's attention to, as if it wished to distract one from its horrifying emaciation by drawing one's focus towards the dark gift it meant to offer. How extraordinary and how powerful, I thought. And how terribly poignant. An unintentional, but certainly visceral, portrait of the paradox that is narcissism: repellent withering of spirit side-by-side deliberate inflation of one's gifts and attempts to draw the eye away from grotesque deficits – from deadness – towards aggrandizement.

The image that I eventually chose for the book cover – of a man whose face is largely intact but whose head appears to be disintegrating – captures, for me, the threat the malignant narcissist faces as he tries to maintain personal coherence while struggling to mediate the forces within him that threaten him with disintegration. The image captures Kernberg's and now my own argument that the rigidity and the grandiosity/omnipotence of malignant narcissistic personality helps protect such people from the identity fragmentation that characterizes borderline states.

These two insights – malignant narcissism as a defense against love and as an enactment of trauma – provided the hinges that allowed me to swing the door open and realize a better understanding of the complex dynamics that define this terribly dangerous human reality, exposing one vista after another for me to try to articulate. As I have said earlier, not a life's journey any of us would choose to take, but certainly one that has proven to be very meaningful. Meaning also helps offset injury, making it easier for one to accept that those aspects of narcissistic wounding that remain unresolved – and there are many – are worth bearing.

After reading my book, my colleague in Ireland Ian Hughes commented that he now understood that evil could be abstracted as envy of love. While, in looking back, I can see that this insight is implicit in much of what I said, I didn't see it. His conception was riveting for me, bringing together some of the core concepts in my work in a very meaningful way. I am grateful to him. I think he may have captured the essence of evil.

References

Kernberg, O. (1984). *Severe personality disorders.* New Haven, CT.: Yale University Press.

Shaw, D. (2014). *Traumatic narcissism.* New York, N.Y. & London, U.K: Routledge.

Index

34, 37, 106, 136, 142, 155, 159–160,
161, 166; narcissist's self-empathy, 23;
poor shame tolerance and lack of, 28;
psychopath's absence of, 27, 200;
reduced under narcissistic state
leadership, 186; sociopath's lack of, 29;
sociopath's predatory empathy, 30; in
treatment, 21
Empire of the Summer Moon (Gynne)
69–70
energy *see* hypervigilance
entitlement 27, 142; enhanced by
depersonalization, 28, 161; supported
by contempt and cynicism, 75, 149;
supported by victimization, 158, 159;
traumatizing narcissists and, 25
envy: evoked in others, 98, 133, 154; of
love, 203; of others, 136, 142, 154, 155
epigenetics 108, 137; *see also* genetics
etiologies 16–18, 137; abuse, 34–37, 46–48,
141–143, 178, 199; adultification,
127–128, 133, 147, 201; brain function,
27, 30, 37, 137, 144, 181; diversity of,
143; diverting attention from damaged
self, 98–99, 136–137, 151, 202;
exploitation, 87, 134, 148, 155; fear of
depletion, 51, 130–132, 133, 134, 148;
genetics 108, 181; importance of
diagnosis based on, 144, 196;
intergenerational transmission, 26,
199; poverty, 35, 36, 73–75, 134, 192;
prevention of regression, 153–154, 159;
of psychopathy, 141; trauma enactment,
202, 203; traumatizing narcissism 22,
25–26, 34, 37, 201; *see also* diagnosis;
fear; parenting
evil 12, 30, 31, 34, 38; as absence of
empathy, 190; banality of, 191; as
envy of love, 203; as nullification of
another human, 36–37; Donald
Trump and, 29
exceptionalism, danger of 194
exploitation 73, 77, 200; bullying to
facilitate, 160; as early contributor to
narcissism, 87, 134, 148, 155; fear of,
74, 105; *see also* manipulation

fame-seeking 17, 149
family *see* malignant narcissists, children
of; malignant narcissist relationships;
malignant narcissists, spouses of;
malignant narcissist, victims of

fascism 97; *see also* Germany;
totalitarianism
fear: of abandonment, 174–175, 178; of
annihilation of grandiose self, 10, 21;
boldness from low reactivity to,
105; cognition diminished by, 109,
161–162; of dependence, 129, 131,
178; of depletion, 51, 130–132, 133,
134, 148; of depression, 102, 178;
diminished self from, 181; early
development diminished by, 36, 37, 44,
56, 91, 94, 100; elicited in others, 52,
57, 59, 96, 100, 183; of exploitation,
74, 105; fight-or-flight reactions, 28; of
intimacy, 158, 175; mobilized by
paranoid leaders, 32; of shadow self,
97, 174; of vulnerability, 74, 75, 198;
of weakness, 105, 113; *see also*
anxiety; hypervigilance; Post
Traumatic Stress Disorder; trauma
fragmentation *see* identify fragmentation
Friedman, Henry J. 32, 37
Fromm, Eric 8–14, 27, 30, 31, 38, 194

Gandhi 164
Garden of Beasts (Larson) 59, 181
Gartner, John 30–31, 38
gas lighting 28
generosity: aversion to, 54, 106, 155;
self-serving 74, 129
genetics 107–108, 137, 141, 181
Germany: post-World War II, 188;
World War II, 53, 181, 185, 193; *see
also* fascism; Hitler; malignant
narcissistic governments
Gilbert, G.M. 190
Gilligan, James 33
government *see* malignant narcissistic
governments
grandiosity 133, 163; from adultification,
127, 147–148; charismatic narcissists
and, 22; to counter self-condemnation,
16; group, 24, 35; lying to confirm,
156; of narcissistic leaders, 19, 29, 30,
31, 33, 35, 184; to prevent identity
fragmentation, 197–198, 203; as shield
from criticism, 10; traumatizing
narcissists and, 25; *see also*
omnipotence; self-aggrandizement;
superiority
greed 98, 132, 149
group narcissism *see* social narcissism

group self 23; *see also* society
guilt 16; lack of, 22, 29, 30; other-blaming
  to protect against, 28; *see also* remorse
Gynne, S.C. 69–70

Handbook of Psychopathy (Patrick)
  104, 140
hatred 16, 18, 32, 37, 53; from fear of
  exploitation, 62; *see also* contempt
The Heart of Man (Fromm) 8
Herman, Judith 29
history: narcissist's projected view of, 76;
  psychoanalytic knowledge to help
  explain, 23
Hitler 10, 19, 27, 30, 165; *see also*
  Germany; malignant narcissistic
  leaders
Hughes, Ian 33–36, 37, 38, 192–193, 203
human beings: ability to modulate
  empathy, 69–70, 132, 190; contempt
  for, 16, 57, 63, 96 , 131–132, 134, 149,
  161, 165; desire for belonging, 190,
  193–194, 197; drive for love, 37, 197;
  evil's nullification of, 36–37; need for
  empathy by, 96, 197; receptivity to
  leadership, 193–194; susceptibility to
  malignancy, 8, 192; yearning for
  safety, 189–190, 191–192
humiliation 82–83; contempt as justification
  for, 75; sadistic, 160; societal, 36, 183; *see*
  also bullying; sadism; shame
humor: lack of self-deprecating, 151;
  sadistic, 54
Hussein, Saddam 25; *see also* malignant
  narcissistic leaders
hypervigilance 74, 87, 103, 113, 133, 149
hypomania 104

idealizations 135, 150, 198; *see also*
  grandiosity; self-aggrandizement
idealized superego 22
identification with aggressor 59, 88; *see*
  also malignant narcissistic leaders
identity fragmentation: Bipolar Disorder
  and, 198; grandiosity to protect from,
  18, 197, 203
immigration 20–21, 167, 195
impulsivity 28, 29, 30, 59–69, 88, 161;
  defined, 104; to protect against
  depression, 104; and psychopathy, 140;
  see also disinhibition
incestuous symbiosis 13–14

inequality, social 35, 36; *see also* poverty
infidelity 65, 155
intelligence, reduced *see* thought
  degradation
intimidation 59, 82, 86, 113, 183; *see also*
  bullying; domination
isolation 10, 29, 79, 132, 148, 168

Jhueck, Diane 33
Jong-il, Kim 19, 25; *see also* malignant
  narcissistic leaders
Jong-un, Kim 27; *see also* malignant
  narcissistic leaders

Kernberg, Otto 16–21, 30, 37, 38,
  197–198, 200, 201
"kiss ass up, kick ass down" mentality
  180, 185
Kohut, Heinz 21–23, 37, 38, 201

"Labyrinth of Lies" (2014) 188
language, degradation of 61, 80, 118,
  162, 163; *see also* thought degradation
Larson, Eric 59, 181
leaders *see* malignant narcissistic leaders
Lee, Bandy 29
life, love of 12, 13–14
life-and-death instinct 14, 15; *see also*
  death instinct
life instinct 12
loneliness *see* isolation
love: in early development, 26–27, 36, 37;
  evil as envy of, 203; human drive for,
  37, 197; narcissistic defenses against,
  64–66, 74, 96, 131–133, 136, 148–149,
  152, 158, 202, 203; in psychotherapy,
  26–27; as respect of another's
  subjectivity, 27
lying 28; to confirm grandiosity, 156;
  driven by envy, 154; under narcissistic
  state leadership, 186; to test acolytes
  loyalty, 156; *see also* contrivance;
  pretense

machismo *see* masculinity, hyperbolized
Major Depressive Disorder 101; *see also*
  depression
malignancy, human susceptibility to 192
malignant narcissism: as an enactment of
  trauma, 202, 203; characteristics of,
  9–10, 15–20, 27–31, 34, 197–201; as
  defense against love, 202, 203;

For Product Safety Concerns and Information please contact our EU
representative GPSR@taylorandfrancis.com
Taylor & Francis Verlag GmbH, Kaufingerstraße 24, 80331 München, Germany

www.ingramcontent.com/pod-product-compliance
Lightning Source LLC
Chambersburg PA
CBHW070324270326
41926CB00017B/3745

* 9 7 8 1 0 3 2 1 6 0 5 9 7 *